DOROTA MASŁOWSKA: FOUR PLAYS

DOROTA MASŁOWSKA: FOUR PLAYS

No Matter How Hard We Tried
(or: We exist on the best terms we can)
Między nami dobrze jest
translated by **Artur Zapałowski**

A Couple of Poor, Polish-Speaking Romanians
Dwoje biednych Rumunów mówiących po polsku
translated by **Benjamin Paloff**

How I Became a Witch
an autobiographical play for grown-ups and kids
Jak zostałam wiedźmą
translated by **Artur Zapałowski**

Bowie in Warsaw
Bowie w Warszawie
translated by **Soren Gauger**

Edited by Frank Hentschker with Tomek Smolarski

Martin E. Segal Theatre Center Publications
Frank Hentschker, Executive Director
Martin E. Segal Theatre Center Publications

New York © 2020

Library of Congress Cataloging-in-Publication Data

Dorota Masłowska: Four Plays. Translations into English.
(Plays. Selections. English)
Edited by Frank Hentschker with Tomek Smolarski
ISBN: 978-1-953892-11-9

DOROTA MASŁOWSKA: FOUR PLAYS
with introduction by Frank Hentschker and Krystyna Lipińska-Iłłakowicz

No Matter How Hard We Tried (or: We exist on the best terms we can) / Między nami dobrze jest
translated by Artur Zapałowski

A Couple of Poor, Polish-Speaking Romanians / Dwoje biednych Rumunów mówiących po polsku
translated by Benjamin Paloff

How I Became a Witch / Jak zostałam wiedźmą
translated by Artur Zapałowski

Bowie in Warsaw / Bowie w Warszawie
translated by Soren Gauger

Four Plays by Dorota Masłowska © in arrangement with Authors' Syndicate Lit & Script Agency, Warsaw, Poland 2023. For inquiries please write to: info@syndykatautorow.com.pl

A Couple of Poor, Polish-Speaking Romanians, in the translation by Benjamin Paloff, was first published by Seagull Books in the anthology *Loose Screws: Nine New Plays from Poland;* edited by Dominika Laster, 2014.

No Matter How Hard we Tried, in the translation by Arthur Artur Zapałowski, was published first by Seagull Books, India as part of the *(A)ppolonia* anthology, edited by Krystyna Duniec, Joanna Klass and Joanna Krakowska in 2014.

Edited by Frank Hentschker with Tomek Smolarski
Cover design and artwork by Kalina Bańka
Layout & typesetting by Kamila Widz

© 2020 Martin E. Segal Theatre Center

CONTENTS

ACKNOWLEDGEMENTS

Grateful acknowledgment is made to The Martin E. Segal Theatre Center for making this publication possible.

A very special thanks to Agata Grenda; Paul Bargetto; Joanna Klass, Joanna Krakowska, Krystyna Duniec/(A)pollonia; Grzegorz Jarzyna, Roman Pawłowski, Agata Kołacz/ TR Warszawa; Agnieszka Glińska, Natalia Korczakowska/Studio teatrgaleria; Kalina Bańka; Jay Wegman; Xavery Żuławski; Stephen Willems/MCC Theater; Dan Safer/Witness Relocations; Anna Podolak; Beata Pilch, Nicole Wiesner/Trap Door Theater.

INTRODUCTION

"The feeble winter sun, like a crappy little coin, had long since fallen beyond the horizon. There were bodies of run-over dogs and animals cast all over the highway. Last year's ice-cream ads, faded by children's lustful glances, swayed on the wind over the cheap bars. I saw the darkness. I touched it."

Driver, A Couple of Poor, Polish-Speaking Romanians

I remember a beautiful, sunny morning in Central Park before The Time of COVID. It was one of these hot days in New York City, when a presidential quarter coin will sink into the sticky, smelly, black asphalt if a car runs over it. And you can't get it back out. Not a cloud in the sky.

Seeking refuge in the shade of Central Park I passed by Cleopatra's Needle, a 3500-year-old obelisk, once commissioned by Pharaoh Thutmose III for the Temple of the Sun in Heliopolis—modern-day Luxor, a city that counts within its limits the ruins of what the Greeks called the City of Thebes.

With that in mind I passed Turtle Pond, an old reservoir in Central Park. I came across a stunning sight: the larger-than-life bronze statue of Wladyslaw II Jagiello—a King of Poland in the 15th century—got a power wash from the Park Department. With the legendary water pressure of New York City hydrants the Polish King seemed to be floating within the water jets against the blue, sunny sky. The cloudy mist and liquid crystal water drops of the municipal champagne reflected the rainbow colors like a kaleidoscope. The splashing noises made the scene seem like Neptune himself had jumped out of the Hudson River to enjoy Central Park for the day and play with its statues like a kid in his back yard.

Originally, the impressive equestrian sculpture of the Polish King in battle— with large swords crossed over his head—stood at the Polish pavilion in the 1939 World's Fair in Queens. It was the same year the Nazis invaded Poland, making it impossible for the monument to return to its homeland. The exiled Polish government in London asked New York to safeguard the stature—and ultimately donated it to the City that displayed it prominently in Central Park in 1945, overlooking Turtle Pond.

But what does the King's stature really tell us about Poland, and its King who was a pagan Lithuanian? And about its people? What they were thinking, what did they love or hate? What did they desire? What jokes did they tell? What does the sculpture tell us about medieval Kraków, the Battle of Grunwald in 1410, about Warsaw in 1945 or Poznań in 2021? And what does the obelisk really tell us about the life of the Egyptians, in Alexandria, Thebes, and Heliopolis in 1475 B.C.? The memory of these old seats of power seemed at the time as invincible as the White House in Washington today. The obelisk fell face down in the sand and the writing in the stone was protected—but just a century of New York City pollution and acid rain almost completely destroyed the hieroglyphs on the obelisk that celebrate the military victories of Ramses II, after surviving 3,000 years in the open air of Egypt.

Heiner Müller reflects on theatre, time, memorial statues and revolution in his Hamletmachine: „The scenery is a monument. It portrays a man who made history, a hundred times life-size. The petrification of a hope. His name is interchangeable. The hope has not been fulfilled." In his revolutionary play, Müller calls for "Tearing up the photograph of the author" in the stage directions.

Müller is of course referring to Brecht's fundamental question about the representation of reality on stage. Brecht believed that epic theatre plays could teach us about history—and what we do not learn from history. That the theatrical experience can transfer knowledge, represent the world in all its complexities and ask us at the same time to be an active part of the change we want to see. Brecht famously said: "Always the victor writes the history of the vanquished. He who beats distorts the faces of the beaten. The weaker depart from this world and the lies remain."

This is where the work of Dorota Masłowska comes to the rescue and fulfills the promise of truth where the great monuments fail. "I saw the darkness. I touched it," says The Driver, in her great play A Couple of Poor, Polish-Speaking Romanians. Masłowska experienced the opening of the Berlin Wall and the fall of the Soviet Empire; the upheaval and social unrest of post-communist Poland. The resonance of the promises of hope and truth and justice from Poland's early-eighties ties with the Solidarność movement still ringing in her ears.

Like the obelisks Masłowska's work connects heaven, earth and the underground of contemporary Poland; its past, present and future. With her writings she scratches the skies of Polish history, and her words shine like the once gilded pinnacles of the Egyptian sky needles. She tells us stories about the weaker ones, whose faces were beaten—and the lies of those who seems to have won. Masłowska records the defeats and illusionary victories of everyday life—all with words just printed out on paper from a computer screen— but as powerful and lingering in our minds as hieroglyphs hammered into stone. Like a Polish warrior Queen Masłowska comes galloping in her plays at full speed. Armed with sharp dialogue she is slicing through the social fabric of post-communist Poland, a country now taken to court by the European Union for the violation of the democratic oath. A nation that now seems to be nostalgic for the lost kingdom of Wladyslaw II Jagiello. Masłowska's characters are dangerous, provocative, and they don't take no for an answer.

Her play How I Became a Witch is as much a children's story as a Grimm's fairytale. In the mask of the witch she shares with us her experience of modern-day Poland that seems to be at "the world's edge":

Witch
When I'm walking home, all wet, cold and mean,
I look into the windows that I pass with a leer.
I live at the world's edge, so the walk takes two years.

There's so many windows, and all of them lit,
and wherever I look, I see people sit:
some sitting on sofas, some on their parents' knees, but they're all staring
blankly at flat-screen TVs. They're checking to see if they have more more
more, or too little—as little as they had before.

It has been a great honor for the Segal Center to host the very first reading
of Masłowska's work in the Americas. I remember her sitting on our black
wooden chairs, her legs dangling in the air; answering questions from a curi-
ous New York audience after a brilliant reading. Her words and lines appeared
on stage as cool, clear and translucent as water bursting out under pressure
from a New York hydrant—refreshing for an audience that was thirsty for real
European stories on stage. As much as I loved looking at the dazzling bronze
statue of Wladyslaw II Jagiello in Central Park, I was so much more impressed
by this young Polish writer and her unique style; her pressing themes; her
craft; her love for her country. For the questions she asked and for the answers she refuses. She represented Poland so more truthfully, sophisticated and knowledgeable than any bronze of stone monument. Like an obelisk
Masłowska's work stands out and is a testimony to eternity and immortality:
of Poland as a nation and, as the great Polish performance philosopher Andrzej Wirth always pointed out—as an interim superpower of theatre.

Now it is an honor again to publish the first anthology of Dorota Masłowska's
work in the Americas. I would like to thank my Polish friends: the brilliant
Agata Grenda for first making me aware of the playwright's work for the stage
during my trip to Poland, which was supported by the Polish Cultural Institute in New York; the wonderful Tomek Smolarski, who keeps the flag of the
Institute up during the Time of Corona. It was over a cup of coffee when he
and I thought it would be a good idea to publish a book with Masłowska's
plays at the Segal Center.

If you want to know about Poland's post-communist young generation—what
they were thinking, what they loved and hated, what they dreamed about—
just read these plays. So much easier to decipher than the meaning of hieroglyphs or crossed swords on monuments erected by those in power—and so
much closer to the truth.

Frank Hentschker

INTRODUCTION

A Witch:
There's so many windows, and all of them lit
And wherever I look, I see people sit:
Some sitting on sofas, some on their parents' knees
But they're all staring blankly at flat-screen TVs.
They're checking to see if they have more more more,
Or too little – as little as they had before.

(*How I Became a Witch*)

In 2002, Polish literary circles witnessed an explosion: Dorota Masłowska, a nineteen-year old writer from the provinces and not part of the literary establishment in Warsaw published her first novel: *Polish-Russian War Under the White and Red Flag /Wojna polsko ruska pod flagą biało-czerwoną/*. The bizarre, baroque, and provocative title was translated into English by Benjamin Paloff as *Snow White and Russian Red*.

The book shattered the readerly circles of Poland because of its rough, visceral, crude language almost directly quoting drug users lingo and this way reflecting on the poisonous (drugged) political situation in the post-Communist country on its way to capitalism. The book's language sounded even more blasphemous to the readers who knew that the author was still a high school student and wrote the book while studying for her final high school exam, the *matura*. That same year the young author received the prestigious *Paszport Polityki* prize awarded by the acclaimed Polish political/cultural weekly *Polityka* to young, promising writers as a "passport" to the world.

Dorota Masłowska was born and grew up in Wejherowo, near Gdańsk, in the Kashubian district of northern Poland. Today she lives and works in Warsaw and occasionally spends time in the country. Apart from prose and theatre she often publishes editorials and gives interviews in the leading magazines (in Poland and abroad) commenting on almost all forms of the Polish, and perhaps not only Polish, twenty-first-century life style. Even while Masłowska tries to maintain her very private, low profile position, her voice continues to resonate strongly on all social platforms, no matter whether she comments on universal questions like loneliness, the lack of social bonds, poverty, happiness or more down to earth topics such as fashion, life in the city versus life in the country, or just prosaic every day work. Since the publication of her first novel, and even more so, from the performance of *No Matter How Hard We Tried / Między nami dobrze jest/* (2008) she became an iconic figure mercilessly, even sometimes brutally, diagnosing the ills of the world in which almost everything can be bought and manipulated. Her misleadingly innocent, smiling face looks at her young (and older) audiences from liberal Polish TV programs, or the leading Polish popular magazines such as *Twój Styl*, or *Wysokie Obcasy*, while her tongue stings and ridicules. As the book-long interview with Masłowska by Agnieszka Drotkiewicz (*Dorota Masłowska. Dusza Światowa / The World Spirit*), 2013 shows, her message is complex and always independent - she undermines national icons such as the "fight for freedom", but at the same time looks disparagingly at semi-blasphemous (often anti-religious) artistic gestures, such as her reaction to desecration of religious symbols at the concert after Maja Kleczewska's *Babel* performance.[1] Indeed, within the first two decades of the twenty-first-century Masłowska became the most prominent presence on the Polish cultural scene. Apart from participating in all forms of writerly culture she also tried live performance and produced a CD *The Society is Unpleasant /Społeczeństwo jest niemiłe/* (2014) with her own text and hip-hop /rap type recitation. She also performed herself in the film version of *Snow White and Russian Red*. Recently she has published another text for theatre, *Bowie in Warsaw /Bowie w Warszawie/*, that premiered in fall 2021 in Teatr Studio in Warsaw.

Now the uproar around the young author has subsided, but the excitement still remains. Dorota Masłowska is an accomplished writer creating dazzling, momentous, and often even subversive statements about the state of commercialized, dehumanized contemporary culture. In 2006 she won another prestigious prize – the NIKE award- for the best literary achievement of the year for her second novel *The Queen's Peacock /Paw królowej/*. The title is a pun connoting two meanings of "peacock" in Polish: it translates as "peacock" but also as a "puke." And indeed, the book written in rhythmical, almost rap-like prose, is close to a "puke" while depicting the disgusting and ugly existence of its protagonists, who live totally senseless, inhuman lives immersed in their own toxic reality. That reality metaphorically reflects vicious political fights, lies, scandals accompanying the transformation of the economy from socialist to market driven, and the constant meddling of the Church into politics. Again, as in the case of her first book, the young author was praised by some writers and critics and damned by the others because of her aggressive for some "improper" language and corrosive subject matter.

That same year (2006) marked Masłowska's theatrical debut - the publication and the subsequent staging (2007) of *The Two Poor Polish Speaking Rumanians /Dwoje biednych Rumunów mówiących po polsku*. The next play *Między nami dobrze jest / No Matter How Hard We Tried* (2008) was commissioned by TR Warszawa and Berliner Schaubühne am Lehniner Platz and opened in March 2009 in Berlin under Grzegorz Jarzyna's direction. The play immediately won critical acclaim and established Masłowska's position as a prominent theatre voice of the young, post-Communist generation. And the subsequent generations still embrace Masłowska'a voice as their own. In 2022, twenty years after the author of Snow White and Russian Red was awarded the *Polityka* prize, a young Polish film director Aleksandra Terpińska received this same award for the film version of Masłowska's 2018 book *Other People / Inni ludzie*.

---

1 Dorota Masłowska. Dusza Światowa. Rozmawia Agnieszka Drotkiewicz. Kraków: Wydawnictwo Literackie, 2013, p. 99.

Why is Dorota Masłowska such a meaningful presence among the population of young Polish playwrights? Why does every publication of her prose or theatre production trigger strong emotional and intellectual reactions among diverse groups – young and older, intellectuals and the popular public – within Polish society, stimulating an avalanche of press and media discussions? I think that one of the reasons is the young author's unusual ability to "hear" all kinds of "tunes" and voices in the surrounding cacophony of overlapping cultural narratives. Once, in a similar way Stanislaw Ignacy Witkiewicz (Witkacy), already as a little boy, was able to "hear" the disparity between "what is said" and "what is done" creating bizarre names and absurdist situations thus attempting to express something that was evading straightforward expression.

At the beginning, especially after the publication and then filming of *Snow White and Russian Red* (2009 dir. by Xawery Żuławski), the critics often tried to label Masłowska's writing and related to it as the so-called *powieść dresiarska /tracksuit novel/* - a novelistic sub-genre about young social outcasts, drug addicts, or punks always wearing tracksuits. But such critical attempts missed rendering the multi-layered complex texture of Masłowska's texts that are funny and at the same time serious, seem simple yet constitute a high level of complexity, they present regular people, but these characters are quite bizarre, they seem to represent specific social groups such as drug-addicts and social outcasts, but in fact, they relate to everybody and everyday situations.

What strikes the reader immediately when confronting Masłowska's prose or theatre is the unusual, malleable quality of language and the patchy, disjointed, non-linear narrative patterns. Her characters, no matter whether they are two Polish-speaking Romanians, Strong and Angela from *Snow White and Russian Red* or Mrs. Nastka from *Bowie in Warsaw*, often speak brutalized and twisted language, full of lame, sometimes pretty harsh, sloppy expressions, often shaky grammatically. At the same time we immediately perceive this language as humorous and witty ironically referencing a reality that truly went awry. In rhythmic rap-like cadences and everyday vernacular taken from advertisements, all kinds of store sale slogans, crossword-puzzles, and popular magazines, Masłowska's prose and theatre present the world in transition, or the world already experiencing the commercial shock in which traditional values and norms, the distinction between good and evil, moral and immoral attitudes, social and family bonds are emptied of meaning. In this world, history, memory, or tradition no longer resonate. The same is true about words such as patriotism, honor, and honesty. Nothing holds. All these words/concepts have been used and over-used by politicians and the media and became smeared and desecrated with lies and contaminated with the germs and dirt of commercialization. The world Masłowska's texts depict is ugly and the language rendering it must be also ugly, full of abject images; it is like the puke from the *The Queen's Peacock/ Puke (Paw królowej)* and a prominent metaphor from her other texts.

The world contained in this "ugly," twisted language is, in some ways, two and not three dimensional – it is flattened and lacking a traditional perspective in spite of the specific references to everyday landscapes, cities, roads, stores such as Tesco or IKEA, apartment buildings *(bloki)*, or TV programs. It produces a parody of our contemporary, commercialized, dehumanized and totally commodified world, but at the same time all these spaces overlap, crumble and create a fluid, unstable reality. We enter such cramped and cluttered and yet perfectly malleable space when confronting the opening scene of Bowie in Warsaw:

The 1970s, Warsaw. The dead of night.
Interior of a small apartment in a large building.
This is a single space crammed with many spaces.
In the darkness we see the outlines of a life's accumulated clutter.
Baby carriages, scooters, ferns, crystals; wobbly piles of laundry on wall unit shelves.
A piling and contamination of shapes which turns into monsters in the night.

The present volume brings to American audiences four texts of which three are written explicitly for the theatre: *The Two Poor Polish Speaking Rumanians / Dwoje biednych Rumunów mówiących po polsku/* (2006), *No Matter How Hard We Tried/ Między nami dobrze jest* (2008), and the most recent *Bowie in Warsaw / Bowie w Warszawie* (2021). The fourth *How I Became a Witch/ Jak zostałam wiedźmą* (2014) is a kind of rap dramatic poem. All these texts have often been performed in and outside of Poland. *A Couple of Poor, Polish-Speaking Romanians* was for the first time presented as a reading by TR Warszawa, directed by Przemysław Wojcieszek. Later, the play was shown in many major theatre venues in Poland and abroad. In the United States it premiered at the Trap Door Theater in Chicago in 2009 (dir. Max Truax) and it was later performed in New York at the Abrons Arts Center directed by Paul Bargetto in 2011.

Dorota Masłowska had a real presence at City University of New York Segal Center. In 2007 she was invited by the Segal Center director Frank Hentschker to come for the first time to the Americas with her very first play *A Couple of Poor, Polish-Speaking Romanians* just one year after the opening in Warsaw at TR Warszawa. The Segal Center commissioned the translation in collaboration with Agata Grenda from the Polish Cultural Institute in New York. In 2014 Masłowska, now famous in world theatre, came back to the Segal Center's PEN World Voices Festival with her international success *No Matter How Hard We Try*, again directed by Paul Bargetto. The legendary Judith Malina from the Living Theatre performed brilliantly in the reading. In 2016 the Segal Center presented the American premiere of Masłowska's video project *Mister D x Anja Rubik – Chleb + Mister D – Hajs* at the Center's Film Festival on Theatre and Performance.

A Couple of Poor, Polish-Speaking Romanians and *No Matter How Hard We Tried* were also presented to American audiences as readings in 2014 as a part of New York Theatre Workshop's event *(A)pollonia: A Festival of Readings of*

New Polish Plays (November 21-25). During that festival *No Matter How Hard We Tried* in Artur Zapałowski's translation premiered at La MaMa, directed by Dan Safer from Witness Relocation Theatre.

Bowie in Warsaw and *How I Became a Witch* appear for the first time in English; the first one in Soren Gauger's and the second in Artur Zapałowski's translation. *How I Became a Witch* subversively subtitled as "an autobiographical play for grown-ups and kids" was adapted for the stage and directed by Agnieszka Glińska in Warsaw's Teatr Studio in June 2014. The success of this performance was to a great extent due to the fact that the author's nine-year old daughter served as her language consultant during the process of writing the text and this collaboration surely led to its enthusiastic reception by both older and younger audiences.

Bowie in Warsaw premiered in December 2021 also in Teatr Studio under Marcin Liber's direction. It only tangentially references the famous British musician's stroll through Warsaw in 1976 when he was traveling from Moscow to Berlin, when the train stopped (for longer than usual) Bowie supposedly visited a bookstore at the Paris Commune Square (Plac Komuny Paryskiej) where he bought a CD of *Śląsk* (Polish National Song and Dance Ensemble). Even though the Śląsk song "Helokanie" echoes in the Polish version, and Bowie's composition Warsaw (1977) ends the play, the real focus of this text is the present-day Poland rendered through the language and the imaginary view of Warsaw of the 1970s. The grey, hopeless, and often abject reality of the communist era, in fact provides a proxy for the play's commentary on the fractured contemporary society dragging its past complexes and animosities into the post-communist times. As Masłowska stated in one of her songs, "the society is unpleasant" – indeed, its members are entangled in futile little battles and are manipulated by senseless media stories, only inspiring hatred, anger, and fear leaving no room for hope, human bonds, respect, or love.

All four pieces present a discombobulated, disjointed twenty-first century world in the characteristic Masłowska style of patchy, bizarre, jumbled, and messy narratives. *A Couple of Poor, Polish-Speaking Romanians* and *How I Became a Witch* use a journey and a road as a main narrative pattern. *No Matter How Hard We Tried* takes place in a city space infused with the sounds of "gurgling pipes ...trams, cars, horns, and airplanes flying past across the low-hung sky and setting the bottle of stale knock-off vermouth in the drinks cabinet rattling." (Blocks of flats -*blokowisko*-is another beloved Masłowska space.) The realities these texts present are muddled and often wild and through linguistic contortions they display the perplexing, but also specific, detailed elements of our modern consumer culture. The Little Metal Girl, a character in *No Matter How Hard We Tried* dwells amidst the language of TV commercials and recipes from old popular magazines, her mother Halina, and the neighbor Bożena cherish leaflets and advertising slogans perpetrating the rhetoric of consumerist joys relying on saving every penny and savoring every scrap of cheap, unhealthy food. Boguś, a plump boy that the Witch from *How I Became a Witch* wants to catch and cook in her hearty soup, cannot live without his iPhone and a bag of chips. His consumerist mentality is forged by his mother, the owner of the company More & More & More & Co. and the father whose only creed is also to have more. This is how Boguś describes his father:

My dad's the CEO.
He brings me more home from the office, so I have plenty more:
more in my room, more in the kitchen, more in the garden shed –
there's so much more, I sometimes wish I had much more instead …

From the beginning the fairy-tale structure of *How I Became a Witch* introduces the reader/viewer into the reality in which all rational laws are suspended and we follow the blending, meandering, overlapping worlds that unfold before us and neither time nor space hold to traditional norms. This aspect of Masłowska's texts was beautifully rendered in the cinematic version of *Polish White and Russian Red* making the viewer confused whether he/she is following the imaginary or the "real" world. But there is nothing more misleading than to seek the so-called real world in Masłowska's texts. All the realities - the imaginary, reflected, or refracted blur and overlap. Identities and traditions dissolve in the fluid trashy *Everyday*. History mingles with the present – Granny from *No Matter How Hard We Tried* still lives in 1944, the time of the Warsaw Uprising, the Little Metal Girl traverses all the spaces, and the TV personalities dwell in some undefined time and space.

The combination of twisted, lame language with tacky, often abject images produces a humorous effect. During the performances of these texts I noticed the audiences burst in cascades of laughter. Yet something lurks underneath this bizarre world. People laugh, but amidst that laughter falls a terrifying, ominous silence. And when the laughter turns into that deep, penetrating silence we feel that the words from the stage touch on something hidden, some still unhealed wounds, complexes, prejudices, inhibitions, unfulfilled dreams. Thus, all these texts, although overtly light and funny, strike a deeply tragic note and express the drama of the contemporary desensitized, dehumanized, trashy world.

Masłowska is not the only voice sounding from the Polish stage, there are others such as Małgorzata Sikorska-Miszczuk, Paweł Demirski, Magda Fertacz, Przemysław Wojcieszek, Danuta Łukasińska, Joanna Owsianko, or Tomasz Kaczmarek whose work makes up *Pokolenie Porno (A Porno Generation)/ Made in Poland* – the two volume anthology of new Polish theater (2003/ 2006). The authors of this collection (Masłowska was not a part of it because her theatre debut took place in 2006) Roman Pawłowski and Henryk Sułek collected the texts that expressed the preoccupations and dilemmas of the post 1989 generations of Poles. The publication of their texts triggered heated discussions and sometimes even outrage because they opened up a Pandora's Box of disturbing subjects relating to taboos such as alcoholism, drug addiction, poverty, the crisis of religion (abuses of Church authority), disintegration of family and social life – issues that were never discussed nor disclosed in the communist era. Many of the new theatre texts transgress social norms and historical traditions, such as the veneration of Polish martyrdom and patriotism, and dispel cultural myths and stereotypes. In a shocking way, the harsh language and images, often referring to real events (in docudramas), display the crisis of (Polish) identity and the break with tradition pointing to uncritical acceptance of certain moral values (such as patriotism and honor) often pushing for a re-evaluation of the Polish historical experience. The young generation of theatre authors especially highlight the experience of transition and change taking place in the Polish mentality and identity as a result of travels and contacts with other cultures. At the same time, their texts present a harsh critique of the nascent capitalist and consumerist attitudes.

A similar spirit of rebellion, sensitivity to change, and sense of transition informs Masłowska's theatre, but there is also a specifically "Maslowskian" element in it, mostly contained in her innovative approach to language and the way her texts situate themselves vis-a vis the surrounding reality. Her verbal/linguistic dexterity and authorial intuition seem to me comparable to her great predecessor, Witold Gombrowicz, who lightly and playfully clad his complex struggles with Polish cultural megalomania and complexes masterfully juggling with the grammar and lexis of the Polish language. Masłowska's belief in the potential of the author's struggles with one's own shortcomings and aesthetic/word choices ("nieumiejętność jest potencjałem"/inability is a potential)[2] and the necessity of taking the risk to express[3], places her close to Gombrowicz's notion of "imperfection" and the famous Beckettian perspectives.

Masłowska's theatre work apart from Bowie in Warsaw has already appeared in two American anthologies (A)pollonia: Twenty-First-Century Polish Drama and Texts for the Stage (Ed. Krystyna Duniec, Joanna Klass, and Joanna Krakowska), 2014, and Loose Screws: Nine New Plays from Poland (Ed. Dominika Laster), 2015. Now American readers receive all four texts together in the Segal Press edition. These texts, I think, appear in very good translations rendering the playfulness, flexibility, and uniqueness of the original Polish. It seems that the cultural barrier that stopped such writers as Gombrowicz from being translated into English has been overcome and the translators Artur Zapałowski, Benjamin Paloff, and Soren Gauger deserve special credit for their courage and skill in rendering the twists and turns of A Couple of Poor, Polish-Speaking Romanians, No Matter How Hard We Tried, How I Became a Witch, and Bowie in Warsaw into American English.
One of Masłowska's recent books, Honey, I Killed the Cats /Kochanie, zabiłam nasze koty/, translated into English by Benjamin Paloff (2019), takes place

---

2 Dorota Masłowska. Dusza Światowa. Rozmawia Agnieszka Drotkiewicz. Kraków: Wydawnictwo Literackie, 2013, p. 108
3 In the same interview with Agnieszka Drotkiewicz, Masłowska confessed: "I think that everything I wrote up to now is an outcome of the risk and the inability to do something. And this feeling of anxiety and the risk and the uncertainty whether I am able to do what I have to do, to accomplish it. /Ale myślę, że wszystko co pisałam do tej pory, zawsze polegało na ryzyku i na nieumiejętności, na tym, że czegoś nie potrafiłam zrobić, i sprawiały mi przyjemność niepokój, ryzyko i ta niepewność, czy potrafię, czy to skończę./ (Dorota Masłowska. Dusza Światowa p. 108.)

in New York, but as the author explains – it is really about Warsaw. So, perhaps the recently published texts for theatre, even though they directly relate to Warsaw, Polish roads, apartments, advertising, and TV programs could also "speak" in an American context, to American directors and audiences the same way they speak to other world audiences. After all, iPhones, iPads, IKEA, and many other icons of the contemporary European and global cultural landscape are the same everywhere as are companies such as More & More & More.

Krystyna Lipińska-Iłłakowicz

No Matter How Hard We Tried
(or: We exist on the best terms we can)

No Matter How Hard We Tried
(or: We exist on the best terms we can)

Między nami dobrze jest
translated by **Artur Zapałowski**

CHARACTERS

LITTLE METAL GIRL

HALINA

GLOOMY OLD BIDDY IN A WHEELCHAIR

BOŻENA

MAN

ACTOR

TV HOST

EDYTA

MONIKA

ACT ONE
SCENE 1

An old multi-story human tenement in Warsaw. A one-room apartment.Two doors: one looks onto a courtyard with recycling bins, the other barely muffles constant toilet noises, burbling water, and gurgling pipes. Spinning all the while outside the window is the wild, all-consuming merry-go-round of the big city with its trams, cars, horns, and airplanes flying past across the low-hung sky and setting the bottle of stale knock-off vermouth in the drinks cabinet rattling, the elaborate pyramids of chipped and leftover-encrusted pots and pans on the kitchen counter shaking, jittering the image on the ever-flickering TV, and short-circuiting the crackling overhead bulb. The interior looks as if it were built on a fault-line or were in the process of being bulldozed: Little Metal Girl in a sailor-suit and a rampant bow in her sparse metallic hair, and her wheelchair-bound grandma, Gloomy Old Biddy, with the tangled wiring of her braids or cobwebs dragging across the carpeting behind her, are inside it like passengers on a sinking ship – teetering between panic and boredom, mindless activity and mindless torpor, claustrophobia, and fear of open spaces. As is typicalwhen dealing with people doomed to one another's company, it is hard to tell whether they are chasing or fleeing one another, or, weary of both, remaining stock-still. Between their alternating fits of inertia and hyperactivity, the girl's mother, Halina, performs her daily chores with the placidity of a mechanized beast of burden, and is currently taking out the trash

GLOOMY OLD BIDDY IN A WHEELCHAIR
I still remember the day the war broke out…

LITTLE METAL GIRL
The what broke out?

GLOOMY OLD BIDDY IN A WHEELCHAIR
The war. Back then, I was a fair young lass, my face like the spring, heart aflutter in my youthful breast like a quail caught in a…

LITTLE METAL GIRL
In a pail.

GLOOMY OLD BIDDY IN A WHEELCHAIR
I could still walk on my own two feet back then. God, how I used to walk.

LITTLE METAL GIRL
You and your "how I used to walk."

GLOOMY OLD BIDDY IN A WHEELCHAIR
Of course I used to walk. I remember how...

LITTLE METAL GIRL
You must be all walked-out, what with walking so much, gran. Now you can finally NOT go somewhere. Jeez, if I was you, I'd sure love to not go somewhere; my English class, for one.

GLOOMY OLD BIDDY IN A WHEELCHAIR
Back and forth, back and forth. My, how we used to walk places before the war. To the cinema, for waffles and cupcakes, down to the river. Across the sand, over the ground, down to the river. On the grass, on velvety violets, down to the river on hot summer days, when its thick, clear current, etched by sunbeams like a crystal decanter...

LITTLE METAL GIRL
What river are you talking about?

GLOOMY OLD BIDDY IN A WHEELCHAIR
What river? The Vistula, of course.

LITTLE METAL GIRL
That shit-stream? Jeez!

GLOOMY OLD BIDDY IN A WHEELCHAIR
What shit-stream? The Vistula: right here. Clogs on your feet, a slice of bread in your hand, and off you'd go to bathe, bask and daydream, dream the sweetest, holiest dreams of youth, pure as the tears down your cheeks...

LITTLE METAL GIRL
What's bread? Nah, just kidding. I love swimming in the Vistula too – it's a timeless thrill. Whenever I climb out onto the bank, spluttering gasoline with gusto, I get fistula, typhoid, and cadmium poisoning, and I'm dead, and I get a sick note so I don't have to go to school.

GLOOMY OLD BIDDY IN A WHEELCHAIR
We used to catch minnows, small and sprightly. How they'd flap about, the little rascals, smudging our hands with their oily silver scales.

LITTLE METAL GIRL
You don't say, gran. We catch johnnies too sometimes – used condoms, that is. How they squirm and struggle to be free! It cracks the guys up, but I see red when I realise how many wily, opportunistic potential Polacks wriggle out of existence every day.

GLOOMY OLD BIDDY IN A WHEELCHAIR
They all said that Hitler, Father said that Hitler fellow...

LITTLE METAL GIRL
And how they squirm! As if they thought the Vistula veered straight off to America somewhere in mid-Poland, so that they could be born over there with a hundred-and-fifty-dollar bill in one hand, and a three-hundred-and-fifteen-dollar bill in the other, while we'd be left to toil all alone in this potato field. Born, they'll be born, all right: with a broom and a dustpan, and a gnawed Christmas turkey drumstick from the garbage. Or rather they won't be born, cause of us plopping them in the you-know-what...

GLOOMY OLD BIDDY IN A WHEELCHAIR
Nobody believed in Hitler back then. We were young, hearts thrashing about in our breasts; thrashing about like a...

LITTLE METAL GIRL
... condom in a pail!

HALINA
What pail?

Enter Halina, with a freshly-emptied dustbin dangling dejectedly at her side, carefully wiping her slippers in the threshold. Pleased with herself, she carefully wipes her slippers on the doormat, and hangs the key on a hook. She could also be bringing coal or preserves from the cellar, or a child's sled, so useful for hauling laundry from the mangle in winter, but, most importantly, under her arm she has a freshly-unearthed treasure: a woman's magazine scavenged from the recycling container and read halfway to shreds.

HALINA
What's that about a pail? Mind your language!

LITTLE METAL GIRL
You're in such a huff, mom. It's as if I'd been conceived by means of your straddling a filthy seat on an InterNoCity train.

Halina bustles around in her kingdom – a kitchenette crammed to the ceiling with a veritable festival of charred, grungy pots and pans, recipes torn out of calendars, Tesco leaflets, carefully-preserved flyers from language schools, canned-food labels, and piles of carefully-washed used yogurt pots. Behind her, drooling hungrily and peeking over her shoulder, Little Metal Girl tries to get her hands on the sugar-bowl. Halina slaps her dirty mitts away.

HALINA
Had your lunch?

LITTLE METAL GIRL
Lunch? What's for lunch?

HALINA
Dry chuffs with vinegar.

LITTLE METAL GIRL *(lifting the lid of a pot)*
Dry chuffs, my favorite. What's that stink?

HALINA *(grabbing the pot away from her, and slamming the refrigerator door shut)*
Don't bother about that, I'll warm it up for my supper.

GLOOMY OLD BIDDY IN A WHEELCHAIR
And then the Germans entered Warsaw. Me in just my summer frock, nothing but my handbag, my handbag with only...

LITTLE METAL GIRL
Germans, Germans? I heard something about some kind of Germans... Oh yeah, they're the ones who yodel!

GLOOMY OLD BIDDY IN A WHEELCHAIR
Me with just my handbag, wearing only the frock with the roses...

LITTLE METAL GIRL
Wilted, I bet. Dried, that is!

GLOOMY OLD BIDDY IN A WHEELCHAIR
I was walking home from the Vistula because it was quite a hot day, my eyes still blue from gazing into the sleepy, cool, soapy, limpid...

LITTLE METAL GIRL
... filthy warm greenish foamy virulent currents of that shit-stream...

GLOOMY OLD BIDDY IN A WHEELCHAIR
... when suddenly...

LITTLE METAL GIRL WITH A SATCHEL ON HER SHOULDERS
When suddenly BANG!

GLOOMY OLD BIDDY IN A WHEELCHAIR
Beg pardon?

LITTLE METAL GIRL
Smoke, fire, flames. Did you see them, gran?

GLOOMY OLD BIDDY IN A WHEELCHAIR
Did I see what?

LITTLE METAL GIRL
It burning?

GLOOMY OLD BIDDY IN A WHEELCHAIR
What's burning?

LITTLE METAL GIRL
The bicycle. The bicycle.

GLOOMY OLD BIDDY IN A WHEELCHAIR
What bicycle?

LITTLE METAL GIRL
I dunno. The burning-bicycle smell was deafening, I'd know that particular stench anywhere.

GLOOMY OLD BIDDY IN A WHEELCHAIR
No I didn't see it.

LITTLE METAL GIRL
But I did.

Unperturbed by the family squabbles, Halina, after clanging the pot-lids a while to perk herself up a bit, brushes invisible crumbs off the table-top with her hand, which she then wipes on her cardigan, and, sighing to the heavens, settles down to read the newly-acquired magazine.

LITTLE METAL GIRL
What've you brought me-mom-mee? The latest discount coupons?

HALINA
No, it's Not For You magazine. Saw it lying in a wastepaper bin. Free, so I fig-ured, why not, I can afford it.

LITTLE METAL GIRL
Not bad.

HALINA
It's from last April. Just the thing not for me.

LITTLE METAL GIRL
They've even done the crossword for you.

HALINA
Now I know the hidden phrase without having to do it myself: "Springtime têteà-tête."

LITTLE METAL GIRL
Show-me-mom-mee. Springtime tête-à-tête... Hang on... Springtime snogging by the shit-stream?

HALINA
Has grandma not had her dinner yet?

LITTLE METAL GIRL
Gran, have you not had your dinner yet?

GLOOMY OLD BIDDY IN A WHEELCHAIR
What was for dinner?

HALINA
Lecso.

LITTLE METAL GIRL
Lecso. All sorts of gunk with paprika and Hungarian space-jizz. See also: soup of the week, soup of the month, waste not want not, World War II, famine.

GLOOMY OLD BIDDY IN A WHEELCHAIR
Oh, that. No, I haven't.

LITTLE METAL GIRL
Gran hasn't eaten.

HALINA
Why's that?

LITTLE METAL GIRL
The hell should I know? The hell should... I KNOW! I bet she's slimming. I'm slimming, too.

HALINA
Has grandma not been out anywhere today?

LITTLE METAL GIRL
Me! Me! Me! I didn't take gran out anywhere.

HALINA
Good. Now I don't have to not take her anywhere, not that I would anyway, because I won't be home from work until 11 PM.

LITTLE METAL GIRL
The thing is, gran's stuck in a building without an elevator all day long, with noone to talk to, so when I get back from school and watch TV 'till late, I don't have the time to wheel that old turnip around anywhere! Perkily did my pig-tails bounce in the breeze when we were out not strolling through the autumn park. She was telling me those gripping stories of hers, like when she went off to that concentration camp. I'd say she's ripping off scenes from The Great Escape and 'Allo, 'Allo, but whatever... We've got postmodernism after all.

HALINA
What are you on about? What kind of word is that?

LITTLE METAL GIRL
I don't know either, I just downloaded it. So there we were, not strolling to our heart's content, to and fro down lanes burnished by autumn, when all of a sudden, this nasty man starts bugging us. Come to think of it, he might have been German – all very debonair, he even bowed to us, clicked his heels and said: "Good day, Arzheimer's the name," but his name has slipped my mind. Some well-known name, starts with an A... Never mind. Anyway, I'd barely for-gotten his name when another man showed up. He also knocked, very debo-nair, with a wig on, and said: "I'm the renowned German philosopher..." You know, what's-his-name? The one who wrote the Critique Of Pure Reason, re-member? Because I can't... Yes, I. KANT. That's him! How the pair of them start-ed rambling on and muddling things... I felt my continued absence in gran's lack-of-a-room was beside the point, and awkward to boot. So, not wanting to disturb them, I went to my own lack-of-a-room, and sat here watching TV with you until it got dark.

Halina settles into the position of someone reading the paper and watching TV at the same time, a task hindered by the old biddy idling all over the place in her wheelchair.

HALINA
Your old man's a glassmaker, yo momma's a pane! You keep thinking you're transparent, mom. Why don't you have some of that gunk with paprika? Who did I not make it but kept pouring from pot to pot all week for?

LITTLE METAL GIRL
Bet she's on a diet; she doesn't want to be slim any more, just transparent.

GLOOMY OLD BIDDY IN A WHEELCHAIR
My, how we used to walk places before the war, did we ever run... to the cinema, for waffles and cupcakes, down to the river.

LITTLE METAL GIRL
Well, if you keep eating those waffles, eggnogs and such, then good luck. You'll never lose weight that way.

GLOOMY OLD BIDDY IN A WHEELCHAIR
Across the sand, over the ground, down to the river. A slice of bread in your hand, and off we'd go...

LITTLE METAL GIRL
You need to kiss the bread good-bye, especially white bread – it makes you fat. And you need to get around more. If you keep sitting in that wheelchair of yours, you'll never get any slimmer. You need to get about more, or push yourself around more at least. Quiet, I hear knocking. Knock-knock.

GLOOMY OLD BIDDY IN A WHEELCHAIR
Who's there?

LITTLE METAL GIRL
I'll open it and see. No... I thought it was World War II coming.

HALINA
What are you on about this time?!

LITTLE METAL GIRL
I swear. Well, never mind. Must have been some model airplanes flying past.

SCENE 2

The apartment and everything are as before. The biddy is in a stupor, the girl is bored and playing with a chicken push-toy. Eventually concluding the activity to be futile, she starts using the toy to push her granny around the apartment. Halina, half-peeved by the pushing and shoving, and half-inured to it, sinks back into her magazine, while catching, with acrobatic dexterity, various objects falling off the shelves and cabinets. People might be wandering round the courtyard throwing refuse into the relevant containers. Lurking among them might be the morbidly obese Bożena, who, commando-like, is keeping out of their line of sight behind containers incapable of concealing her offensively huge bulk. Gloomy Biddy manages to break free of the hijinks and hurriedly lock herself in the toilet amidst the soothing burbling of the pipes.

HALINA
"The primroses are in flower, and spring is well upon us, stirring us with its balmy breeze. You're more inclined not to go on invigorating walks; it's time not to break out that bicycle you don't own. Sunny afternoons are just made for physical activity, and seeing friends, whom you don't see because you have none, as well as for throwing picnics, and getting thrown out of restaurants, if you know what I mean. It's high time you spring-cleaned your wardrobe! So it's not back on the hanger with those greys, browns, bulky tights, thick sweaters, coats and jackets. Dare not to wear those breezy dresses you don't own and the fine tights you don't own either. Most likely you don't have any lighter jackets, but the one you do have certainly won't fit your fat frame. Not to worry. We have last year's tips to keep you from landing squarely on the sidelines with your finger on the sphincter of springtime trends."

LITTLE METAL GIRL
"Shake the moths out a little, spray on a little deodorisant, wash it a little, don't wash it a little, don't bother to wash it all a little. Don't take out of the closet and put on what you've slept in, and sleep in what you wear. Now just have nothing to wear a little and you're done! It takes absolutely no effort, and has just as much effect."

HALINA
"Skirt: Tesco, 28 zlotys. The grease stain lends it mystique. T-shirt: out of the closet, faded at the tits. Greys, browns and urine yellows, grease stains, and threadbare patches, are all in vogue this season, just like any other season. Sweat stains, our top tip: they'll show up on their own sooner than later. Men's socks – from the Russian Market: 17 pairs for 10 zlotys. Shoes – imitation leather. Everything for five zlotys – 12 zlotys. Accessories – plastic carrier bag. Onefifty, Lidl. Huge and hefty; capacity – 10 kilos of potatoes, five bottles of vinegar, chicken-feet, yesterday's issue of freebie Metro daily, with room left over for a little purse. Sink-washable.

LITTLE METAL GIRL
Last spring's treatments for complexions made gray by the winter, ruined by cigarettes, a bad diet, and coronary heart disease.

HALINA
Wash your face with soap and apply Nivea cream or plain old margarine. Scouring it with a towel will also work wonders.

LITTLE METAL GIRL WITH A SATCHEL ON HER BACK
Our tip: if you want your Nivea cream to last longer, don't use it.

HALINA
Don't wash one side of your head with your regular shampoo, or the other

side either, for that matter. Our top tip — the more you don't do this, the more apparent your hair-loss will be, and that disturbing shoe-cabinet and sweatin-glard aroma will linger longer in your locks. Last April is finally the time for the springtime sun not to glint in your dull and lifeless strands.

After a suitable interval, Biddy ineptly wheels herself back inside the apartment to the sound of flushing water.

LITTLE METAL GIRL
Don't oil your wheelchair: the shrill squeaking will be the perfect way to let others know you've just trundled in to resume your endless prattle...

HALINA
Will you look at that, mom, I could have sworn you went there for the peace and quiet, and, gracious, was I ever right (still engrossed in the magazine, she vigorously pushes the old biddy's wheelchair so it doesn't block the view of the TV set.

LITTLE METAL GIRL *(pretending to be reading to the Biddy)*
"In April last year, everything will be the way it was. You will get a mysterious letter: it might be a reminder from the gas company! Meaningful dates: the 15th. A windfall of mothballs awaits you. Meaningless dates: all the rest of them. Your lucky colour: transparent. Your lucky stone: the gallstone."

HALINA *(goes back to her reading)*
Phew! Right! "Now that you've got your wardrobe in order, it's time to sit back and wait for the lack of compliments, indifferent glances, and a slap on the kisser from time to time. Now you can relax and wait for World War II to come again, and for those yogurt pots you've been collecting so assiduously all these years to finally come in handy."

LITTLE METAL GIRL
Knock knock!

HALINA
Who's there?

LITTLE METAL GIRL *(peeking into the pots)*
It's just me, World War II back again. I see that not only do you have lots of yogurt pots, but that you've whipped up some delicious biohazard, too. I'm impressed.

HALINA
What are you on about? Go to your lack-of-a-room!

LITTLE METAL GIRL
I seem to be right here, but let me double-check. Hello? Hello! Where am I? Right here. Right here? Then go right here and stay there. Right away.

SCENE 3

Enter Bożena, sans knocking, with the agitation typical of someone who has nothing of import to impart, yet laboring under the delusion that they do. She is morbidly obese and mobility-impaired. Unable to shut the door behind her, she rips it off its hinges and puts it to one side. Puffing, grunting, and holding her aching back, she hurriedly staggers towards the armchair, onto which she immediately plops, as if unable to stand on her own two feet. Everything in the apartment rises by 40 cm.

BOŻENA
Sorry for not calling your mobile before I came, but I don't have a mobile – why should I when I'm fat as a pig? So I just dropped in.

HALINA
I'm not saying this just to be polite, but... God, you're so fat, just like a pig. You'll pant me out of house and home.

BOŻENA
Thank you. I can see it in your eyes. All the same, you could carry on showing contempt a bit longer, so as to spare me any doubts that I'm a fat pig, who shouldn't obnoxiously wobble around in other people's field of view. People should have the right to choose what makes them puke.

Taking advantage of Halina's preoccupation with lighting the stove, Little Metal Girl, bustling about the place in search of something to break or rip up, intercepts the magazine and starts reading it innocent as you please.

LITTLE METAL GIRL
"Star-sign: Fat Pig. Last April, Fat-Pigians can expect many wonderful surprises. Biedronka will launch a new, affordable luncheon meat – *Ye Olde Poultry Loin*. Ingredients: water (97%), pork rinds, dishwashing liquid, windowcleaner, gelatine, spices; as well as a new brand of out-of-date cream – *A Few Days Off*. Ingredients: water, gelatine, white coloring, thickener, thinner, decalcifier, detoxifier, live salmonella cultures. Wash down what others won't eat with what they won't drink. It's time you accepted who you are and reinvented yourself. So try and get out a lot and go for walks because, like all Fat-Pigians, you ARE a fat pig, but don't go out for walks, especially in other people's field of view: they have the right to puke for better reasons than that."

Virtually unnoticed, she puts down the magazine. Bożena glances at it with thinly veiled curiosity, but doesn't dare lay her hands on it.

BOŻENA
Ooh, what a lovely mag – *Not For You*.

HALINA
That's right, *Not For Us*.

BOŻENA
It's very nice.

HALINA
I bought it in the waste-paper bin today. It was a bargain: for free, and the crossword was solved to boot. Such a lovely surprise, as if I had the time to do crosswords!

BOŻENA
Now that I'm performing the duties of a filth removal specialist in personal private premises, like I always have, I simply have no time for that sort of thing. The work's by no means demanding, but it's tiring and unsatisfying.

HALINA
I can relate to that, because, as a specialist in charge of shifting palettes in the tried-and-tested manual fashion in the retail sector, I have to get up before I go to bed, and I come home from work much later than I get up for it the next day. But, in the future I don't have, I'll be up for promotion to manager in charge of electronically determining the real weight of goods in the fruit and vegetable section; so I figure, why not give it a shot?

BOŻENA
Sure, you've got what it takes. Language skills – Foreign. Job experience – Street-corner advertising material dispatcher; national scent ambassador via direct frottage in buses and trams for Old Bag fragrance, with its dominant note of sweat, subtly complemented by hints of musk, mothballs, and old soup...

HALINA (*fussing around in the kitchen, blending impressive expertise with total futility*)
I keep thinking about the holiday I won't be having. I've been reading up on it, and I've finally decided: no way, we're not going on holiday again this year.

BOŻENA
You don't say!

HALINA
That's right! We're not going again this year.

BOŻENA
So where is it you're not going to?

HALINA
Nowhere.

BOŻENA
Naturally, where else? We're not going to the seaside this year. God, it's just so unaffordable! We haven't got the money! Besides, I'm fat as a pig and shouldn't obnoxiously wobble around in other people's field of view.

HALINA
Sure thing, you bet.

BOŻENA
On our way, we'll not stop off in Kobyłka, where we've got a cousin, and we'll be going nowhere straight from there!

HALINA
I guess I'll see you there, then – call my lack-of-a-mobile, you've got the number. Nowhere, good old nowhere: all the memories it brings back! But it's getting crowded there lately. I mean: my brother-in-law, sister-in-law, brother, uncle, cousin and sister are all there already...

BOŻENA
How dark and cozy it is in here!

HALINA *(vigorously pushes Old Biddy's wheelchair which is blocking her view and stopping her from simultaneously talking, following the TV show, and pawing at the magazine)*
Your old man's a glassmaker, yo momma's a pane! Mom, if you think you've turned transparent, better think again. And you, go to your lack-of-a-room!

LITTLE METAL GIRL
That's where I seem to be right now, but let me double-check. Hello? Where am I? Ah, here I am. Just where I thought I was.

Little Metal Girl once again intercepts the magazine without anyone noticing.

LITTLE METAL GIRL
"Unlike the apartments designed nowadays, in which family members fruitlessly call to one another for hours down spacious corridors, halls, and separate bedrooms, trying to figure out their own whereabouts, not to mention those of their nearest and dearest, these claustrophobic, cramped quarters give an impression of smallness, and it's here that the whole extended family

eat, sleep, excrete, can't sleep, toss and turn, vomit and get the shits, don't live, and die, all without ever having to look for one another, but nevertheless still find themselves there. This effect has been achieved with a simple architectural trick: the apartment has been cleverly partitioned so that Little Metal Girl's lack-of-aroom, the gloomy cripple's lack of peace and quiet, and the anxieties of Halina (51) all fit into the same room, where all day long they make no room for one another. It's hard to believe that they've also managed to fit in an entire authentic 1970s (fiberboard) furniture set. Over the years, its surfaces have been finely buffed, scratched and utterly covered in children's scribbles. Moreover, a blend of foodstuffs, hard drinks and bodily fluids has veneered this King Mieszko set with a remarkable, grime-like palimpsest. The edges of the wallpaper have been slightly moistened and torn, while the mildew on the wall, covered by a wall-hanging, isn't there at all. An old halva box, the tastefullyframed lid of a Solidari-Tea tin, a plastic ribbon pinned to a potted asspidistra, the odd vegetable-peelings and chicken bones strewn here and there, quaint, fluffy dust-balls, a year's worth of freebie Metro daily, a 'casually-placed' tube of periodontal paste, yogurt pots... It's not that the local brats have knocked the trash over, it's just..."

HALINA *(irritated, snatching the paper and putting it back in its safe place on the table)*
She won't give me a moment's peace!

LITTLE METAL GIRL
But I am in my lack-of-a-room!

SCENE 4

In the kitchen, Halina is scraping at her pots and pans, Little Metal Girl pushes the wheelchair until it gains momentum then nimbly hops on the back and scoots around the TV until the wheelchair falls over on its side. At this point, all the pills stashed in the blanket on Biddy's lap could come cascading, Pachinkolike, onto the floor. Unable to return her grandma to an upright position, the Girl leaves her lying on the carpet, mopes around in search of something to do, then starts scratching varnish off the furniture with a nail. The recumbent old biddy braids her hair or knits a ten-meter snood. She then puts away the needlework and starts wriggling in a desperate attempt to sit up. In her armchair, Bożena plucks up the courage to reach out for Not For You *magazine. With trembling hands, she turns a few pages, then starts leafing through it with increasing confidence, and even hazards a comment.*

BOŻENA
This personality quiz hasn't been done yet.

HALINA
Well there you go.

BOŻENA
I'll do it so it doesn't go to waste. "Are you a: spontaneous excursionist, a hearth-hugging stay-at-home, a sexy vamp, an overworked workaholic, an imaginative troublemaker, an inveterate globetrotter, a fat pig, or a cut-price frozen panga from Liddull?"

HALINA *(wiping her hands on her sweater, and looking over Bożena's shoulder)*
I'm an inveterate globetrotter, me.

BOŻENA
That's right, "A" – same here. "All A's – you're an inveterate globetrotter."
Why don't I tick one "B" just to mess with them. There, finished!

HALINA
Do mine in a different colour, so we don't mix them up. Seems like a silly game, but it's right on the nail.

BOŻENA
Isn't it just! Remember how I didn't go to France and how I'll never set foot there again? French fries and French bread – they really go for that over there, but it's just like Wrocław White, worse even. The monumental outline of the famous Eyefull Tower that's supposed to be so tall, they say, but in the paper it looked about so big, shorter than my finger.

HALINA
That's nothing, we didn't go to Italy, but I wasn't at all happy that we didn't go. What a waste of time! Food's nothing to write home about: Sardines, Roman lettuce, Italian meatballs, Neapolitans, and their pizza's just cut-price Tesco deep-freeze, with mildew, no less! I had one, couldn't waste it, but the digesting part didn't go down too well, so the trip ended up in York, if you know what I mean. Besides, what's the point of going to Italy, now that the Pope's no longer the man, but a Ger-man. Good thing I didn't go there and didn't take any photos. Now I can not show them to you.

GLOOMY OLD BIDDY IN A WHEELCHAIR *(rolls up in her creaking wheelchair)*
Until Warsaw was invaded by the Germans...

LITTLE METAL GIRL
Germans? Oh yeah, they're the ones who yodel!

HALINA *(edifyingly)*
Germans are people who live in the Federal Republic. They never reuse their

plastic bags, but just throw them out; and as for yogurt pots, they don't even bother with those. If they have any chicken skins left over, what'll they make their aspic in, I wonder? And when World War II comes again, they'll have to come running to us.

Bożena produces, from God-knows-where, a charred and slobbery photoalbum.

HALINA
How fat you are! How untanned! My, my! It's a wonder you fit inside the frame.

BOŻENA
This is where we didn't go. We didn't go here either. And that there's not us. I would have shown you if I had the album (pockets the album as quickly as she had produced it)

HALINA
Some people have it good. Dead lucky they are.

BOŻENA
Sure. Takes luck to be dead.

SCENE 5

The stagnation continues. Halina and Bożena are lost in thought, their hands folded pensively on their midriffs. The creak of Biddy's wheelchair, the scratching of Little Metal Girl's nail on the cabinets, or the grating and crackling noises as she stabs at the wiring.

HALINA
Would you like something to eat? I found a great recipe here – "LECSO: Take *Ye Olde Luncheon Meat* from Tesco's; don't throw it out, just scrape off the mildew; sauté it when it turns slimy, then cut it into a few slices of prosciutto. Grate some mock-cheese into Parmesan once its consistency has started to resemble chewed plasticine, otherwise it might still be good for something. Add it to a pot of old mushroom soup, which should have acquired a pearly glaze by now..."

BOŻENA
Where do you get the soup from?

HALINA
Cook it the week before.

BOŻENA
That IS simple. What are those bitter, rancid thingies sprinkled on top?

HALINA
Pine nuts.

BOŻENA
Pine? What kind of nuts are those?

HALINA
Never heard of them myself, but they're quite good, kind of like bargain-bin peanuts – one and the same actually. My tip is: they don't taste rancid at all if you don't eat them. You can also add bread wrappers, gristle and veins... Don't throw them out, fry in suet, boil in chicken-foot stock, mince, then refry, don't throw it out, just add more salt, store in yogurt pots, reheat, heat up, refry, eat. If it starts frothing – puke it up... (not that you really have to) and voilà! They might laugh now, but next time World War II comes around, they'll be wolfing it down like so many Hoovers.

BOŻENA
Thank you. Look at me: so fat and still gorging myself. Gobbling it up like a Hoover, I am. Dig in, piggy, dig in! It'll put hairs on your chest. I'd serve it with breadcrusts.

HALINA
I'm sorry it's all make-believe, but I ate everything before it spoiled.

BOŻENA
Right. Well, never mind. I'll be off now. Tomorrow I have to get up before I go to bed.

HALINA
When I get home much later than I'll get up, I'll still have to clean the lake with newspaper.

BOŻENA
I'm out of here.

HALINA
If anybody asks, I'm out of here too.

Meanwhile, Little Metal Girl sneaks up again and starts reading the women's magazine.

Little Metal Girl

„The air of apparent chaos and bric-a-brac haphazardness pervading this beautiful old, utterly devastated apartment has been achieved thanks to genuine chaos and haphazardness. The overall mess could well be mistaken for a real mess, which it actually is. Now it's over to our resident interior decorator: 'This miserable dump is actually a beautiful pre-war apartment, but, despite the ongoing failure to renovate the premises since the war ended, or thereabouts, it still lacks the tidiness, dryness and spaciousness so fashionable of late. There are two possible ways out of this annoying nightmare: The first, yet rather expensive, option is to convert this hole into a wine-cellar, and move into a luxury apartment. Graceful shelves and stands, if properly placed, might permit the storage of several truly tasty vintages here! Or, more affordably: the family members all kill one another to return in more fitting incarnations – or simply never get born and don't live at all, which is far better for all concerned, especially for all the others concerned. As for the building, it would be best if it were bombed (preferably during the war, as bombing might prove hard to do later on), the rubble giving way to a fairly elegant high-rise building, in which normal people could buy apartments, furnish them with RIKKA sofa-beds from IKEA, STAKKA tables from IKEA, ROSTE vases, HAMMA flowers, in LIKKE water, GRETTA ambient air, and their own SELVVES, and, while paying off their mortgage for the next 40 years, they could drop by for a snooze after work, wash their butts, and go back again.'"

ACT TWO
SCENE 1

The same interior with the same two doors and window, outside of which the city leers ravenously; the same gurgling in the pipes, and sounds of soccer coverage and sexual intercourse heard through the walls, with the same environmentally friendly garbage cans outside. A Man comes into the apartment: elegant, scrubbed, and stylish, he looks around and scowls at the moldy plaster, the peeling wallpaper, and the scuffed wheelchair-marks on the carpet. Neat Swedish workmen from IKEA come in behind him bearing cardboard boxes, which they put down in the places the man indicates with his foot. The man uses spit to stick several stylish heirloom pictures from IKEA on the walls. The pictures either immortalize the beauty of his ancestors, or depict gerberas and sunflowers in extreme close-up (oil on canvas). The man takes a laptop and a bottle of wine out of his briefcase, and starts drinking.

MAN
They've shut up at last! I totally can't focus on my feature film screenplay e titled "The Horse Rode Horseback" which caused quite a buzz and scooped up all the awards! It takes place in Poland, in places like Łódź or Wałbrzych, or a mining village in Lower Silesia, but it's partly shot on location in Lithuania, and partly in Katowice. The hero, whom I'm calling JASIEK for now, lives in a radioactive block of flats. One day, his drunken father, a coal-miner, staggers into a glass-fronted sideboard left behind by the Germans, breaking both his arms and legs. Jasiek's family falls on hard times. To support his cancer-stricken family, the boy is unemployed and falls in with the wrong crowd. Violence reigns amid gloomy run-down residential housing, leaking batteries, burning bicycles, and CGI slag-heaps, on one of which our hero sees the deaf and blind but still passable MONIKA, dejectedly using a stick to rummage through the shifting pixels. He befriends her. Together they pick scrap in the radioactive rubble of the run-down Gdańsk shipyard so perfectly recreated for us in Chernobyl. Monika teaches him to see the things that our hectic, weekly lifestyles prevent us normal people from noticing. Until one day, Jasiek's brother falls ill with leukaemia. Undaunted, Jasiek takes fate into his own hands.

Not bothering to knock, the Actor enters the room making anguished gestures.

ACTOR
I don't want to live in this apartment building anymore!

MAN
To make matters worse, there's this queer always hanging around, whom everyone treats with intolerance in this Polish den of bigotry, though he turns out to be a normal guy, who's simply well-groomed and not tolerated.

ACTOR
I want to live in some other apartment building!

MAN
The penultimate scene: Jasiek's parents' apartment. It's stuffy, typically Polish: cramped and squalid. Jasiek's mother is washing her feet in the sink, his under-aged sister, still a baby, is playing with fish-bones wrapped in a greasestained Polish flag. The camera pans across the trembling father sprawled in delirium on the couch and drinking dirty brake-fluid through a hose coming out of a flagon, which makes him throw up blood violently onto the scruffy carpeting. Pan to window. A solitary stray sunbeam plays upon the grimy, stillnot- double-glazed window. Digital zoom through the pane: In the courtyard paper-recycling bin, a sweet mongrel puppy is frolicking with a discarded magazine such as FOR YOU, on the cover of which is a pretty smiling young woman's face. Now let any of those two-bit critics tell me I don't leave the audience any room for hope!

SCENE 2

Enter the TV Host with a sheaf of papers flying every which way. She stuffs the brand-name tags dangling from her apparel up her sleeves, and, without so much as a look at her interlocutor, sits down in an armchair, twisting her legs into a graceful braid. She starts reading from a piece of paper, as if her mind were on other, more important things. The actor's replies can be spontaneous, but he can also be glancing at a magazine, or reading haltingly from a prompt sheet, or playing a cassette and lip-synching to it.

TV HOST
You play Jasiek in the exciting and talked-about film "The Horse Rode Horseback." Why don't you let us in on your secret? How do you manage to look so great?

ACTOR
I drink a liter of regular real liquid water a day. I also eat fruit and vegetables made out of organic fruit and vegetables. I try to avoid sweets, fast food and cigarettes because they have 1100 calories. I work out regularly; I trim my nose and ear hair. My wife even laughs at me and calls me a poof. Not that she has anything against gays, mind you. She just makes fun of that endearingly comical, distasteful effeminacy of theirs.

TV HOST
I see. *(She puts her notes in order, crosses out something, then stares at something else. She reads from her notes hastily and with some difficulty).*
Your character also goes through a life-changing experience. Set against the backdrop of a Poland that time forgot, in an age of transition and rampant

capitalism, our homespun "here and now," our homespun "over there and no sooner than 2045," our homespun "the West is there already, and we're not," our homespun "how I hate the Kaczyński twins," our homespun "and off I dive into my piggy-print sheets where I... snore-snore." What made you go into acting? What do you have?

ACTOR
I have a car, a regular one for driving, and an off-roader for driving off the road, and I have an apartment, and a wife with whom I share my great love of me. I have a daughter, and I want to spend as much time as I can with her... but sadly, I drink a bit, and then I snort coke, and then I get sleepy and agitated, so I have to snort more, until I get incoherent and the only prescription is more coke, so I snort on the set, off the set, before rehearsals, before the show and after the show. Even before this interview I had to chop out a line this long in order to get that rapturous feeling of me being me and the happeningness of things happening; I don't feel a thing, I've stopped sleeping with the wife, and I don't give a shit about my daughter. I've sold both my cars and the apartment, but I'm through with that crap now, and I've started drinking to unwind a bit, and at night off I dive into my piggy-print sheets where I... snore-snore... I'm such a... What? A sleepyhead!

TV HOST
As a child, you were said to be short, but that changed as you got older. And now for my last question. Can you describe your average everyday day?

ACTOR
It was a very demanding part, very demanding. A lot of scenes were actually shot in Poland. We stayed in the local hotels, some didn't even have shampoo, soap or separate foot-towels. That's why I'm in need of peaceful total silence, rest, meditation, and a new off-roader. I also want to go to Peru and drive a quad through the cradle of our civilisation. Then another week on vodka, a week of coke, a couple of days' detox, psychotherapy, and three days as a tampon in a Hellinger Constellation. I also mean to get around to reading all the titles and the last name of the author of books by that famous Hoolybeck. And then off I dive into my piggy-print sheets where I... you know what. I'm such a... sleepyhead. I also enjoy fine wine: I like drinking it, and pissing it out. Of an evening, I like chilling to this smooth-jazz compilation that came free with Knorr soup... *(Saying this, the actor opens a door in the wall unit, revealing a cabinet resplendent with bottles of wine, which he proceeds to take out and place on the table).*

TV HOST
Not familiar with it...

ACTOR
It's a very well-known soup. Wine, wine, wine is like a prayer. You have no idea what an arduous, complex, intricate, all-but mantra-like process goes into its making. Each and every bottle in my cellar has a vivid tale to tell, like a symphony of elaborate processes, procedures, formulae, and people's hard work, patience, knowledge of the rules, and time, time, time. Just picture this, if you have the imagination for it...

The two of them abandon their armchairs and assume positions traditionally associated with weather-persons.

ACTOR
China – little Feng-Shui stands by the production line, making grapes. His serial number in this huge European fruit factory is 1,760,182... which numerologically adds up to a Six, and that means... He sticks pips into the pulp and wraps it in skins 32 hours a day, in peril of his life, for which he has no break, and no hope. He doesn't loaf around – there are 15 million other fouryear-olds just like him, waiting to take his place. He works quickly and gives it his all, not wanting the foreman to notice his exhaustion otherwise he might get transferred to a less inspiring job, such as assembling blackberries or attaching stems to blueberries. At night, he goes back to his shed made of twigs, eats Korean-flavoured Chinese pot noodles, and dives into his pile of discount Chinese bras and panties, and... snore-snore.

TV HOST
Meanwhile, an old Indian woman named Delhi is scurrying about, wearing those incense-reeking blotchy rags she got practically free down at the Oriental shop. For breakfast today, she'll make do with a little curry powder. She hurriedly lowers the branch to bar the door of her car-tire hovel, and rushes to sift grains of sand: only the roundest and most symmetrical ones can be made into bottles.

ACTOR
Now it's time for the Polish economic migrants: Jan from Tłuszcz, with a PhD in social sciences, is shaping soil into lumps and painting them black. Back in Poland he was a jack-of-all-trades. Maria, a downsized weaver from Łódź, is devotedly helping him out. Into the lumps she weaves imitation earthworms, artificial beetle grubs, and roots painstakingly braided around real roots. Now it's time to go to her second job: after hours she cuts out serrations and paints tiny veins onto leaves. No wonder – she was always artistically gifted, and has a graphic arts degree from the Academy. She looks after every penny, and thehard-earned money will allow her to buy a ticket back to Poland, plus the airport taxes. Meanwhile, political prisoners from Russia are wiping the air clean of exhaust fumes. And children in Uzbekistan are selecting the prettiest sunbeams...

TV Host
And then chop-chop, hocus-pocus, the wine goes onto the racks, into the boxes, crates, and trucks. Along the way, several not particularly attractive Bulgarian women by the roadside will manage to fill their pails with foreign condoms, or maybe not. And then there's the checkout girl from Tesco who breaks a bottle and, to pay for it, takes out a loan without guarantees, endorsers, or her husband's consent. Unable to repay it, she hangs herself on her handbag strap. Her desperate deed makes the photo-feature section in many a tabloid. Exactly how the quick-witted photographer managed to capture the suicide as it happened will remain forever unremarked by the horror-struck readers, but will strengthen their reluctance to leave their houses after 4:30 PM.

Halina and Bożena appear out of nowhere, coming back from either the basement or the toilet or somewhere else altogether, and quickly take their erstwhile places: Bożena in the armchair with her hands folded on her gut, and Halina by the cooking range with the tabloid spread out in front of her.

Halina *(reading the tabloid)*
"She hanged herself on her handbag strap! Before that, they killed and raped her, rolled her up in a carpet, and braided its fringes. They were ruthless!"

Bożena
You don't say?

Halina
Look at the pictures! They cut off her head and used it to play ball with her legs! Me, I never go out after 4:30 PM anymore because it's dangerous, and besides I don't leave work until 11 PM.

Bożena
Me neither, I don't go out after 4:30 PM or any other time because I'm fat as a pig, and I shouldn't wobble around in other people's field of view. It's their field of view and they have every right to puke for better reasons than that.

Halina and Bożena quickly walk off, or leave the stage in some less obvious way. The Actor and the TV Host sit back down in the armchairs. The changeover is very fast. The Actor sits down at the table, and starts handling the bottles and stroking their labels with undisguised pleasure. He wipes the glasses, inspects them under the light, and pours the wine.

Actor
So you see, this ridiculously expensive wine is truly worth the price, and today, in the Vistula, your urine will really blow away other people's urines. Have a sip. Well?

TV Host *(tasting, sniffing, smacking her lips, swirling the liquid in its glass)*
Well... Nice glass.

Actor
Exactly. That's because I drank it all. And this is my cork collection: I drank this one. I drank this one. I drank this. I drank this. I drank it! This one I didn't drink. My wife necked it out of sheer delight, when she realized whose wife she was.

TV Host
Well then, you can be sure that when World War II comes back, your corks will really blow away the flames in the fire.

Little Metal Girl appears in the doorway, gracefully swinging her pigtails.

Little Metal Girl
Knock knock!

TV Host
Who's there?

Little Metal Girl
It's me again, World War II, I've brought some flames along. Nobody here but us flames. Wow, did you really drink all this? What splendid corks. Mind if we lick at them?

Actor
Not at all. Frankly, I do it myself sometimes.

TV Host
Society has many problems. Your character comes from a dysfunctional family, his father drinks... Thanks for the interview. Best of luck. Goodbye.

SCENE 3

Edyta is pacing the apartment, unable to find a place for herself. Well-dressed, with a handbag and a face puffed up with tears, she is chain-smoking slim cigarettes, and holding a dismal pair of soggy and flaccid lace panties. Halina takes out the garbage, while Bożena crouches commando-like behind the garbage can.

EDYTA
Ohmigod, how I cried watching that film, I was so moved! You could wring the discharge from my panties. I guess I'll have to throw them out and buy a new pair, because these are out of fashion anyway! It was all so moving, so cruel. I keep moaning about my problems and complexes and that my titties

are as small as socks, but now I see that, with the grace of God, other people have it worse, and life is just so real! I can still see the mother rinsing her privates in the washbasin, and her father the miner drinking brake-fluid through a hose coming out of a flagon and vomiting onto the carpet. I haven't been so afraid since Freddy Krueger and that rollercoaster, because we're blinded by our selfishness. After all, we could have been born as someone else, not us. It wasn't bound to be that way.

BOŻENA
A word of advice to the characters in the film: if your husband or boyfriend drinks brake fluid, I'd wholeheartedly recommend RUBOLEUM flooring – vomit and blood mops up easier, and it stinks less, while people with cataracts, and especially the blind, might even take it for a parquet floor. But I won't say that, because I'm fat as a pig and won't go imposing my point of view on people.

HALINA
I didn't like that film at all. Nothing but cursing and cigarette-smoking. I like films about pretty ladies, them dancing, them singing, them not living and not shitting. A film about horses. Horses! What do I care about horses?! Incidentally, that's just my subjective opinion, because I haven't seen the film.

EDYTA
Ohmigod, I was so afraid today when I saw the checkout girl at Tesco. Ohmigod, I was scared to think that someone could let herself go so much. Ohmigod, it scared me; all she needed was a few minor tweaks: a good hairdresser, a touch of makeup and at least five hours' sleep instead of two, and she'd look like a normal person. Ohmigod, I was scared that might not be enough, and she'd still need a hair graft, a face transplant, and possibly a whole new body and personality, a new set of ancestors going back four generations, plus a brand new wardrobe, and she should also change her date and, above all, her country of birth, and she might be able to look like a normal person. I haven't been so afraid since Freddy Krueger and that rollercoaster. I haven't been so afraid since "Critters." Life is just so real, injustice is just so unjust, the disadvantaged are completely disadvantaged, and social sensitivities are so sensitive. Today I swore that as soon as I found a river, from which I could save people from drowning, or a fire, from which I could save people from burning... Though that might not be so easy, because disasters are hard to find in peacetime, when all the wars are in other countries, and that limits your options for performing out-and-out good deeds. So at least I'll buy a kilo of nice sweets and I won't take them to an orphanage, I'll just eat them in the car myself to calm my nerves – munch munch munch. Why don't I just take all the handouts by the underpass and wait until I'm round the corner before I throw them away. Or else, instead of hanging around in underpasses after 4:30 PM, because it's dangerous, I'll sort out the junk in my handbag: plastic with plas-

tic... paper with paper... lipstick with lipstick...

Edyta fussily takes stock of the contents of her handbag. She leaves the room, and meticulously segregates all unnecessary items and throws them in the appropriate containers. Bożena makes to grab the magazine, but Halina is nimbler and more assertive.

EDYTA
Would you believe this mess? It's last April's FOR YOU magazine, with the crossword puzzle done! Into the waste-paper bin with you! What a mess, everything's laying around, the environment's dying, and whenever I look for anything, all I end up with is dirty fingernails!

HALINA
Oh, it's last April's NOT FOR YOU magazine. Lovely! It's cheap, for free, I can afford it.

Halina leafs through the magazine. Little Metal Girl rides up on a squeaky kid's bicycle and ventures a glance at the glossy pages.

LITTLE METAL GIRL
Not bad at all.

HALINA
It's from last April. Just the thing not for me.

LITTLE METAL GIRL
They've even done the crossword for you.

HALINA
So I know the hidden phrase without having to do it myself: "Springtime tête-àtête."

LITTLE METAL GIRL
Show-me-mom-mee. Springtime tête-à-tête... Hang on... Springtime snogging by the shit-stream?

SCENE 4

All the characters are in the apartment: the Man is sitting at his table, now strewn with wine-bottles, smoked cigarettes and half-snorted lines of dope, his heirloom paintings of ancestral gerberas have long-since come unstuck and fallen off the walls. Halina, Bożena, Gloomy Old Biddy, and Little Metal Girl are sitting in their natural positions and avidly following the action on TV.

MAN
Cut! Obviously that wasn't the end, but just the beginning, a brief overview of the out-takes that didn't make it into the final cut of the film, as a goodwill gesture towards the 4 million punters who didn't come to see the film, because they wouldn't fork out 20 zlotys for a ticket, not to mention the "Buy 8 Get 2 Free" nachos, M&M's, sugar-frosted nuts, Coke and seven beers, just to get a glimpse of dumpsville and listen to fake barfing in Dolby Surround, as if they didn't get the real thing in Dolby Surround every day. So I had to agree to some minor concessions, a man's got to make a living somehow, I've got a mortgage to pay off too! Monika is tired of being blind and deaf...

HALINA
No wonder, you'd have to be blind to want to be deaf!

LITTLE METAL GIRL
She might not be blind or deaf, but she's too fat. She ought to lose weight.

BOŻENA
She ought to lose weight and change her outfit. Dressed like that, I wouldn't even go and buy vinegar from Biedronka!

MAN
... Monika decides to break with her dead-end life and give it her best shot. She sells the rotting coop with her favourite pigeons and buys a ticket to Warsaw. There, she moves into a computer rendering in an advertising brochure for a gated community...

GLOOMY OLD BIDDY
Is that really Warsaw? Solec Street? I don't recognise it...

LITTLE METAL GIRL
Oh gran, it's that building, you know, the one they haven't built yet.

GLOOMY OLD BIDDY
I was walking down there the day the war broke out...

HALINA
Some people's noses get longer, others blow smoke, while others still can do it with a deadpan expression, but, whatever the method, it's all: Strictly Bullshit!

LITTLE METAL GIRL
It's not nice to keep nicking someone else's life and passing it off as your own in stories to slobber on your pillow to! All my life, ever since I can remember, gran never walked anywhere or went to any con-densation camp either.

MAN

... Where she finds a job with an advertising agency as an up-and-coming copy-writer, in a reputable law firm as a successful solicitor, and in a design studio as a gorgeous architect. She works a lot professionally, and has a fax machine, but after work she feels lost, because she has no kids. She goes down to the Photoshop where she sips Knorr soup...

HALINA

Monika, don't overpay! You can get the same soup, only worse, in Biedronka for half the price.

BOŻENA

Soup on its own won't fill you up: you'll just get hungry again! Try adding noodles, or some bones at least.

LITTLE METAL GIRL

Don't make her add noodles! She'll never lose weight. She'll stay fat, and obesity is an illness.

BOŻENA

Maybe in that backward Poland of yours. Things are completely different back home in America. That was just a thought, because I'm fat as a pig and I won't go imposing my point of view on people.

MAN

There, she meets Max: they touch lips naked in the toilet and then in the elevator. Nonetheless, they run into problems. Monika is fed up with the emptiness and lack of values, while Max turns out to be an irresponsible slacker who doesn't want to start a family, but keeps a cabinet full of cut-price brown flour next to his Knorr soup...

HALINA

He's overpaying. Regular's much cheaper.

MAN

... Hot on his heels are three heavy-set, sloppily self-tanned Colombians from the Russian mafia, a sexy policewoman, a bungling, Tramal-addicted gumshoe, and a gay hairdresser. The latter, though not tolerated, turns out to be a good guy and saves a poor child from a fire, because in fact he isn't gay at all, just a normal guy who's simply well-groomed and not tolerated.

LITTLE METAL GIRL

I hate intolerance. Seriously. I also hate those Vanilla Swirl and Malt Creme chocolates from selection boxes. Rock on!

MAN
Monika gives birth to a husband and kids, a boy or a girl, and feels very happy and fulfilled as a woman. She has frank chats with her toilet-bowl about the new Domestos. Looming on the horizon are three computer-simulated sky-scrapers, and they walk off laughing hand in hand. The End. That would be the last scene of the film, if I ever got round to making it.

TV HOST
Hi. Just recently she was digging through pixels on a slag-heap, and today she's a big star. She sold her rotting pigeon-coop, and took the one shot she had, and today she'll be openly laying bare the contents of her handbag.

MONIKA
In my bag, I normally carry the items I need most: a magnetic lasso tool plus Alt, a polygonal lasso tool, an eye dropper tool, a paintbrush, brightness/con-trast, colours, gradients, masks, a Shift key, and I'm never without an eraser – it's especially handy for pubic hair, which is so easy to come by these days.

TV HOST
So the life of a star is not all as one would think – whee and coochie-coo with a polyester cat on a red carpet, but...

MONIKA
Honestly...? ... It's hard work. There were times when after a whole day of mo-notonous non-eating, non-drinking, followed by non-pissing and nonshi ting, and non-sweating in between, I was so squashed, stretched and weary that I'd lie down on the Photoshop couch, too weak to go to the house I was too tired to remember I didn't have, because I didn't exist, and for days and nights on end I lay there waiting for someone to come along and unsquash and un-stretch me, not to mention the phantom pain I had after having my navel re-moved. And yet I owe a lot to not existing and not being. On the one hand I'm nobody, but then again, I'm not Polish.

TV HOST
If that's the case, your Polish is excellent – you speak it with hardly any accent at all.

MONIKA
It wasn't easy. I was born here as a little baby, entirely by chance. You see, this is where my great-great-grandparents, great-grandparents, grandparents, parents, siblings, uncles, aunts and cousins lived, blown here on the winds of fate, naturally, always longing for the West, whence they came. They say that at first I cried a lot and waved my tiny fists. Even then I wanted to go back where I came from, to the West, that is, but being a helpless infant, I wasn't able to speak a word of Polish, let alone book a ticket. They didn't even have

the Internet in 1970's Poland. What could I do, I learned Polish willy-nilly and now I speak it without an accent, but still, I can never remember the meaning of certain long words, not that it stops me from saying them. I must also confess that the local water and air disagree with me, I don't like the landscape, the architecture, and I don't like the people, all so glum, unhappy with their lives, and insecure.

SCENE 5

Edyta with her wet panties bundled up in her hand, Halina, Bożena, Little Metal Girl.

EDYTA
Ohmigod, I was so unsettled and upset, all this makes me want to go home and have a Lausanne salad, a goat-kid pâté, and a bucket of Parmesan, and if that isn't enough, I'll have a bushel of carrots, wash it all down with a liter of makeup remover, and another kilo of nice sweets, that I won't take to the poor orphans in the orphanage, but eat them in the car myself to calm my nerves, and once I've stopped by the gym along the way, to fight the flab, I won't be able to bear the fact that there were no rivers en route, from which I could save people from drowning, and no fires, from which I could save people from burning, so I couldn't... And the fear that the doors of existence might slam shut behind me without the same bang without which they opened, will get too intense, so I feel I should shout it out loud and clear. I'll shout it out, straight and calm. I'll say it forcefully, but not too sharply, or maybe I'll just whisper it into my own ear – pssst, or think it, poker-faced, not letting on, otherwise they'll blame me for not shaving my beaver again. The film "The Horse Rode Horseback" perpetuates and sugarcoats the stereotypical role of women in the morass of pseudo-bliss, objectifying, squashing, stretching and denying them their natural navels.

BOŻENA
Well, I'm no feminist. I'm a fat pig.

HALINA
Nobody's talking me into having an abortion! I would never let them kill the tiny wee babe sheltered in my womb! Where would I get the money?!

BOŻENA
How would I get the money for it?

HALINA
I can't afford to be a baby-killer like that.

LITTLE METAL GIRL
I'm no lisbian either!

HALINA
What are you on about? What kind of word is that?

LITTLE METAL GIRL
I don't know either, I just downloaded it.

ACT THREE
SCENE 1

In his apartment, the Man is furiously putting his papers and wine bottles in order, rolling up cardboard boxes, and folding the pictures of gerberas.

MAN
What's all the fuss about? Tell the one in glasses to shave her beaver and buy some contact lenses, then she can give birth to a husband and kids, have all the Domestos she wants, and stop thinking about this nonsense. Because of them I totally can't write my screenplay entitled "The Horse Rode Horseback", which caused quite a buzz, scooped up all the awards and single-handedly revived Polish cinema, which is in a sorry state, not to be confused with a united state. Because of them I totally can't write my screenplay: as if it weren't bad enough that I drink and eat too much, drive quads through the cradle of our civilisation, frequent Egyptian swimming-pools and New York boutiques, and when I come back wanting to make a film about present-day Poland and its disadvantage and deracination, its fraying social fabric, poverty, intolerance, unbalanced national identity, and the other dreadful problems that Hoolybeck wrote about so convincingly... – not that I'd know, never read him; that stuff doesn't concern me – ...I simply can't, I don't know how. When I fly back to Warsaw, to this potato patch blighted by sick systems, sick concepts and sick relations, and the Metro going whoosh, the trams going vroom, the planes going whizz, the polluted shit-stream going glug glug glug, I want to have a life and I still have to pay the mortgage on my apartment, which, honestly, would make a much better wine-cellar.

Exit. The Biddy fiddles with the radio dial. Eventually, an announcer's voice comes out of the static and drone of the airwaves.

RADIO
In the old days, when the world still lived by divine laws, everyone in the world was Polish. The Germans were Polish, the Swedes were Polish, the Spaniards were Polish, everybody was Polish, simply everybody. Poland was a fair country to behold back then; we had magnificent seas, islands, and oceans, a fleet to sail them all and discover ever-new continents that also belonged to Poland. There was the famous Polish explorer Krzysztof Kolumbus who, predictably enough, was later renamed Christopher, Chris, or Isaak, or something. We were a great power, an oasis of tolerance and multiculturalism, and everyone not coming here from another country, because, as we've said, there were no other countries to come from, was welcomed with bread...

Little Metal Girl rides up on her bike. She circles nervously around the radio, as if jealous that something had elbowed her out of the soundscape.

LITTLE METAL GIRL
Bread, bread; I've heard something about inbreds once.

GLOOMY OLD BIDDY
Bread.

LITTLE METAL GIRL
Bread or bred, I don't know what it means, but if it's that white, flaky crap from Tesco's, we should have told them that it's great for drawing on asphalt. And it doesn't wash off in the acid rain. But it's very fattening.

RADIO
... and salt. But our nation's heyday eventually came to an end. First they took away America, Africa, Asia and Australia. Polish flags were defaced and painted with stripes, stars, and other squiggles. Polish was officially replaced by fancy-pancy foreign languages that nobody knows except for the people who speak them, so that we Poles don't understand them and feel like right sno-trags...

LITTLE METAL GIRL
Whatever. I download subtitles off the Net and understand everything.

RADIO
Next they took Egypt, France, Italy and Brazil away from us, and then they took Germany...

LITTLE METAL GIRL
Serves us right! Where else would we find work otherwise?

RADIO
... the Poles living there were immediately Germanised and forced to yodel. And last of all they carved off Russia, where the Polish populace was made to speak in some outlandish dialect. We were left with a sandy parcel of our beloved native soil. The Vistula sliced through the fields of blood-red mallows like a silver thread, and the golden wheat ripened, our daily bread...

LITTLE METAL GIRL
Then tell them to get that white flaky crap from Tesco's, they're great for writing on the asphalt, only they're lethally fattening, and Gran will never get to be transparent!

RADIO
Until Warsaw was invaded by the Germans who said Poland would no longer be Poland, and that Warsaw would no longer be its capital, but just a rubble-filled hole in the ground...

LITTLE METAL GIRL

That's right, a hole! A godforsaken hole. I hate this city! The Metro goes whoosh, the trams go vroom, the buses stink, and wherever you go, it's always over someone's dead body!

RADIO

... and that we would no longer be Poles...

LITTLE METAL GIRL

Damn right! Damn right! I'm no Pole either, why should I be? That's a choice I couldn't make, not even subconsciously. I'm a European.

RADIO

... we're not Poles, but Germans or Russians – or their corpses, to be exact, and those who aren't corpses yet will soon be ones anyway...

LITTLE METAL GIRL

Exactly. I fully agree with that radio. Why bother being Poles?

GLOOMY OLD BIDDY

O Poland, glorious land, I can still see your beauty dying.

LITTLE METAL GIRL

If it was dying, it should've popped a couple of aspirin! Everybody knows Poland's a stupid country: it's poor and ugly. The architecture's ugly, the weather's gloomy, the temperatures are cold, even the animals have run off to hide in the woods. The shows on TV are bad, the jokes aren't funny, the prime minister looks like a pumpkin, and the president looks like the prime minister. In France they have France, in America they've got America, Germany in Germany, and even the Czech Republic is Czech, but in Poland all you get is Poland. In France they have baguettes, England's got toast, the Germans have rolls, but in Poland it's bread, bread, bread. In France, they all speak French, they speak English in England, but in Poland, I curse, like everybody else does, in Polish, which nobody understands. I've long since made up my mind, that I'm not Polish, just European, and I learned the language from records and tapes left behind by the Polish cleaning-lady. This here's not my mom, but our personal salesperson from Tesco. She brings Tesco to our house on a forklift and we just point at what we don't want and she takes it back again, and how she skids round those corners! This is not our neighbour, but our private leaflet dispenser. She brings the underpass to our door and hands out leaflets there, she ignores them for us and throws them away round the next corner! She's so fat we keep her locked up at home. Won't have her wobbling around in normal people's field of view. And this here is not my gran, she's our cleaning lady. She's so old and transparent because she just rode in from Ukraine today in this wheelchair. And we exist on the best terms we can! We're no Poles, just normal folks! We came to Poland from Europe to get good bio-organic potatoes grown in real soil, not like those watery ones from Tesco's, and we learned Polish from records and tapes!

Static on the wire, a broken connection, a humming sound; the Little Metal Girl turns the dial on the radio, and big-beat music comes blasting out.

RADIO
The horse rode horseback and hollered whoa, the fish took a ship, the fridge went brrr. The horse rode horseback, a pre-shut door, blood in the bloodstream, watch it flow...

GLOOMY OLD BIDDY
Knock it off! I remember the day the war broke out.

LITTLE METAL GIRL
The Cola war?

GLOOMY OLD BIDDY
Me with just my handbag, with just the floral-print dress on, walking home from the Vistula because it was quite a hot day, my eyes still blue from gazing into the sleepy, cool, soapy, limpid current... My leather shoes clicked jauntily along the boulevard...

LITTLE METAL GIRL
...dragging cattails, old rubbers, sanitary pads, and a soggy plastic bag stuck to their heels...

GLOOMY OLD BIDDY
Then I was back in our courtyard. I'd just opened the gate, and was by the door of our building, reaching out my hand to my little brothers and sisters, when I happened to notice that, while strolling down by the river, something had got stuck to the heel of my shoe. I stopped by the rubbish bins to scrape it off, and I can still remember that...

SCENE 2

Change of lighting. By the recycling bins, Gloomy Biddy – without her wheelchair, and wearing her floral-print dress – and Little Metal Girl are painstakingly trying to remove the trash stuck to Biddy's shoe.

LITTLE METAL GIRL
That it was a big old empty lunchmeat can, with a few soggy Tesco leaflets, a degradable bag, a tampon applicator, a body-bag, and a McDonald's takeout with nearly all the fries inside, that, despite lying in the water for over

a year or even two, retained their shape and aroma, so I nommed a couple even though they're very fattening, and I can kiss being transparent good-bye if I don't get a grip on myself...

GLOOMY OLD BIDDY
When all of a sudden...

Sirens wail, planes roar, bombs are dropped.

LITTLE METAL GIRL
When all of a sudden BANG! This stench seems familiar. We'd better run, there's a bicycle burning here.

GLOOMY OLD BIDDY IN A WHEELCHAIR
The whole sky, the whole sky grew dark...

LITTLE METAL GIRL
That's because of the incoming model aeroplanes. Why don't you fall down the stairs into the cellar, gran, and break your arm and crack your skull on the bricks lying there!

Gloomy Old Biddy and Little Metal Girl tumble down the stairs

GLOOMY OLD BIDDY IN A WHEELCHAIR
The whole sky, the whole sky...

LITTLE METAL GIRL
They rented the whole sky for a model aeroplane show. Somebody must have been busy with the glue!

GLOOMY OLD BIDDY IN A WHEELCHAIR
A terrible noise, my heart was a-flutter like a quail...

LITTLE METAL GIRL
... being bashed with a pail.

GLOOMY OLD BIDDY IN A WHEELCHAIR
And then silence, a silence so cold and echoing...

LITTLE METAL GIRL
Let's go, it stinks of potatoes and soggy cardboard in here. I'd rather puke at the sight of Auntie Bożena.

GLOOMY OLD BIDDY IN A WHEELCHAIR
Stop, don't go!

LITTLE METAL GIRL
Oh, what a surprise. I could have sworn that our building was just where all this flying rubble, stones, glass and loosely-scattered pixels are hanging in the air nowweren't here just now, where! I recognise these splintered drawers, but I could have sworn they were intact, in a chest-of-drawers. We used to have splinters exactly like the ones flying there, only they were chairs. These here teeth are the spitting image of the ones that we had in our combs back home. These shreds are just like shreds of our photos, except that ours were whole. And those Poles whizzing past used to live nearby, but the ones we knew were alive and in one piece, not some unidentified remains flying every which way. Could it be that I'm so drunk that not only do I not remember ever drinking anything, but that I can't even find my own house? The one that's collapsing now bears a striking resemblance to it, and in fact it is. How strange.

GLOOMY OLD BIDDY IN A WHEELCHAIR
It all fell down and piled up in layers. I shut my eyes even tighter, and when I opened them it was all lying there: rubble, bodies, dust, bodies, grit, bodies, rubble, bodies, like some kind of ghastly lasagne.

LITTLE METAL GIRL
Whenever mum doesn't make lasagne, that's exactly the way she doesn't layer it. Cool slag-heap! It's great for poking through the pixels. They rummage in the rubble.

GLOOMY OLD BIDDY IN A WHEELCHAIR
I don't know how long it's been: I forgot my wristwatch when I left the apartment that autumn. Exhausted and famished, I wandered for a long time through a huge heap of rubble. Bread!

LITTLE METAL GIRL
Just as long as it's whole-grain, and not that radioactive crap. I don't want to be slim, I want to be transparent.

GLOOMY OLD BIDDY IN A WHEELCHAIR
Bread!

LITTLE METAL GIRL *(keeps on digging)*
Did you see that bicycle burning, gran? There it is, at last! There it is, at last! I recognise the cracked peephole, it's ours... The door to our apartment, what a relief! Knock knock! Knock knock! You need to knock harder; knocking on a pile of ash doesn't make much of a sound.

GLOOMY OLD BIDDY IN A WHEELCHAIR
I suppose they must all be in their rooms. Wipe your feet. This is where the doormat used to be. And hang up your coat. I saw a hanger lying around near

that broken crockery.

LITTLE METAL GIRL *(running to meet him)*
Uncle Maurice! Uncle Maurice! Uncle Maurice, I've found your leg: it was standing in the living room. Where's the rest of you, uncle? And whose mouth is this? Who left it lying so carelessly under these burnt shelves of charred books, making that repulsive smacking sound from under the embers?

GLOOMY OLD BIDDY IN A WHEELCHAIR
Daria! I'll tell mother – if I ever find her face, still reflected in the mirror clasped in her severed hand, that is.

LITTLE METAL GIRL *(still rummaging in the rubble)*
Well, what's this? Some perfectly good arms; only one of them's broken. It must have broken when you fell into the cellar, gran. But I'll have to pry them loose, because they're clutching on to something! Aaargh! They're clutching real hard here! What could it be? All bloody, mangled, and dead. It must've smashed into those bricks! In America, they give you rubber gloves for this sort of thing. Ah, here we are. Isn't that your face, by any chance? And isn't that all the rest of you, gran? Oh what a tangled bundle of nerves, if you can find the tooth of a comb, we'll straighten them out, because you look like a shredded parachute *(drags all of her grandmother from beneath the rubble)*. You really should take better care of yourself, gran. Is this is that famous frock you've been blathering on and on about; so these are the roses? All gone to seed and broken. You are what you wear! Nettles, balding dandelions, some bloodied bandages, do you think we'll be able to get the stains out? What have they embroidered on it? Spent cartridges, lurking earwigs, barbed wire: all that's gone out of style, couldn't they have just gone for little skulls instead? Jeez, you should have called mom. Everybody knows you can't programme the washing machine, gran: it's better to ask someone to do it for you than to end up breaking it again.

SCENE 3

The Man's apartment. The layout is exactly as it was before, only there is no more trace of mold, wall units, wall-hangings, or yogurt pots under the IKEA pseudo-glitz. The only trace of their existence is a heap of pixels sifting around by the garbage cans, running around on top of which Little Metal Girl in a thoroughly mouse-eaten sailor-suit with wasps' nests in her hair, and – if possible – making dramatic gestures out of a medieval epic: Roland on a hilltop, thrusting his sword in his Adam's apple. Off in the distance, on their sunbleached armchairs are Halina and Bożena in couch-potato mode; moping about next to them is Edyta, not knowing where to hang her emotion-drenched lace panties and a bag full of mixed chocolate wrappers, and Monika, still in search of her missing navel.

MAN
And this is where the audience realises that grandma died in that air-raid. But the girl still says:

LITTLE METAL GIRL
Gran! Gran! Get up, gran!

MAN
And then she turns on the water-works, because she realises that not only did her beloved grandma die in the air raid, but that, consequently, her mother was probably never born either, which would not only make her an orphan, but mean that she too doesn't exist, and never has, which is far better for all concerned, especially for all the others concerned, me most of all, because now I have peace and quiet and a room all to myself.

LITTLE METAL GIRL
Bread! Bread!

MAN
Cries the girl in the last scene, as she starves to death on a heap of rubble. The audience feels moved, and ponders their life in peacetime, when all the wars and famines happen to occur in other countries.

LITTLE METAL GIRL
Bread!

HALINA
Have those mildewy crusts I put out for the birds on the windowsill. Why let them go to waste?

BOŻENA
I'll have them! I didn't go down to Tesco's today because I can't go wobbling around in other people's field of view. After all, they could be puking for better reasons than that.

EDYTA
Would you care for a sweet? They're very nice. I've got some left over in the car that I didn't eat when, after seeing that film, I got too emotional to take them to the orphanage.

MONIKA
Me, I don't eat anything because even nothing makes you put on weight and gives you navels.

LITTLE METAL GIRL *(to herself)*
Bread! Gran, did you see that bicycle burning? *(bangs on the Man's door with her fists)* Bread!

MAN *(looks suspiciously through the peep-hole and opens the door)*
Get out of here, you filthy brat, I don't have any bread to give you. Bread, huh! Give them bread, and they'll waste it all on vodka and drugs.

THE END

A COUPLE OF POOR,
POLISH-SPEAKING ROMANIANS

A COUPLE OF POOR, POLISH-SPEAKING ROMANIANS
Dwoje biednych Rumunów mówiących po polsku

translated by **Benjamin Paloff**

CHARACTERS

BLIGHTY AND GINA: A COUPLE OF POOR, POLISH-SPEAKING ROMANIANS
(Blighty and Gina are both Poles pretending to be foreigners.)

DRIVER
(Male, in middle age, nervous.)

WOMAN

GEEZER

POLICE OFFICER

BARTENDER

HALINA THE HATCHECK GIRL

ROSCOE

Martini and Rossi, Martini and Pickup, Martini and Spit up.
Martini and Rossi, Hyundai Sonata, Los Trabantos, Buenes Aires.
Suzuki Katana, Cinquecento, Seicento, Fellatio.
Volare, o-oh, Cantare, Romy Schneider, Coffee and Tea.

He's belting this shit out, and she says, Shut up. And he says, But this is our Romanian national anthem, babe. Don't renounce tradition. And they left some doodles back here, because they were all over each other, and as soon as I got going, they just scratched away. And that there's metallic black paint, the most expensive there is.

This weird thing happened when I was driving from Warsaw to Tczew...

And these two people, they were acting all crazy, and they introduced themselves... We're from Romania: I can show you the flag. What flag? What flag???

I said to them: What do you mean, do I have any scraps of meat? What the fuck is that, scraps of meat? Put your chick in the car, give me your address, and I'll send you your scraps of meat. You'll finally get that Chick-fil-A sandwich you've been dreaming about. Now fuck off.

My wife and I stopped off at the Texaco, and these two people came up to us acting all weird. One of them, the woman, she was pregnant, and they're passing themselves off like they're Romanians who speak Polish. The wife's in chemo. She's missing a tit. I can never remember if it's the left or the right, and...

But the girl, I mean, she was like one of those girls who holds on to the door and doesn't want to let go, even when I'm moving. And I was like, No. No fucking way.

It's an abomination. Unacceptable.

I said no, because I can't let them into my car, you know, seeing as the car's registered to my business, and you can see the screen in back, and you know, I can't take them, so they say...

And they just stood there staring, all crazy. She had that exact same expression on her face like, you know, a fish in jelly. My husband said that unfortunately there was no way we could take them with us. When we refused, they started crying and cursing up a storm.

I said: No. Because no means no.

So if that no-good broad lies down on the ground, that's her fault. You're just going to lie there, oh, I said: That's a new one. Come over here, slut, I'll lay you out right good. And oh yeah, I'm heading right for her. Boy did she take off. She blew up dust. Like she was all jacked up on something.

I filled up, went inside to pay. When I get back my ten-year-old son asks me if there's such a thing as Polish-speaking Romanians. I say of course there isn't, because he's an anxious kid, sort of talks too much, kind of slow for his age, and he thinks up these stories.

They were like so nice, like so nice, but when I saw their teeth, whoa, I totally said no to giving them a lift. I'm not saying that it's such a big deal, but these days it's no problem, all you have to do is stop by some five-and-dime and buy yourself the cheapest toothbrush they have, and give yourself a good cleaning twice a day, brush-brush, rinse, straightedge for life, and that's it. You got to take care of that. It's called manners. Amen.

ACT 1
SCENE 1

Winter. A gas station. The two poor Romanians pile into the Driver's car.

BLIGHTY:
My wife's called Gina.

DRIVER:
But this girl, about twenty, pregnant, she didn't say a word. She just sat there, but I figure she's an accomplice to the murder. Whose murder? Me, my murder, get it? Though that may seem unrealistic.

BLIGHTY:
Just call her Gina. Gina, what's your last name?

DRIVER:
He asked her last name, and she still didn't answer. Just sat there. But her name was Gina, which was probably short for Regina, and that's the bloody glove right there. Now they can catch these murderers, because that's an uncommon name, and that's what I'm demanding, that they arrest these killers in the name of all taxpayers, who could very well find themselves assaulted and killed by these two.

BLIGHTY:
She doesn't have a last name. Just Gina. A beautiful name for a girl like that. Actually, both a name and a first-name-last-name, and at the same time a stage name. Gina's a good girl. No stealing, no barfing. The child she's carrying in there is living proof. You know, that's life. We're poor, honest Romanians who happen to speak Polish. The wife's pregnant, she's going to a doctor in Wrocław, to a specialist, because she's got some metastases, some cysts, because it's just a mess there in her belly. And so on. So we'll all go where you're going, huh?

DRIVER:
To Wrocław! You hear that, Detective? And this is on the road to Gdańsk!

BLIGHTY:
To Wrocław. But we're not picky. Maybe Gdańsk would even be better. They have all kinds of specialists. The sea, iodine, mussels, ships. Maybe Gdańsk, then. I don't want to argue.

DRIVER:
I told them I'm going nowhere. Just to Elbląg. And anyway, then I'm coming

right back. I was all calm about it, because that's the way I am, calm.

BLIGHTY:
Well, then, to Elbląg, or wherever, and then she'll make do. She always makes do. Always. We Romanians, whoaaaa, we're feisty. She'll even sing you something when she straightens herself out a bit, huh, Gina? You'll be alright, dear. A very nice girl. Well, sit yourself down. Yeah, come on, pookums, is everything alright? Is that a new hair band? Now when did you buy that? Just now? I don't believe it. You're too cute, you know that? What are those, chicory blossoms, those stones?

DRIVER:
It's actually hard to say how it happened. It just took a minute.
The man she was with, I knew his face from somewhere: he was definitely one of those famous mob guys. Knuckles, or that other one they show, and I'd just turned away, because he yelled at me: Look out! The Romanians are coming! or something like that. And I turned around, and of course it was a set-up, and he stuffed her into the front seat, with all her crap, her bags and stuff, and I say, Hang on there!...
And he says, Gina. This is Gina.
I was worried, Detective, which I think makes sense. I say to him, Hey man, what Gina, what's this about Gina now, what do I care about somebody's wife named Gina? That's what I asked.
She could be named Slim Shady, for all I care, but get her the hell out of here. I'm in a hurry. I'm on my way to work. What the heck kind of nonsense is this?...

BLIGHTY:
Actually, her name's Novalgina, but she tells most people to call her Gina. Novalgina, Aspirin, Caffeine, for us these are traditional Romanian women's names. Saint Novalgina, in Romania she was, you know, the patron saint of drunk girls coming home in the dark. Right? That sort of thing happens. Girls such as she. But she tells most people to call her Gina. I don't know, sort of a caprice on her part. Please don't call her Novalgina. Just call her Gina. Show some respect for the feelings of this perhaps great artist.

DRIVER:
But what's it to me? Get out, you...Romanians. Because I'm about to call the...
All this time the pregnant girlfriend I was just telling you about, she was pretending not to be listening. But I had this little scented pine tree, and she was playing around with it, probably planning a way to steal it undetected. So then he tells me to look at how pretty she is, and what on earth does that have to do with me, if she's pretty or not. All I know is that she smells like frying oil, like some awful deep-fryer, and just get away from me, shithead, and take your princess and her brat with you!

I'm not going anywhere.

GINA:
You said you were.

DRIVER:
Did I? My mistake.
I was being ironic. Because I was already getting irritated with this antagonistic and unnecessary circumstance.

GINA:
This thing's fucking awesome.

DRIVER:
And the girl-shithead was playing around cynically with the pine tree, trying to change the subject.

GINA:
Did you buy this, or did you make it yourself?

DRIVER:
What do you mean, make it myself? Make it myself?! Lady, you can buy these anywhere. Just go into the station, and there are tons of them! What planet are you guys from, anyway?

BLIGHTY:
Just look how pretty she is. Oh, you little rapscallion. Well, her teeth need a bit of work. But that's from a hard life, right, dear? We don't have it easy in Romania. In fact, we've only eaten butcher's scraps our whole lives, and that's murder on the old bones. And, you know, zirconia. Chicory. And for dessert we like Pepsid. You know, for heartburn.

DRIVER: And he tells me about his cosmic odysseys, how they have it there in Romania, how they ate bones, weeds, rocks. Well, maybe so, but HEY, we had marshal law here, too. There was rationing, and HOLY COW, WHAT'S ANY OF THIS HAVE TO DO WITH ME! Please stop talking to me! Because I'm not listening to you! I'm not listening to this anymore! I'm not listening.

He covers his ears dramatically.

GINA: Or vanilla-sugar, dry. For example. Some AquaFresh, but very rarely, very rarely, only when mom pawned something, like the family crystal. We had tons of that, because she whittled veggie sticks all over Romania and was very famous.

BLIGHTY:
Anyway, I'm not going to hide the fact that the pot is calling the kettle black. That's a saying back in Romania. Because I don't have such great teeth myself. A nice cover of teeth, but with some blank spots, yes indeed.

DRIVER:
And he shows me his teeth, these foul brownish pegs, just like cigarette butts. I nearly lost my lunch: How can you have teeth like that and still procreate?... And the girlie with that little pine tree, is that any way to behave?

GINA:
Oh Jeez, I'd like to have one of these...

DRIVER:
And he says:

BLIGHTY:
Well then just take it, he has two. You're not going to be offended anyway, right?

DRIVER:
You get that? He said for her to take it. My private property, mine. Foreigners, who I'm laying eyes on for the first time in my life.

GINA (*trying to hang it around her neck*):
But where should I put it?

BLIGHTY:
You know, it's not easy with her, once she insists. She won't relent, because she's, you know, relentless. Why don't you just give it to her? Please, do it for me. We don't have these little pine trees in Romania. We don't even have anything like a pine tree, just other kinds. Oak. Bloke.

DRIVER:
Bloke! Have you ever heard of a tree like that, Detective? Because I haven't! Please get away from my car. And leave me be. I'll take appropriate measures. The girl, too. Take your old bag and fuck off. This is my car, and I don't have time for this. And I tried to drag her out of the car. And get the fuck out, bitch! And let me tell you, that brought her around.

GINA: Oh yeah?!!

DRIVER:
And she grabbed her bag and hit me with it here, right in my neck bone...

GINA:
Bully! Get your big paws off me!

DRIVER:
And I have this boil right near there, and that could have caused an irreparable threat to my health and my life. I started to scream: Somebody! Anybody! Help! Because I wanted to call for help, but they prevented me, they terrorized me, and then they wanted to kill me.

BLIGHTY:
Hey, man, what's up? Have you lost your mind? You want to beat up a pregnant woman, a big man like you? You don't see she's smaller than you? She's all skin and bones; she doesn't stand a chance against you. You just stay where you are, Jean Genie. Undo your boots. That's right, my little sunflower. You know you got a little booger in your nose? Other side. Well, my little Gina likes to walk around with boogers in her nose. Know what I mean? The little whore. But she's a sweetie. Let me get that for you.

GINA:
Nooo, I'll do it myself. I'll do it!

BLIGHTY:
No, let me do it. *Let me do it.* Come on!

DRIVER:
And he's all cool and shows me her gunk, her disgusting snot from out of her nose. You see, I'm sensitive to that sort of thing, I... It reminded me of when I was in grade school, when the other boys, with their spit, wet willies, you know, they lit their farts... I'm not going! I'm not going anywhere! I'm staying right here! I'm staying here! I'm staying! I'm biding my time! Because I love the cold!

BLIGHTY:
Fine, have it your way. So now I'm just going to have to kill you...

Blighty shows him his pocket knife.

DRIVER:
And that's when he first threatened my life.

BLIGHTY:
I'll kill you, though I don't really know how. I don't have the technique down, so maybe it'll hurt more than anything you've ever felt before. And then after that you'll go to hell, and I wish you all the best. And you'll do your time in hell, your nuts will burn off, you won't like it, and you'll think to yourself: It

wasn't worth it. Oh, how it wasn't worth it. And in the end I'll get to Elbląg anyway, and now fuck. They throw an innocent man—meaning me—in jail...

GINA: And he was such a big shot, like he was too cool for school. And all you had to do was flash him your vegetable peeler and he shits his Underoos.

BLIGHTY: And you don't even know where this knife has been. Maybe I scraped the walls of an aquarium. Or maybe I cut some dog shit into slices, huh? Or maybe it's dull. Because maybe I use it to open envelopes. With letters inside. From my relatives in Romania. Letters they write on tree bark, with urine and feces. And Easter-egg dye. Little cousins all begging for me to send them a piece of paper. Laszlo wants a Snickers, and Dickwad a Mars, and Bam-Bam a Twix, while Cincinatti's dreaming about this cardboard French-fry holder, you know the kind. And you think I send them this stuff? I do. It really means a lot to them. A whole lot.

Knife in hand, he opens the back door and gets into the car.

Get in. I said get in. Stop fucking around: Get in, get in, get in. We Romanians have a lot of patience, but any Romanian is eventually going to tell you: Enough. Let's get going.

SCENE 2

Driving.

Gina and Blighty take out some smokes and, in a terrible rush, start smoking two at a time. They cough.

BLIGHTY:
Enough, already. But it's a good thing I didn't kill you. And Christ, I came close close, but I'd have paid for that in the morning. Sure, you know, I went to this party, it was cool, no big deal, but then I killed some strange guy I didn't even know!
It just makes me sick. Faster, friend, faster. Let's show some respect for each other's time. But don't get so upset. Because you're sweating, and you'll catch a chill.

He massages the driver's shoulders tenderly.

BLIGHTY:
Hyundai Sonata. Nice ride, huh, Gina?

GINA:
Like a bullet out of gun, right? No stopping a car like this.

BLIGHTY:
Or a Chevy Cavalier. Now those are some wheels. You know, when we tell
them in Romania how we got there, look out. Our relatives'll burn down our
lean-to, just out of jealousy. Hyundai Sonata. It's not a car, it's a religion.
They're going to shit themselves, you'll see. Why don't you fucking let her
rip! Fuck yeah. Like a hot pussy, you know? Like a hot pussy, you got a car
with that kind of potential, and you let it float there like a sea monkey in
soup. Gina's going to hurl...

GINA:
Now you just hold on there. I don't think I'm that drunk.

DRIVER *(apparently falling to pieces):*
My assailants were constantly humiliating me, egging me on, forcing me
to drive faster and faster, against all good sense and the rules of the road.
I've been driving for fifteen years. I have this little habit: when another car
is coming the other way, I read its license plate. I can't control myself. The
same with road signs, Gdańsk 153 kilometers, etcetera, Iława, etcetera. I add
all the numbers and divide up the sum. I always have this hope that it'll come
out even. When it's even, I'm happy. I take it as proof that, somewhere out
there, there exists something like symmetry and order in the world's most
elementary structures. But the worst is when it doesn't come out even.

BLIGHTY:
I'm going to take my boots off, okey-dokey? Perky? Puerto Rico? Martini
seicento fellatio?

DRIVER:
I keep quiet. I don't say anything. The most important thing with murderers
is not to provoke them.

BLIGHTY:
What I just said, that means "thanks" in Romanian. But I haven't slipped off
my slippers yet. Oh yeah. Like porn. Because it's like, we're here in our own
intimate little circle, huh?

He yawns, settles down to sleep.

DRIVER:
I just keep saying to myself: It's okay. It's okay. It's okay, it's okay, it's okay.
Because maybe this isn't even happening. Maybe it's just a dream, I just
don't know it yet, and I'm getting worked up over nothing... But it wasn't
a dream. And now he's almost asleep, almost passed out, and I was hoping...
I was thinking...

BLIGHTY:
Damn, man, it stinks in here. Gina, did you fart?

GINA:
I didn't fart. It already stank in here when we got in.

BLIGHTY:
Right. But now it's getting nasty. And it wasn't me.

GINA:
Yeah. It wasn't me, either.

BLIGHTY:
Someone let one rip, that's for sure. But definitely not me.

GINA:
Me neither, no way. Not you, not me. Who do you suppose released the hounds?

BLIGHTY:
Piggy. And he was sitting here all quiet like a church mouse, huh.

DRIVER *(falls to pieces):*
What?! IT WASN'T ME!

GINA:
Who, then?

BLIGHTY:
YOU! It was you! It had to be!

GINA:
Stinker.

The Driver throws himself hysterically at his cell phone and tries to make a call.

BLIGHTY: And just what do you think you're doing with that phone? Who do you want to call? Tell us. Maybe the police? What kind of friend are you? Give me that phone. Give it to me.

Pause.

You're driving. That's ridiculously unsafe. I'll dial the number for you: just tell me what it is. Oh my, get over here, hurry, for the love of Christ! A pregnant woman! Frozen! Unarmed! She's sitting in my car! And she's driving with me, and I'm taking her somewhere! I don't know what I'm doing! Help! Save me!

My God! You're fucking useless, a real asshole. How could you?

He settles down with the telephone and falls asleep.

DRIVER:
So then he finally fell asleep. And then I knew that this was my only chance to speak with that Woman: she's a woman, which lent her certain human qualities. Women can never be quite as evil as men can be. As far as I'm concerned, that's the whole basis for the world's existence, since they have to give birth to children, and they're not alcoholics. But that gave me hope, so I say to her: Do you know how to speak, or what?

GINA:
I learned once, you know? But somehow it didn't take. I didn't have a knack for it.

BLIGHTY *(in his sleep):*
We're just a couple of poor, honest, Polish-speaking Romanians... We sailed here on the coal barge Advil... We don't have these little pine trees where we come from. We have other kinds.

DRIVER:
This one here's your boyfriend?

GINA:
Who? Him? No. My cousin. That means he's sort of like my lover.

DRIVER:
Your Romanian here snores a bit, huh?

BLIGHTY *(in his sleep):*
It's the septum.

GINA:
Because of the septum: he broke his nose in jail. Now he has a terrible complex about it. Don't say it too loudly, because he'll get pissed, and he'll cut us down like dogs for fondling each other and plotting against him.

BLIGHTY *(in his sleep):*
No, no, no, no, hold on, what's going on here?

Pause.

DRIVER *(wiping his face with a cloth handkerchief)*:
It's his kid?

GINA:
Whose?

DRIVER:
Your kid.

GINA:
With my kid?

DRIVER:
Well, you know, that thing you're carrying around in there. Is it with him?

GINA:
Me? Oh, Jesus... What? No!

DRIVER:
It's not his?

GINA:
No. I like only just met him yesterday... And what does it matter to you, anyway? My mother keeps asking the same thing, and I tell her: it's a kid, it's just a fucking kid, and that's it, get it? It's my son. And he's mine, be-cause, well, that's how it turned out. It's my kid. I definitely didn't have him with you. And she says: You should take care of him, but no: you smoke, you drink, you party, you pull down your panties for whoever walks by, and then you wake up at 5:30 in the afternoon and are surprised you don't feel good. Why don't you do something about it, like, grab the vacuum cleaner and... But I...
Fine, forget it. It's fine. It's a good thing you reminded me.

She takes out a tube of glue and pretends to sniff it.

GINA:
I'm totally addicted to this shit. To tell the truth, I don't even like it anymore.

DRIVER:
And this monster, this awful woman, I don't even want to call her a woman, she reaches into her crap, into all that garbage, and she takes out a tube of Crazy Glue. And she looks herself over in the label! Like in a mirror!

BLIGHTY *(in his sleep)*:
Gina's an artist.

DRIVER:
And that, uh, that doesn't, you know, hurt the kid?

GINA:
Come on, man… But I keep it under control. Anyway, the doctors said that my kid is already used to it, and if I stop it would be a worse shock than a little Christmas cheer. That is, the kid could come out retarded, and it's better for me to have a sniff than for me to get into a bad mood and the kid to come out all fucked up. In small quantities it's probably even healthy. You should give it a try. It'd chill you out, and then you wouldn't just sit there. Hey, check out those tanks, there's going to be a war.

DRIVER:
Nooo! Never!
I screamed.
The stink was horrible. I started to get dizzy.

GINA:
Know what?
Because the worst fucking thing is that the world wants to turn a person into a gray rag saluting in line, a passer-by passing across the street. A passenger on the fucking tram sucking on a tube, with this face, ugh. Without any features. Without any face. Like you. Cold-cut Man.
I don't want to be like that.
(Terrified.) Hey, what's-your-name? Oh, Jeez! Look!
Tell me something.

DRIVER:
What? What is it?

GINA:
Tell me something, but so that she won't figure it out, you get it? No! Not like that, don't turn around! Is that my mother, sitting there in the back? Just tell me, because I don't want to turn around. Brunette, older.

DRIVER:
Nooo! That's your boyfriend, the one you came here with! Your cousin!

GINA:
That bitch is following me. It's just that I lost all her alimony yesterday, and now she wants to kill me for sure. It wouldn't surprise me if she was sitting right there behind us. I have to keep a close watch at all times, I can't turn around for one second, because she'll pop out of nowhere and say: Why don't you take care of it, that's your son.

DRIVER:
Who is? Him?! *(He points at Blighty.)*

GINA:
My son? Are you out of you fucking mind? I don't feel so good. Maybe I'm having the kid. Call Dr. Lubich.

DRIVER *(almost crying):*
How? Your cousin took my phone!

GINA:
Chill, chill, chill. If that's how it is, I can just hold it in. Hee hee. But relax. I'm just fucking around.

They drive.

DRIVER:
Look, lady, that's no joke. When my wife gave birth, there were some complications. They had to tear out her asshole… Her bladder was damaged. How the woman suffers…

BLIGHTY *(now awake):*
She doesn't have an asshole.

DRIVER:
Of course she doesn't… But I was suggesting no such thing…

BLIGHTY:
Gina doesn't have an asshole. She's not that kind of girl.

GINA:
Shut your pie-hole, alright? Go back to sleep. Don't ruin it for two people engaged in refined conversation.

BLIGHTY:
Shut up yourself. Don't come crying to me about how he's insulted you…

GINA:
Goddamn fucking son of a bitch.

BLIGHTY:
Turdy shit super-shitstorm. Pee-pee. Armpit.

DRIVER *(on the verge of losing it):*
Stop… FOR THE LOVE OF GOD… People… Must you talk to each other like that,

call each other names?! Carry on?! Have you no shame?! Lady, you're pregnant, you huff Crazy Glue, you curse, you stink up the car, that kid hears and sees all of it! It gets recorded in his fetal state! Then he'll say it, like when you have people over! The first words out of his mouth! God...

BLIGHTY:
You hear that, Freddy Mercury? Give her a break, man, she'll calm down. She's a dumb Romanian, a simpleton. Her whole life she's been working away, material girl in a material world, and all that: she's doesn't know how to behave around people. You see what you've done? He's nearly had a heart attack from listening to your bullshit.

GINA:
Yours isn't any better!

BLIGHTY:
Now that's just what I'm talking about...

GINA:
No. No. No, and still no.

BLIGHTY: Right! Exactly!

DRIVER *(bursts into tears and stops the car):*
Stop! I'm begging you... It's yours... I'm done! I'm done driving! I don't want to, I'm giving it to you... The car is yours... I'm giving it to you! I'm getting out... I'll go on foot... I want to take a walk. There's this forest here, that's the place for me, I'll find myself some old root and build a house in it... I'll carve out some plates, spoons, hangers, um, some musical instruments...

BLIGHTY:
No, no, no, my dear, absolutely not. Stop whining. Calm down. Calm yourself this instant. We're under a tight deadline, too. We're trying to get there on time.

GINA:
No, let him cry himself out, he needs the release. He has to let it go.

BLIGHTY:
No, don't defend him.

GINA:
Go ahead, now, cry, it's very cleansing. Now I, for example, when I had a bladder infection, you know how it is, I was moping around, I couldn't find a place to go, I just always felt like I had to pee. I'm running here, I'm dashing

there. I'm letting it out on my legs! I'm sprinting, the hundred-meter dash for Romanian women with bladder infections! I open my fly! I'm already all pissed! I sit on the throne and make three hot, triumphant little drops, and it feels just like someone's pricking me with needles. You know. Like my body's been tossed under a sewing machine. Sort of like an orgasm. Only worse.

DRIVER *(crying the whole time):*
Detective, I owe the fact that I'm alive solely to myself, to keeping it cool, to my control, to the fact that I didn't provoke them, that the entire time I didn't react to their attempts to rob me of my mental faculties, because now I have no doubt about it... And then I saw a patrol car stopped by the side of the road. For a minute I was afraid it might be a mirage, that they were trying to drive me all crazy and insane, that they'd put it there, plotted against me, so it was like it was there to provoke me, to get me going. And then they were laughing at me, making fun of me...

BLIGHTY:
You punk-ass motherfucker, you see what you've gotten us into? No, my friend, this is not how friends behave. What you're up to now, it's scandalous.

DRIVER:
And then I don't even know, it just took a second. Despite the killers' attempts to terrorize me and dump it on me and instill in me a sense of guilt and responsibility for that patrol car and to persuade me to keep driving, I succeeded in turning off and driving straight for that patrol car.

POLICE OFFICER:
What's the problem here? Why are you stopping?

DRIVER:
I was driving too fast, Lieutenant, General, sir. You have to arrest me. I, I was, um... You can't see it back there, but there's a hill. I sped up at the bottom, I crossed the double solid, and I hit someone. You didn't know that, but I confess to everything, even more. I would like you to arrest me. I throw myself on the mercy of the court. Please arrest me, it's all I ask. I'll give you the details a little later...

BLIGHTY:
Daaad... Dad, come back to the car...

POLICE OFFICER:
What's that? What this all about? What's going on?

BLIGHTY:
Everything is absolutely fine. We're a couple of poor, honest, Polish-speaking

Romanians. Dad here has Alzheimer's. There's a whole plague of it in Romania: it makes it driving with him a real nightmare. He's not himself since they let him out of the camp, these horrific bad dreams keep reminding him, the trenches...

DRIVER:
I didn't write down the badge numbers of those two Police Officers, but I'd guess it'd be pretty easy to find them. One's not too tall, the other's taller, blond. If you ask me, those guys are guilty, and they should be suspended from duty for failing to provide assistance to an abducted person, and what's more, for collaborating with thieves and murderers, believing their nasty lies, as if I'd been in the trenches and lost my identity there.

POLICE OFFICER *(to Blighty):*
Is that a problem? Isn't it dangerous to let him drive?

BLIGHTY:
He's doing just fine, General, sir. Is this the right way to Elbląg? That is, are we heading in the right direction? Because Dad's totally confused. My sister and me, we have no idea where we're going, and we're in a hurry to catch a ferry. To Romania, in fact. Actually, it's this coal barge, the Advil. Maybe you've heard of it?

POLICE OFFICER:
But there's no coastline in Elbląg.

BLIGHTY:
Of course not. Because it sails on a lake. Lake Elbląg.

DRIVER:
A coal barge called the Advil. Awful name. Please locate that one as well. Maybe they're still on it.

SCENE 3

Still driving. The Driver is driving, sobbing hysterically, and he's spazzing out behind the steering wheel.

BLIGHTY:
STOP BAWLING!

GINA:
Leave him alone...

BLIGHTY:
He'd better stop, or else I'm going to start bawling.

GINA:
Stop it. Let him cry it out, it helps.

BLIGHTY:
No, Genie, because I can't work under these conditions. I can't stand it when a person is as hysterical as he is.

DRIVER:
The feeble winter sun, like a crappy little coin, had long since fallen beyond the horizon. There were bodies of run-over dogs and animals cast all over the highway. Last year's ice-cream adds, faded by children's lustful glances, swayed on the wind over the cheap bars. I saw the darkness. I touched it.

BLIGHTY:
HEY, MAN. Listen to me. We're terribly grateful that you wanted to give us a ride. It's a long time since we've seen so much kindness from a total stranger who really had no reason to help us out, that kind of sympathy in a tough situation, but who wanted to and did. Such human kindness and sympathy really means so much to us...

He starts to dig around in the mesh bag.

Now we have to get going. It's not far from here to the ferry. Your offer to give us a lift, your doing that voluntarily, you didn't have to do that, but it was a huge help. Thanks to you, we will soon be back in our homeland. Romanians don't mince words, that's our motto. That's why we wanted to reward your goodness and kindness.

The Driver looks in disbelief at Blighty, who removes wads of bills and various other things from a plastic shopping bag.

I'm the Wonderful Wizard of Oz. I came here in disguise to see if people are good and do good deeds. You'll be rewarded to the tune of five thousand, paid in a lump sum. One, two, four, five. And my MP3 player as well. And three Euros. And sunglasses, or maybe not—I'll need these tomorrow. You know how they come in handy. Here you have the controls with the headphones. You download a bunch of stuff from the internet. You transfer it from your computer, and you can take five thousand MP3s wherever you go. Anyway, there are a couple of CDs on there, but I don't know if you'll like them. Actually, I might have thought about it earlier; if I'd known I could have ripped you some, you know, some of that Neil Diamond, Benny Hill. Duran Duran. Monty Python.

So, we're out of here. Come on, Gina, get dressed. That's real money, no funny stuff. Buy yourself something nice. A Cuisinart. I recommend it. Me and Gina, we have one in Romania, and it's worth it. It bakes its own bread. Gina goes out early to the fields, gathers some grain. Then we mix it up in the Cuisinart and we have such fresh bread, with none of those E1939 or E1968 isotopes: now that's what I call LIVING.

GINA:
Hey, are you nuts? I'm as tired as a second-day whore, and all I see are woods. Berry patches.

BLIGHTY:
COME ON.

They walk away.

DRIVER:
And Detective, the worst part was at the very end. He put a knife to my throat and demanded my money and my keys, and she pointed at me with a pistol she took out of her handbag, and the safety was probably off. They wanted to kill me and rob me. They demanded my valuables, all kinds of jewelry, home appliances. They were especially interested in a Cuisinart, which I don't own and have never owned, only my mother-in-law had one once, and I don't keep in touch with her. I don't know how they found that out. How did they know that? You know what I'm thinking is, they had to have followed me earlier. For years I've suspected someone was watching me. And then they fled into the forest without a word, without even thanking me. They didn't leave me any money, not a penny, not a red cent as thanks. And Detective, I would like it to be noted that if they're caught, I hope I'll be able to look them in the eye one more time. But I can't forgive them. I won't. I won't. Not ever. Did you write that down? I won't. Fine, then.

ACT 2
SCENE 1

Evening. Gina and Blighty are walking along the highway, crying, in a total psychological meltdown.

BLIGHTY:
Please. Please. Please. Don't rub up against me while you're walking, I'm oversensitive to that. What? Why?

What do you mean, I gave him five thousand and an MP3 player?! What, like I just gave it to him? To who? To our friend with the screw loose? You got to be kidding me. I gave it to him? For free? But that guy was abby-normal! And you didn't say anything while this was happening? What do you mean, I said I'm the Wonderful Wizard of Oz? I said I was a wizard? Maybe you'd say something like that, but me?

Actually, I remember feeling like a wizard, but it's not like I'd just give something to someone because of that. And you let me do it, you didn't say anything and just let me give him all that stuff?! Five thousand?! Have you lost your mind, woman? You think I found it in my Christmas stocking? I worked my ass off to make that. And I gave it to him? Maybe I sold it? Maybe I sold it to him? No, that's crazy. That doesn't make any sense.

Where's that bag? Sorry. Gina. What kind of name is that, anyway? They couldn't think you up a better one? Are you guys Indians? Peruvians? Regina? What's your last name, Salve? Hee hee. Sorry. I have to hand it to myself, that in the biggest shitpile life has to offer, at rock bottom, I always manage to exude a sense of humor.

No, come on. Let's calm down. Let's be serious. That's what we need here, we need to explain a few things. So there was this party, that's a fact. We got a little fucked up. I understand that that's when I met you. But something was off with those drugs. I don't remember a damn thing. You could tell me whatever you want. But where did I get five thousand? Did I take it out of my savings? Aha.

Impossible, no way. If I'd taken it out, I'd have remembered. And I gave it to him? All of it? And you let me? And there wasn't even ten złotys left?! Look in your bag, there's got to be something. I need some coffee. I need to get my head in the game, to take a shower. Give me a mirror or something. I have to be on set tomorrow at eight. And what about that MP3 player? I gave that to him, too? No way. I had everything on that, all my favorite songs. And where's my phone? What do you mean, you don't have it? Look in your bag, it has to be there. And my ID. What do you mean, it's not there?! Not there?! Give me that. It has to be in here.

And maybe you've fucked me over, huh? Come on, don't get all upset, I'm just asking. I don't know you, I'm laying eyes on you for the first time in my life. I don't trust anyone anymore. I have to be at work tomorrow at eight, I have to be on set at eight, get it? Do you understand what that means? I have to be on set at eight, and if I don't fucking show up, it's going to be my fucking ass. This sucks. I don't believe it. Do you even have a job? Do you know what that means?

GINA:
No.

BLIGHTY:
Then where did you get the money for all those good times, huh? Maybe I gave it to you?

GINA:
I don't know. I got it out of the ATM.

BLIGHTY:
And it just landed there from out of the sky?

GINA:
Nooo, maybe it was the alimony.

BLIGHTY:
What alimony?

GINA:
Well, I went to the ATM. I figured there wasn't anything there, I swear. But there was five hundred. So maybe that was the alimony, I guess. So I bought myself a hot dog and a couple other things, then that party...

BLIGHTY:
Right, fine, but what alimony? Like, child support?

GINA:
Well, yeah, child support.

BLIGHTY:
And what the hell did you do with the child?

GINA:
With what child?

BLIGHTY:
I don't know, with your child. You said you had a kid, right?

GINA:
Oh yeah, I did...

BLIGHTY:
Oh yeah. Oh yeah. You have a kid.

GINA:
I left him somewhere. Wait. So maybe I took him to preschool?

BLIGHTY:
When?

GINA:
I don't know. In the morning.

BLIGHTY:
What morning? Which morning?

GINA:
Well, yeah. Exactly.

BLIGHTY:
That's right.

GINA:
Day before yesterday, maybe. No, maybe yesterday, it was yesterday. No. Because I don't think it was today.

BLIGHTY:
So, what? He's still there? Hah hah.

GINA:
Listen, you have anything to drink?

BLIGHTY:
Just relax, don't freak out. I'm just asking. I don't give a fuck, lady, I don't even know you.

GINA:
I don't know, but how should I know? Maybe my mother picked him up. Sometimes she picks him up when I can't.

BLIGHTY:
Well, that's just great.

GINA:
Well then don't ask me questions when I can't do anything about it now.

BLIGHTY:
You're right.

GINA:
The main thing is that he doesn't get bored. All you have to do is turn on his "Heroes of Might and Magic" and he has fun. He mostly keeps to himself.

BLIGHTY *(starts to shout)*:
Exactly! Exactly! He keeps to himself! And I just got fucked out of five thousand, and that's that! Enough, goddammit, I've had enough. Enough with these parties, enough with the drugs, enough of those fucking awesome parties that end in such a fucking stupor I give five thousand to some neurasthenic ass-backward grandpa. And I wake up dressed in a cardigan from the Salvation Army, pulled off some corpse back in '72, and it's just fucking swell. Eight hours I've been pretending to be a Romanian who speaks Polish, and I'm talking about the detrimental effects of eating butcher's scraps all the time, only all of a sudden it turns out that I'm a Pole coming down, a fucking Pole coming down and speaking Polish. And I wake up in some field, on some berry patch in East Bumblefuck, on the border with Kazakhstan, in a Kazakh cardigan that reeks of moths, and with my teeth all done-up with marker that I can't even wash off. And I have to be on the fucking set tomorrow at eight, because it just happens that I play Father Ted in a respected and beloved TV show. Father Ted. In top form, as always.

Pause.

BLIGHTY:
But these drugs are really bad. We... I just want to ask you one more thing. It's very important. Maybe it's stupid, so pardon me. Did I, that is, you and me, did we have sex? I'm just asking.

SCENE 2

The Tasty Grub. The Bartender and Halina the Hatcheck Girl are watching TV. From outside we hear the approaching turmoil and commotion. Enter Blighty and Gina on the verge of a breakdown, all sweaty, on the edge of madness.

BARTENDER
We're sitting there minding our own, and just then I hear this sort of screaming, like a scuffle. So I say, Now what's it going to be, Bulgarian chicks shooting worms out their cunts and all screaming like that? And I go check it out. And then the door opens, and this two-man isolation ward walks in, I don't know, drunk or fucked up on something, or they escaped from the nuthouse, them and all their paper-or-plastic. They come in. Oh yeah, and that countess there is all pot-bellied. And yeah, so they come in.

Can I help you?

GINA:
I would like a lot of boiling water. I'm having a baby. Have granny strip the bed.

BARTENDER
And she points me to Halina. Granny! And she was tossing her handbag around. So I say: We don't have anything like that, boiling water. There's coffee, tea, we got borsht, French fries. Just what it says here.

GINA:
I'll have the croquette.

BLIGHTY:
No no no—she's such a kidder! None of that. None of that, if you ask me. Out of the question. Please excuse us for a moment.

Look there. Hold this. Turn around and look there, and hold this, and don't say a word, I'll do the talking. You stay here and look there and don't move.

I beg your pardon on behalf of this unstable individual. My friend is sort of coming down. She's not even really pregnant, you know. She just has this pillow stuffed in there, oh, hah hah. And stop laughing, stupid, because this isn't even funny anymore. A psycho-junkie, this one. But those drugs'll fuck you up, if you'll forgive my saying so.

I'm terribly sorry, but something's happened, and I'm in a bit of a pickle. Might I kindly ask you ladies: what is this lovely town we find ourselves in?

BARTENDER
What town is this, and where are they! That's what he asks me!
Ostróda.

HAT-CHECK GIRL:
It's Ostróda.

BLIGHTY:
Oh, Ostróda. Really, it's lovely. So is that more to the south, the north, the east? Because I can't really place it.

BARTENDER
Well, it depends.

BLIGHTY:
Uh-huh.
It depends. Quite right.

You see, because we're in this unfortunate situation: we ended up here by accident. It's not our fault. We're from Warsaw, and we wound up here, well, it's just...

BARTENDER
Uh-huh. I'm from Warsaw, too. Halina, too, she's from Warsaw. We're all from Warsaw. We came here on vacation. We just got back from sledding.

BLIGHTY:
Well then, there you have it. A fine thing, sledding. It's lovely weather for a sleigh ride together with you, as the poet says. You know, the great poet.

But to business, my ladies, because all joking aside, this occurrence, well, it occurred, that is, it's really unclear to me, hard to explain how it all happened. In fact, it might sound a bit unreal. In a word, I found myself here under mysterious circumstances, and tomorrow I have work at eight, but sadly I don't have my phone on me. And I have to call.

What this basically means is—I don't know how to prove this—I don't really look like this. I don't look like this. I was just fooling around, dressing up, having fun, and you know, it all ended badly, real...badly. I'm a professional actor. I play Father Ted in that TV show. I'm sure you've seen it, Father Ted, oh yes, that's me. I was wondering: What time is it?

BARTENDER
But, sir, this is a disguise, too. That there is Princess Diana in disguise, and I'm Danielle Steele. It's ten pm, as you can see right there on the clock.

BLIGHTY:
Ten pm. That can't be. No time to sleep before I have to be on set. What a fucking nightmare. Goddammit, Gina, do something. Say something to them.

Tell them who I am. You know.

GINA:
We'll have two orders of stew.

BLIGHTY:
NOOOO!

HAT-CHECK GIRL:
Hey, Roscoe!

BLIGHTY:
No, come on, what do I need this Roscoe for? And who is this Roscoe, anyway? For the love of God, you ladies don't have any appreciation for the fix I'm in. And who is this Roscoe? What's he to me, this Roscoe? *People!* People. For the love of God. I'm Father Ted. Help a fella out, I have to be at fucking work tomorrow at eight.

BARTENDER
At eight, for what, collecting cans?

GINA:
We Romanians are a feisty people.

BLIGHTY:
Would you please shut up? Not a word—keep quiet. Turn around. Turn around. Turn around now. Please shut up. You left your kid at preschool. Now stay there and think it over, whether that's a motherly thing to do. She left her kid at preschool. Three days ago. Went to get herself a hot dog. A psycho and a junkie, this one.

BARTENDER
And what did she say? That you're some kind of Romanians or something? Great.

GINA:
But I'm sure my mom picked him up, for sure.

BARTENDER
The cheapest phone card is fifteen seventy.

BLIGHTY:
But I'm broke!

BARTENDER
Fifteen seventy.

BLIGHTY:
Come on, lady, all I need is one call's worth. Just enough to yell: Get me the fuck out of here!

BARTENDER
Roscoe! Come here! We have a bit of a problem.

BLIGHTY:
LET ME MAKE A CALL! FUCK! ONE CALL! ONE CALL! IT'S JUST A FEW CENTS!

BARTENDER
Just a few cents, sure, but the cheapest card is fifteen seventy. I don't know if you're some kind of troublemaker, a priest, or even a Ted. That's how much the card costs, and that's money, and it's not like any old head-case can mosey on over from the funny farm and call wherever he pleases. That's what I said, right, Halina? And then Roscoe came in.

ROSCOE:
So what seems to be the problem here?

BARTENDER
It's right here. This is Father Ted. With his wife, the nun. And their kid, the altar boy. Hee hee.

ROSCOE:
Alright, what do you want?

BLIGHTY:
Greetings, Mr. Roscoe, sir. So here's the deal: I'd like to make one phone call, and these ladies here are all for it. They just say I still have to check with you if it's okay...

ROSCOE:
And you have to make such a ruckus?

BLIGHTY:
Certainly not, but...

ROSCOE:
And do you have to make such a ruckus?

BARTENDER
But what the hell, for an hour now this con artist's been telling us stories about how he's some rich actor from Warsaw, but he can't buy himself the cheapest phone card, because he can't spare the money. They're junkies or something. But I know that mug from somewhere. Hey, wise guy, you're the one who steals the eggs from my henhouse.

BLIGHTY:
That's not true, I... Fuck you! To hell with you, to hell with you all! I fucking curse you! That your fucking microwave blows you all to hell!

SCENE 3

BLIGHTY:
It's worse than Romania. A nightmare, a nightmare in waking life.

But that's poetry. I'm speaking poetry.

GINA:
Getting back to the kid. But I'm sure my mom picked him up from preschool. When was that? Wait, the day before yesterday. Thursday. I took him to preschool. I definitely remember that, because he was just wailing, like, blaaaah. I swear. But did I pick him up? You don't know? I didn't say anything about that, that I picked him up?

BLIGHTY:
Hold on, let me concentrate. I'm thinking about something else right now.

GINA:
Try to remember. I didn't say anything?

BLIGHTY: I don't know, dear, because on Thursday I didn't know you.

GINA:
True that, true that. Right. I think she must have picked him up, because she always picks him up, because, for example, I can't. You're right. And that's what happened. That's it. He was standing there and screaming. Boo hoo. What do you think? Maybe that's what happened. Maybe she wanted to spite me and didn't pick him up.

BLIGHTY:
Does he have house keys, just in case?

GINA:
He does.

BLIGHTY:
So then he went home.

GINA:
You think so? *(Pause.)*
He doesn't have keys, he's four years old. Idiot.

BLIGHTY:
Sorry, but don't "idiot" me, we're not at that level of intimacy, pal. But you're kind of right, though: How could I just give someone five thousand? No way, there's no way. Five thousand, you know how much money that is? For five thousand people would eat their own shit, for that much you could buy a whole field with a house, a fence, a villa in Białystok.

GINA:
Actually, I'm not even sure I dropped him off. It's quite possible that maybe he stayed at my mother's. Entirely within the realm of possibility. He plays "Heroes of Might and Magic," he likes his Lego's. He'll manage to keep himself occupied.

BLIGHTY:
Stop getting off the fucking point. Enough already, because tomorrow at eight I have to be on set, and that's the most important thing we have to do now.

GINA:
I'm not making the call. Just get lost, alright? Don't even try to convince me, I'm not going to call. So that she can tell me what? I can say it myself. She tells me all kinds of shit. Yesterday I blew all the child support. She's not going to let that slide. She'll make me get a real job.

SCENE 4

Night. A field. A woman in smeared makeup, forty or fifty years old, heavily slurred speech, stops her car, gets out, opens the trunk, takes out a bottle of vodka and drinks, then puts it back. Meanwhile, a couple of poor, Polish-speaking Romanians run up to her car, losing their shoes as they throw themselves on her hood.

BLIGHTY *(in tears)*:
Warsaw plates... Are you going to Warsaw?

WOMAN:
Warsaw.

BLIGHTY:
You miracle of God, you. The Almighty of the Universe, that's what you are. I called for you and you came. Promise me you're not a mirage! A miracle. Miracles happen. To Warsaw, how far is it from here?

WOMAN:
Huuuh?

BLIGHTY:
How far is it to Warsaw?

WOMAN:
About a hundred kilometers.

BLIGHTY:
A hundred! A hundred. That's what I was saying. A hundred kilometers is like, oh, it's as easy as taking a stick and beating the shit out of dog. We're rescued! Saved! Madame. Queen. You're beautiful. We're coming with you! We're coming with you! Oh, it's so warm in here! So nice! We're normal people! We just look like this. Please. We'll behave like cultured folk! No breaking wind!

WOMAN:
Please. You're a godsend. This isn't even my car. It's a Cavalier. Press that there, and you're all set.

BLIGHTY:
So my friend can come too, right?

WOMAN:
What's it to me?

BLIGHTY:
Come on, Gina, she's going to let you come along, too. I set it up. I vouched for you. She DOESN'T STINK. She just looks like that.

Driving.

BLIGHTY:
So what's up? How's life? Weather's not so good this year. Terrible winter harvest this year.

Silence.

WOMAN:
Of course. The weather. The pressure. Super-duper.

Silence.

BLIGHTY:
And do you always drive this fast, Ma'am? To be honest... Perhaps you could go a little straighter?

WOMAN:
But over there... If you see anyone coming at us the other way, you just let me know. I took my contacts out and put them somewhere over here, but I can see just fine. So? Where are you going? Students, you're students? What do you study? Don't worry about me, I'm not drunk. Don't worry about a thing, just let me drive.

BLIGHTY:
We're not students, we're Romanians who speak Polish. We're lesbians, fags, Jews, we work for an ad agency. Like I was saying, you know how it is, we're going to Israel to plant trees, the goddamn people out here don't want to give us a ride, not one centimeter. I'm Father Ted from the Presbytery. I have to be on set at eight. I still have to get some sleep so as to be in shape tomorrow, have a bath.

WOMAN:
And does one of you maybe have a driver's license?

BLIGHTY:
Well, to be honest, um, no. Aaah. Maybe she has one, but I doubt it. Look out!... Jeez, lady, what are you doing?

WOMAN:
Well, if you don't, what the hell do you want with me? I thought you did, and that's why you came along. Shit.

No, it's fine. Don't get upset, we'll just keep going. The Lord gaveth, the Lord takethed away. No doubt about it... Or maybe I'll show you: here's the clutch, here's the shifter, and you're all set. Or no, I'll drive. It's a car, it's a ride, it's all on credit... Fine, cool, everything's under control. Fuck, I'll tell you. I'll tell you, but I'll tell you. You're so happy, so young, and this car cost fifty thousand. For fifty thousand it can't be bad.

GINA:
Sorry—this is an embarrassing question—but you got anything to eat?

WOMAN:
Oh fuck. Hungary, Romania, Turkey, I know, really beautiful country. Everybody says, Romania's a mess, shit everywhere, sewage, Islam, kids eating shit

from pine trees. That guy, the dictator, Cincinnati, he's in charge, and people eat rocks. But it's a great country, they have peppers and fruits, and vacations, and my husband and I go skiing there. Just great. You go. No things, no lugggage, no credit cards, no money, you just keep going, you'll be free from all that food and all that crapping all the time. You have no idea what a mess it is.

GINA:
You know, sometimes we find something in the garbage. These days people throw out such great stuff, like whole chickens, hot dogs. Garbage cans. Sometimes when I'm on my way to the garbage something tempts me, so, you know. So that when I take out the garbage, I'm in no hurry to let go of the bag.

WOMAN:
That's right, they just throw it out. Garbage is a sacred thing. Once I even found a Secession lampshade. Everybody asks about it.

Silence.

GINA:
Well that's all well and good. But I want to take a leak.

WOMAN:
What? You can let it out wherever you want. This is my husband's Cavalier. I don't give a shit, I'd be glad. Adieu.

Pause. The Woman drives increasingly in zigzags. The Romanians are starting to worry.

BLIGHTY:
Hold on there, Countess. You know, you're a great driver. A fine conversationalist. But if you were to bust out some coffee, we'd be grateful, huh?

WOMAN:
What? You can't tell me what to do, sweetie, because I picked you up, because I thought you had driver's licenses. So no complaints.

They keep driving in a zigzag.

BLIGHTY:
But you see, the coal barge Advil, which is supposed to take us certain places, including Israel, is sailing soon... I have to be on set tomorrow at eight, and you're really going out of your way with these zigzags. And it's just that we'd prefer to live, which is just a matter of... A couple days ago my friend

here left her kid at preschool. To this day he's probably sitting there, playing with his blocks.

GINA:
And why did you have to remind me, asshole? Too late. I'm reminded.

BLIGHTY:
He's sitting there, no bedtime story, no cap, in undies that need changing. It's just tragic. We're going to rescue him. If we don't get back she's going to get told off by her mom like you've never seen, boy.

GINA:
Asshole. Stupid prick.

WOMAN:
But hold on there, now, kids, and listen. I'm not having anything to eat, because it's a fact that me, I'm feeling a little fucked up. I admit it, I'm fucked up, but there's no sense you getting out. No, because this is wild Polish wilderness, there are marshes out there. Something will come up, like a gas station, civilization. Then you can get out, but here, I just don't have the heart to let you go.

She takes a bottle out from under her legs and drinks, and she passes it on.

Bottoms up, hah.

BLIGHTY:
Lady, I can't believe you. Keep your head in the game! What the fuck is that, no bottoms-up now, just get some fucking focus, because my nerves are shot. Me, an old Romanian who's seen a thing or two. Where the hell are we? Białowieska Forest? Stop the car. I said, stop the car!

WOMAN (*stops with a screech of the tires; it is the middle of the forest, and there isn't a single light or sound*):
Go ahead. Walk into the forest. We aim to please. All you had to do was say so. Send me a text message tomorrow or sometime, if you find some mushrooms.

Hah hah.

They keep driving; the woman drinks straight from the bottle.

Just a second, someone's calling me.

The phone is ringing; she answers.

Yeah. Yeah. Yeah. And. And. Nooo, I'm not drunk. I'm driving. With my friends, if you have to know. What are your names?

BLIGHTY:
Laszlo Shambo. And this is Regina. Last name Salve.

WOMAN (into the phone):
Regina and Shmeges, my friends. No. No, I'm not crazy. They're just very nice, easygoing, cool young people. No, I'm not drunk. Come on! You've been waiting for me for three hours? No, I'm not drunk. And who's that talking in the background? Nobody? Is that her? Well you don't have to be all secretive about it, some girl just dropped in to play around on the computer, and you're talking for hours on the telephone, and she's getting bored, naked and sad, and cold, catching a chill, so go to her, go lick her cunt. No, I'm not drunk. I'm not. And maybe I am, so what if I am? I don't know where I am, because there's no signs here, to tell the truth. But there's some field, some woods, actually. Branches and blueberries: maybe it's Norway? I'll be there presently, you go ahead and make me some dinner. Dinner. You burnt it and used too much salt. So it's burnt. And too salty. But that's the way I like it. Because if I don't fucking kill myself, I might come home very hungry. Bye. Adieu.

BLIGHTY:
Gina, you hear? We'll be there soon. Not long now. I'll make it to the set. Could I borrow that phone? I have to make a call.

WOMAN:
Watch the hands. Sorry about my husband. He's terribly worried I'll fuck up his car. I get it. His lover is there, he was supposed to have a romantic evening, she was making up a class after school, she changed her diapers and came right over. You know how it goes. It's true love, he has her on the phone pretending he's Valentino. He's all furious, pacing from window to window with his limp prick, and he says to her, Sit down here, love, you need to trim your nails. Sorry. And he stands there in that window and shits his pants that his Cavalier is going to pull up, first one wheel, then another, and I'll carry in the rest in a plastic bag. Hah hah.
Hee hee hee.
AAAAAAAAA!!!

There's an accident; the car hits something in the dark.
The Woman, bloody, is lying on the airbag, and nothing has happened to the Romanians. A wild boar is lying in front of the hood.

BLIGHTY (outraged):
Now what? What the hell is this?

WOMAN *(losing consciousness):*
Hedgehog.

BLIGHTY:
A hedgehog... A hedgehog! I'll show you a hedgehog.
Hey, lady, come on, wakey wakey. Jeez, the Countess has bought the farm.
Now we're really out on our asses, in the middle of nowhere, in the god-
damn sticks.

GINA:
So, give her first aid.

BLIGHTY:
Me? And you think it's as easy as apple pie? I don't have time; I'm in a hurry.
She's probably done for, right?

GINA:
How do you know?

BLIGHTY:
Is she alive? She's alive. Life's the first thing. She'll be fine now, she has
charisma, see for yourself. She sort of has a moustache. The kidder.

GINA:
Maybe you're right. There's no point now. What are we doing?

BLIGHTY:
You see her phone anywhere? I have to call and let them know I might be late
to the set.

GINA:
Maybe it got fucked up.

BLIGHTY:
What?! No way.

*He throws out a smashed telephone, looks under his legs, pulls out the Wo-
man's bottle of vodka and drinks deeply.*

You want a swig? There's a little left. I can't get fucked up, because I have to
have my shit together tomorrow.

Come on, let's take her watch. You have yourself a lovely watch, dear,
a Seiko. Those little diamonds are the height of fashion. Don't think badly of
me; I'm desperate. Twelve-fifteen. That can't be; maybe it's stopped. So it's

around eleven, so there's still a chance I'll make it.

He puts on the watch, digs around in the Woman's purse.

Alright, she has a purse, so maybe she has some cash. I need to buy a phone card. No, you dig around in there. I'm just sick about this, morally. I've never stolen anything in my life. Except maybe for some dalliances in preschool. You know. No, give it here. I'll look. I can't trust you: you're a nutcase and a junkie.

Gum—we can split that. Birth-control pills—that's gross—you want them?

GINA:
Get that away from me.

BLIGHTY:
Well, take them, they'll give you great hallucinations.

GINA:
Leave me alone, you jerk. Take them yourself: we definitely need to cut off your gene pool.

BLIGHTY:
So take them. You can use them. Aw, fine, I was only joking. Anyway, this bitch has already sucked down half. An old drunk hag like her, and you can still call her Miss Jackson if you're nasty? That's gross.

GINA:
Will you shut up?! I can't listen to you anymore, you idiot. Fuck off, and put down her purse. If she's already lying there dead don't rummage around in a corpse's purse.

BLIGHTY:
What. Maybe she's not fucking around, maybe she takes them for acne? You think? Calm down. Makeup, scribblings, markers, eyeshadow: I'll take that for you, it's all good. Trust me, you could use it: you don't know what you look like, but I see. If you don't want it, give it to someone else. Wait, maybe she has another phone. There's a wallet. Thirty złotys. She has THIRTY ZŁOTYS! Jackpot. When we get to a gas station we'll buy ourselves some Q-TIPS.

To the Woman.

You douche bag. You've drunk all of it. I'll show you.

SCENE 5

The ditch. They get out of the car and start to hobble through the total darkness.

BLIGHTY:
No mother, no father, alone at last to the bitter end. Well, I'm on board. Some drunk hag picks us up, hits a boar, but of course there are boars in the forest. He could have attacked us. But people have no sense of responsibility. She could have killed us. People are hopeless. I have to call, or there's going to be trouble.

GINA:
Would you just shut up? Shut up, shut up. That's all I ask.

BLIGHTY:
Fine, great, you shut up. I hate you. I always hate the girls I screw when I don't love them. It's disgusting, disgusting, sex without love. It's porn. Strip down and bend over.

GINA:
What? What did you say? I didn't fuck you. I already told you. I didn't fuck you.

BLIGHTY:
And how can I believe you, how can I believe you, why should I? Lady, you have amnesia since I don't know when: now you remember, now you don't, the Lord giveth, the Lord taketh away. How do you know if you slept with me or not, when I don't even know? Please. Don't make me laugh. I had a suspicion I slept with you because now I feel like shit, and it's probably because of that, because of that, that's how I know. I hate mechanical, industrial sex with strange women for whom I don't even feel contempt, just blinding zero and zilch. Some strange body under my hands, it may as well be some strange animal's body, a strange, faceless body, bam-bam, and after it's all over you just lie there. You lie there. Breathing. Your breath like a passing car, like a siren going by, like a shadow falling. It's all so ridiculous. Spit and sperm dry up like rain. Because those are the juices of love, the juices of love. Spit! Sperm! Egg whites! And water mixed with potato flour!

GINA:
I didn't fuck you. No way, no way. I told you. Definitely not.

BLIGHTY:
Of course we did! You took advantage of my being unconscious and unarmed!

They walk in silence.

BLIGHTY *(he can't stand it):*
And what a lovely mother you are. You abandoned your kid. Great, don't say a word about it, I prefer not to think about it. Fucking kid at preschool day and night, even the cleaning ladies have gone home, the janitors have gone home, and he just sits there in a puddle of urine and smashes his Hot Wheels. Because what else is he supposed to do, what now? All the toys reek of him. Okay, okay. Time out. If I cross the line, you let me know.

Pause. They're walking; no one drives by.

BLIGHTY:
Sorry, but I have to say something. Because we're going to fall asleep. And we're going to freeze. I'm cold. This cold is driving me nuts. How did they stand it in these woods back in the day?

GINA:
So lie down.

BLIGHTY:
Very funny. Veeery funny.

GINA:
Don't you think I'm cold, too? Cold as a cold cunt.

BLIGHTY:
So what, now you want to blackmail me into giving you my jacket? No way. Though I'd probably hit the afterlife in about fifteen minutes. You could take part in my beatification.

Pause.

BLIGHTY:
So you think we're going to die? Now? Just like that?

GINA:
Yes.

Pause.

BLIGHTY:
Such hopelessness. What a bummer.
But something is telling me to give up the drugs, not to fool around with that crap anymore. It's everyday stuff for you junkies, but for a normal person it's

really destructive. And please. Someone tells me: it's a costume party, it's called "Poor Whore Score," Eva's inviting you, in Mokotów. So I dress up, I color my teeth with marker, I put on some stinky rags, and the cab driver doesn't want to take me. I get there. I meet this chick, namely, YOU, and it's supposed to be a good time. People are dancing, someone offers me something they've cooked up, and then BAM: Operation Romania! I'm a Romanian! I'm on my way somewhere, I'm handing out my money! Me, decent Father Ted, a bachelor. You're the one who talked me into it. Why did you remind me? Now I'm pissed off for nothing, and everything's come back to me. Late for the shoot—check. Going to die—check. But not like this. This is crazy.

To be honest, in spite of it all, I'm afraid that I won't receive eternal salvation. That is, God knows that theoretically I was more good than bad, and in the best light I was okay. But then the Catholic Church starts fucking me over with its gospels, confessions, fasts, and I'm screwed. Me. They fuck Father Ted.

GINA:
Oh, Jesus—I see a light.

BLIGHTY:
Impossible. It can't be.

GINA:
Is that a house?

BLIGHTY:
A house! We're saved! Warmth! Tea! Not to mention food! A clean bed! I'll call Warsaw, tell them I'm running a little late, but I'll be there for sure.

ACT 3
SCENE 1

Blighty and Gina are standing in front of the door of an unfenced house, which is built in the middle of an open field. They're banging hard on the door:

Help! Help! Hello! Save us! Open the fucking door!

Finally we start to hear the sounds of the opening of many locks, bolts, chains, more and more of them, and the head of an unshaven Geezer pokes out.

GEEZER:
Is that you?

BLIGHTY:
Yeah, it's us. In the flesh.

GEEZER:
Are you alone??

BLIGHTY:
Of course we're alone.

GEEZER *(removes the last chain):*
You sure?

GINA:
Yes, we are.

GEEZER:
Come in. Just hurry.

Inside the Geezer's house. He collects garbage. Everything's dirty: two tubs, shoes, all the garbage in the world. The television is on.

GEEZER *(looking them over):*
Father Ted? But it's the priest!

BLIGHTY:
Yeah, that's me. I'm the guy who plays him...

GEEZER:
What an unexpected and pleasant surprise! At night—at such an hour! Father Ted! At last! The priest has finally come to see me. This is the best, a real

pleasure. And this woman, this girl, who is she?

BLIGHTY:
My friend, an acquaintance.

GEEZER:
An angel?

BLIGHTY:
Yeah. She used to be a prostitute, a junkie. You know how it is, my son. I took her in—we did.

GEEZER:
But where's your cassock?

BLIGHTY:
What cassock?

GEEZER:
It would be pretty cold in the cassock, eh? It's howling balls out there. You came in your civilian clothes.

BLIGHTY:
Alright, old man, give it a rest. I'm blushing. You have something to eat, grandpa? Something warm to drink? I'm freezing my ass off. My girl, too.

GEEZER:
No, no, I don't. I was hoping… I was waiting for the priest to help me do the shopping. I can't go out.

BLIGHTY:
You can't? Why not?

GEEZER:
Don't ask, Father—you don't want to know. As soon as I go out, they come, they come. I'm walking, I'm walking, and I hear scratch-scratch, they're coming. They turn the locks, and they hurt me, they hurt me. They come in and hurt me. Oh, Father, you see. I can never go out, because I have to come right back.

BLIGHTY:
You have a telephone, gramps?

GEEZER:
Somewhere over there. I had one. But they were calling.

He lies down on the bed.

Here are the marks. This is where they hurt me. This is where they hurt me. Here are the marks from when they hurt me. They come, they come and do such terrible things. I can't leave here for a moment, not for one moment, because they come right away, right away. And they hurt me.

BLIGHTY:
Now that's just great.

GINA:
Could we maybe sleep here, grandpa? We'll fall flat—on our faces. We came on foot, all the way from Kazakhstan. From Uzbekistan. We just want to get some sleep. We won't cause any trouble.

GEEZER:
Get some sleep. Forty winks. Seems, it seems... For Father Ted, always. But you have to be careful. They don't sleep. You have to be on your guard. But maybe they'll see, they'll notice it's you, Father Ted, and they'll come to their senses.

SCENE 2

Blighty and Gina are lying on a bed, covered in rags. They look at the watch, chewing gum, in a claustrophobic room filled with garbage and a gurgling sink. Gina is playing with some string.

(The watch is the same one they took from the Woman.—Trans.)

BLIGHTY:
Well? So? You got what you wanted. It's your party, your own private "Poor Whore Score" costume party, which cost me five thousand and my job. Let's have fun! I don't know, let's play a word game.

GINA: A word game.

BLIGHTY:
Don't repeat what I say. I'm not going to make it to the set. I've lost my faith. They'll wait, they'll call, there's going to be this big scandal. They're going to kick my ass out of there, that's for sure. And they'll pick up some ridiculous actor. They'll tell our viewers that Father Ted was in a fire and had plastic surgery and now he looks totally different! What a mess! I'm totally fucked!

GINA:
Fucked.

BLIGHTY:
Where's my cell phone? Where did I leave it? Maybe you jacked it? No. Better you think about your kid. Leave a kid at preschool. What a moral accomplishment that is. Better not to have kids at all. What's his name? It's a boy, right?

Silence.

Well, say something. I'm falling asleep. Grandpa will come in the night with a metal pipe and will think we've come here to hurt him, and he'll kill us. I'll keep watch. But let me ask you: Why do I have to keep watch? What about you? Why, in spite of everything, do I have to be the responsible one? Who the hell are you? What do you do? Professionally?

GINA:
I'm a life-artist.

BLIGHTY:
Oooh. That's exactly what I thought. And what else do you do?

GINA:
Like I know? Not so much.

BLIGHTY:
Right.

GINA:
I used to fill out invoices...

BLIGHTY:
I need to call my agent. He's going to be pissed.

GINA:
My mother set it up. But I went there with a hangover, and I those numbers just tripled before my eyes. Because there were these columns, rows, boxes, and there were these sluts sitting there in their festering sweaters, which they'd crocheted and measured out against me. I'm a hundred percent sure that in those hours of work they put my tits through the photocopier and looked over how they came out.

Oh yeah, and I worked at this stand during the summers. I fried up kiełbasa, fries, you know, by the square meter, me and a hundred-and-fifty-liter vat of three-year-old cooking grease. That's me, Miss Oil. But I always jacked something, ten złotys maybe, and that evening I had ten złotys, TEN ZŁOTYS. And I went to the club for a brew, all proud of myself, and I sat there with my snout all red like canned Spam. Miss Kiełbasa, and the oil dripped from my hair onto the table, and my mother said: finally, finally, finally something, finally.

BLIGHTY:
Well that really sucks. You have to do something with yourself, take something up. Or maybe you just don't have any talent.

GINA:
So then I hang out, I go out and hang out, I go in and go out. Generally I just fuck around with various dickheads like you, though I don't really want to. I just go to their place because I want to get a decent night's sleep, no one screaming bloody murder in my ear when I wake up with a hangover. You know, we have a studio apartment, seventeen meters. If someone slams a teapot or a pan, that's no joke when you're hung-over, when you're dying and your kid brings his toy piano to the bed and starts to bang out "Three Little Indians" or "Baa Baa Black Sheep." And they think I'm going to their place because I want to have the greatest sex of my life in seventeen positions and no mercy. Even if they don't give a shit, they still have to stick it in and pull it out at least once, or else no, no, no, it doesn't count. And in the morning it's: Oh God, where are your clothes, you must be in a hurry, I sure am, are you still drinking that tea? If you want, I'll get you a thermos!

Hah hah. Hah hah. And now I'm on the tram, on my way, just like that. I run up the stairs, I open the door. Where were you?! Look what you're doing! That's your child! Mommy, Mommy, who was Copernicus's father? A better question would be, who was his father, right?

God. Who else could it be?

All day he was playing "Heroes"! And finally he pissed himself. I'm sorry, but I'll take the vacuum. Mommy, baa baa black sheep! Baa baa black sheep! Have you any wool? Yes, sir, yes, sir, three bags full! Mommy! Mommy! But the way I read it, that sheep peddled its ass, too.
No, you'd better listen how he learned to play a hymn on his toy piano! Listen! Every verse! Now backwards! Go get your piano and play for mommy. Not there, dummy. And just look at yourself! Don't you have a home? Did you sleep in a dumpster?

BLIGHTY:
Well, I can't help you there, sweetheart. But that really does suck that you act that way; you should quit it, meet someone who won't treat you like a whore. And have you been tested for HIV? You should. Let's be serious: you have to find yourself a guy who, maybe he loves you, maybe he doesn't, but you can't keep tearing yourself up. Maybe you have some kind of subconscious complex; maybe it's caused by a bad relationship with your father.

GINA:
God our Father.

BLIGHTY:
I, personally...

GINA:
Could you lend me five złotys?

BLIGHTY:
Me? To you?

GINA:
My kid is really dirty. All the other women have their normal kids. Why do I have a dirty kid, and not a normal one?

BLIGHTY:
I hate random sex with women who just think of me as Father Ted. And they think that this way they're affirming their existence in the world, that they've slept with me. I slept with Father Ted, I'm no longer a nobody, la la la. I slept with Father Ted, girls, it was such a turn-on, I thought I'd go crazy.

GINA:
I can't go back. She'll kill me.

BLIGHTY:
I hate it. But the worst part is that they always pull me in with some ruse: we have some albums you'd love, we have a collection of rare stamps, we have various flavors of tea. Come on. These shelves are from Ikea. We have this, and we have that, isn't it COOL?

GINA:
I have to take a piss.

She goes into the bathroom.

BLIGHTY:
We have this, and we have this, and here we have some titties. Don't you peek, now. There's this, and that. And these are our stockings: let's throw them there. And oh, who do you play again, is it this one, or is it that one, because now I'm not sure? And here we have a scar, it's awful, simply an awful scar, but that's fate. Here you have it, look it over, there's this and there's that, and I'm going to take a bath. Oh, I'm back already. Well? Not bad, eh? So now what? You're sleeping in your clothes, are you insane? Come on, I'll show you where you're going to sleep. And to tell you the truth, I'm going to

sleep there, too, with you, can you believe it? Watch. Me and you, you and me, and me and Father Ted, because you're totally wrong that I'm just some bartender at Café Café, just some girl at the newspaper stand on the way to the university. It's absurd that you'd think I'm just anybody, since I'm not just anybody. On the contrary, because you're here and I know you.

And I lie there like a burnt-out whore in a burnt-out house.

I wonder if I left the iron on.

I wonder which tram to take home.

What fucking Romania is this? What solitude.

Oh, you've already shot your wad. That's actually a good thing. I'm overjoyed. Now I'm going to sleep. Oh, I'm up already. You've left already? Where have you gone? The girls will be here any minute to see you. They say you're terrible for me, just terrible! And that a girl like me! And they say, if you're going to be like that, well!

And I take the tram. There I go. No mother. No father. Alone till the end of the line.

And now they've fucking fired my ass. No—they will fire my ass, in three hours. I'm nobody. I'm finished.

In a fresh burst of euphoria, he stands at the bathroom door.

Gina! Gina? Hey.

Now I know what your problem is. I just got it, it's real easy.

GINA *(trying to tie herself a noose)*:
Yeah?

BLIGHTY:
Just don't get offended. You haven't found love! It's as simple as that! It's just that nobody loves you! Nobody loves you, and that's why you're so unhappy. You screw those guys who don't love you, and it's pointless, it's empty, it doesn't mean anything. Love is the most important thing in the world, having someone who won't tell you to fuck off in the morning. Well, you know. Gina? Love will cleanse you.

Hey, now, what are you doing in there?

You taking a bath? What for?

Come out. I don't want to sit here alone. I'm afraid. You went into the bathroom by yourself, and you left me here.

I won't peek.

What are you taking a bath for?

I'm not going to fuck you, and that's that, even if you scrub yourself with boiling water.

Hey, Gina!

I was just kidding, moron.

Open the fucking door.
Open the door!

He pulls on the doorknob; the door opens.
Gina, who in the meantime has hanged herself, is hanging in the middle of the bathroom.

Now what have you done?! What did you do that for?!

How could you?! What is this? What's this? Get down from there this instant.
AAAAAH!

GINA:
So I hanged myself.

BLIGHTY:
So just go on hanging, because I'm out of here.

GINA:
Fuck no, you can't just leave me here by myself.

BLIGHTY:
Save it. I'm gone.

And what's next, and what I'm writing, what would happen then: Blighty runs out, and Gina cuts herself down with the pocket knife and runs after him. Along the way they knock down the horrified Geezer, in his long johns. Praise the Lord, we're rushing to catch our ferry!

The coal barge Advil sails up on the snow. They run onto its deck, where the Romanian crew and the passengers greet them enthusiastically: Finally, finally! They hand out candy wrappers and flyers for language schools, and everyone kisses them on the hand. An ecstatic prom of welfare recipients. The participants eat branches and dirt. They hold droopy old balloons in their hands, and they sing shrill Romanian songs. The waiter says to **BLIGHTY:** *Mr. Bułacz, you do us a great honor. Specially for you and your wife we have prepared an entire pepper stuffed with butcher's scraps! Would you like a taste?*

BLIGHTY:
Of course, but I have to wash my hands. I've been on the road all day.

He goes into the bathroom. Gina is hanging there.

THE END

THE END

HOW I BECAME A WITCH

HOW I BECAME A WITCH
Jak zostałam wiedźmą

Translated by **Artur Zapałowski**

SPONSORED BY BRATCATCHER – professional nets for catching children.

CHARACTERS

WITCH

CORNELIUS THE ROCKING HORSE

PRESENTER 1

PRESENTER 2

VULTURE 1

VULTURE 2

BOGUŚ

BOGUŚ' MOTHER

GIRL

GIRL'S MOTHER

VERMIONE U'RINN

1.

WITCH
When I'm walking home, all wet, cold and mean,
I look into the windows that I pass with a leer.
I live at the world's edge, so the walk takes two years.
There's so many windows, and all of them lit,
and wherever I look, I see people sit:
some sitting on sofas, some on their parents' knees,
but they're all staring blankly at flat-screen TVs.
They're checking to see if they have more more more,
or too little – as little as they had before.

CORNELIUS THE ROCKING HORSE
And every so often one of them will say:
„what's that rumble, could it be that a storm's on its way?"

WITCH
But in fact it's the growl in my gut that they hear
,cause I ain't had a bite in more than two years.
All the checking they do is convenient for me:
not a thing do they feel; they can't hear, they can't see.

PRESENTER 1
And the TV's always playing, like a mean old teacher saying:
„you'll never be good enough
unless you buy more stuff."

CORNELIUS THE ROCKING HORSE
Sometimes a young vampire or some playful ghoul
sticks their claw in a person and pulls out his soul,
whacks that soul ,gainst the wall a couple of times,
then hangs it up in a tree or on a clothesline to dry....
Lady takes down the laundry: „Ooh, an invisible cloth!
Great for washing the windows, I'll get those smudges right off."
While the owner won't even have noticed the loss,
as he stares at new things he should buy on the box...
Then he looks for his soul, all confused and depressed,
not even aware how futile his quest.

WITCH
And I'm walking home, all wet, cold and mean,
looking into the windows that I pass with a leer.
Night falls, dark and cold, in my guts there's a rumble
so loud people shiver and the masonry crumbles.

Human kids make me nauseous, they're truly atrocious!
When I was a kid....

VULTURES
You were never a kid...
You hatched from an egg, and were raised by us Vultures.
You were old from the start, you had teeth and a mustache.

WITCH
Maybe so. But the children were different back then:
„Would you please wash my apple in the river, kind lad?"

BOGUŚ
„To assist you, old woman, of course I'd be glad.
Here's some candy I sucked on, that I'm sure you'll enjoy."

WITCH
„Thank you ever so much, you wonderful boy!"
and though it has to be said that I really hate candy,
I slobber and smile and pretend it's just dandy.

BOGUŚ
„See you later, granny!"

WITCH
„Good-bye," I reply, and walk away quick
because all of that goodness is making me sick.
There were times when a feeling I can't quite comprehend
made me stop eating children for years upon end.
They were so good and clean, so polite and so smart,
I felt sorry for them, I just didn't have the heart.
Though I don't have a heart, badness me, not at all,
in the middle of my chest there's a huge gaping hole,
but, at times, even holes with compassion can tWitch,
so the kids went unharmed by this starving old Witch.

VULTURE 2
She neglected to add, that sensitive hag,
that soup from good kids makes her totally gag.

VERMIONE U'RINN
It tastes horrible!

VULTURE 2
Truly, poison most vile!

VULTURE 1
The very thought of it always makes her retch bile!

WITCH
Be quiet, or I'll zap you with an evil spell!
The kids of today are so snotty it hurts,
„Help me cross this wide street, will you please, little Girl"

PRESENTER 2
„Give me your iPhone, so I can play Angry Birds."

WITCH
„But I'm an old woman, I don't have an iPhone"

PRESENTER 2
„I'm calling the cops if you don't leave me alone!"
„This is my badge, I'm a Fed, and you're busted.
I'll read you your rights, then I'll bring you to justice"

WITCH
Not to mention the times they shot at me with lasers!
Or screamed HE-MAN! at me, or unsheathed their light-sabers,
used karate on me, and treated me rough,
or said: „You can eat me, but first buy me stuff."
No wonder I now treat those kids with disdain,
no wonder my appetite I've ceased to contain.
But when you consider all the junk food they eat,
it's hard to resist: they're so crunchy and sweet.
There's children right here in this theatre now,
they must have sneaked in through the window somehow.
The crackling of chips in the darkness I hear,
if you see a kid, be sure to bring it right here;
when I get home tonight, all wet, cold, and mad
I'll get out my cauldron, boil water, then add
some carrots and the child (I hope it's nice and plump),
two bay leaves, some salt
let simmer, and – done!
I can already smell
the stew's heady bouquet!
It's my favorite dish, it's my FATALITÉ!

PRESENTER 1
Night falls, a wolf howls, all the lights have gone out,
people lie there in bed – what are they thinking about?
Some are fretting, some dreaming (you can tell by their snores):

they're fretting they don't have more more more more
or fretting at being poor poor poor poor.

PRESENTER 2
And dreaming of things they must own own own own,
so pretty they must be shown shown shown shown.
But whatever they buy and whatever they do,
it's never as good as something brand new!
So they moan and they groan, and they clutch at the sheet,
all driven by greed.

WITCH
And I'm famished: it's been two years since I've eaten
and the knock in my gut sounds like old central heating.
So now and then people will wake up and say:
„what's that rumble, could it be that a storm's on its way?"

2.

CORNELIUS THE ROCKING HORSE
The dogs are all howling, and there's one other sound
namely gas-station hot-dogs spinning slowly around.

WITCH
I'm walking down the road, my guts twisted tight,
when I see in one window there's a flickering light.
I break into the backyard, to the window I creep,
there's an uncombed little Girl, getting ready for sleep –
not too big, not too small, not too pale, not too blue,
there'll be plenty of steaks, not to mention the stew.

GIRL
She can't sleep, turns and tosses, squirms all over the bed.
Neither side's nice to sleep on, she could do with a third,
and her eyes won't stay shut like a broken umbrella,
her thoughts spinning around like an airplane's propeller.

PRESENTER 1
And it's like all her toys chose this time to play dead,
Littlest Petshop looks lifeless, Barbie's stiff in her bed,
Monster High's dead already, you can blame them for nothing,
as they lie and putrefy in their fab little coffins.

PRESENTER 2
But the Furby had always been chirpy and pert;

what a shame to see it so cold and inert.

CORNELIUS THE ROCKING HORSE
Off in the distance, trains rattling and rumbling,
and a deep rolling sound like a huge stomach grumbling.

WITCH
When I was a kid, my peers were more cultured.

VULTURE 2
You were never a kid.

VULTURE 1
You were raised by us Vultures.

VULTURE 2
You trembled with fear at night in our eyrie,

VULTURE 1
and we'd tease you and go:

VULTURES
„What big teeth you have, dearie!"

WITCH
I'll turn you into frogs if you don't shut your beaks!
Enough reminiscing, it's making me weak!!!
I climb onto the ledge, my face wrapped in my cloak –
This Girl will be stew!!!
But then suddenly I choke.
„What's that stench?" I sigh, resigned.

VULTURE 2
Could it be a heart that's kind?

WITCH
Let me look at the readings
on my goodness detector.
What a stroke of bad luck, what an utter disaster...

VULTURE 1
Looks like quite a good child, a seven on the scale;
a nine would be lethal to ingest or inhale.

VULTURE 2
A five she can stomach if it's simmered for hours,
but a seven is poison – she'd lose all of her powers.

GIRL
„Who are you?" the Girl asks at the sight of the crone.
„How did you get in, that's what I want to know,
‚cause my mom always makes sure to lock the front door."

WITCH
I plop down on a chair and cough for a spell,
I pant and I wheeze at the hideous smell
of ladybugs, milk, and the pork-chop from lunch that she'd hid on the shelf
„I am....I'm... I'm a good fairy," I say.

VULTURES
„Bullcrap, she's a Witch."

WITCH
Vultures, scram, go away!

GIRL
„You don't look like a fairy. There's a growl in your belly.
Want some food from the fridge? Some fake chemical jelly?"

WITCH
„I'm on a diet. I should eat once every two years at the most"

GIRL
„But you're so thin, you're all skin and bones, like a corpse."

WITCH
„It's a wonder diet, you see, and there's only one rule:
for twenty-four months say good-bye to kid-stew,
nipper-nuggets, brat-broth, even chili con child..."

GIRL
„Huh?"

WITCH
„I was speaking in French." and the Witch sort of smiled.

GIRL
„Yes, Good Fairy, I see," the Girl answered politely.

WITCH
„So, my dear…" (and endearments are something I hate)
„…how come you're not asleep at this hour so late?"

GIRL
„It's this nightmare I had, with a crone gross and old
peeking in people's windows, mean and hungry and cold,
and she stared through my window so it gave me the creeps
and I'm now much too frightened to be going to sleep."

WITCH
„Poor dear…yuck." say I, and I glare at her dollies.

GIRL
„I'm so glad you dropped in. Wanna play Monopoly?"

WITCH
And chattering away, she pulls out a game.

GIRL
„I've seen many fairies, in books, of all places:
golden slippers, pink gowns and beautiful faces,
no bats in their hair, no bumps on their skulls,
guess they must have been fake. You can't trust adults:
they're so easy to fool,
all good fairies should look exactly like you.
Is that a real ‚tache? You mind if I touch it?
I want one when I'm big, very much. It
gives a person such status, and makes them look cool,
like a mailman, a cop, or the sweeper at school.
And I wouldn't mind having fuzzy pits like my daddy,
could you do that for me? One of my teeth's loose already.
But there's one tiny question that's been bugging me:
do you have any Witches in your family tree?
No, there's no need to answer, that question wasn't too nice.
Choose a piece. Who goes first? Why don't we roll the dice?"

WITCH
„It's been ages since I've played Monopoly, you know"

GIRL
„Doesn't matter. Just roll the dice. Here we go."

WITCH
She made me move a piece, buy hotels, avoid jail…

GIRL
„Would you mind if I trimmed your long filthy nails?"

WITCH
In the meantime, I'm browsing Modern Witch and Hag World
for tips on de-gooding a good little Girl.
„To avoid being poisoned by a Girl that's too good,
boil her with a boy who pigs out on junk food."
I hold onto the bed, ‚cause I'm feeling quite dreary.
Where to find such a boy?

VULTURES
It's your move now, GOOD FAIRY!

WITCH
My head's started pounding, I say: „Stop!
This won't do.
It is way past the bedtime of Girlies like you!"

GIRL
„You're just sore ‚cause you're losing. But you like this game too!"

WITCH
„Go to sleep!"

GIRL
„I'm not sleepy why don't you and me look
at the pictures of nice butterflies in this book?"

WITCH
„I have some SleepDust here. Now if you'll just let me sprink-
-le your head, you'll be whisked to DreamLand in a wink."

GIRL
„But it's dust from the vacuum, it's dirty and stinks!"

WITCH
„Don't be disrespectful, or the dust will not work.
I make it from nettles, nail polish and corks,
I add scraps of dreams that I scrape from old pillows,
and some motes of the moon caught in branches of willows.
But my recipe's secret, it can't be disclosed,
or else folks would start making SleepDust of their own."

CORNELIUS THE ROCKING HORSE
For they lie there awake, both the rich and the poor.
Some are fretting, some dreaming (you can tell by their snores):
fretting at not having more more more more,
or fretting at being poor poor poor poor.
And dreaming of things they must own own own own,
so pretty they must be shown shown shown shown.
But whatever they buy and whatever they do,
it's never as good as something brand new!
So they moan, and they groan, and they clutch at the sheets,
if they knew about SleepDust, they would start to compete
to discover its secrets, and they'd descend in droves,
on DreamLand without end, where most anything goes.

PRESENTER 2
The dust would first go to the rich and the vain,
who'd add it to their baths, mix it up with champagne,
and dream all the time till they'd start to complain:
„I don't want anymore of this sleep dust," a spouse
would say to her husband in their palatial house.
„Touring magical realms has become such a bore,
all the jumping off rainbows, all the mystical lore,
it's so hard: sure, I fly, sometimes I even soar,
but whatever I do, there's never more, more more more!
And my bathroom's so full, I can't shut the door."

PRESENTER 1
Her husband would then dump the dust in the litter,
where it would get salvaged by ordinary people.
They'd be happy at first, but then they'd get sore:
„We don't want those dreams of more more more more,
we just want to feel a little less poor.
We don't really need magic mountains of gold,
just drab little dreams of stuff we can't afford."

GIRL
„People sure are weird, but why should that upset me?"
I'll go to DreamLand by car... No, my brother won't let me.
A rocking horse I'll ride, I know!
Cornelius, come, it's time to go."

WITCH
„Before you go, child, I don't mean to annoy:
I'm looking for a child, specifically a boy..."

GIRL
„A boy? I know one –
it's my brother, he's sleeping."

WITCH
„No, no that isn't the boy that I'm seeking.
Your brother's too nice, too kind and too lawful.
The one that I'm after is perfectly awful."

GIRL
„An awful boy.... But where would I find one of those?"

WITCH
„I don't know. Try looking in those darkened rows.
That's the audience, with hundreds of kids and their Ma's.
He's out there munching chips and tapping his phone!"

GIRL
„But how will I find him?" said the Girl with a groan.
„That's easy, my dear. He'll be formally dressed,
clean pants, polished shoes, and a shirt freshly pressed.
He'll have a bag of chips, and another with wafers,
the one chocolate-covered, the other BBQ flavored.
You'll find him with ease, just follow the rustling.
He never sits still, always squirming and bustling:
„Lemme play on your iPhone, I'll show you a cool hack"
but don't give him your phone, or you won't get it back.
He has ADHD, and his rudeness runs high,
and when his mouth's not too full, he screams „Buy, buy, buy!"

GIRL
„But I don't understand what you want the boy for."

WITCH
„There are theatres where people sit quietly at shows:
not a sound, not a crunch, the whole thing's deeply flawed.
They just sit there like corpses, then politely applaud.
Now that's hard on the actors – playing to a dead crowd –
so they mumble their lines, scared to say them out loud.
When spectators don't eat at a play, it's not right
they'll fall ill without snacks to get through the night.
That's why I need that boy: theatres need such boys
to shatter the silence with their fidgety noise."

GIRL
„That makes sense, but what shall I do when I find him?"

WITCH
„That's easy: you nab him, and then tightly bind him."

GIRL
„But I'm no good at nabbing..." the Girl starts to fret.

WITCH
„Don't worry, I'll lend you this professional net.
No child can squirm free of its wafer-proof clutches,
it's certain to catch every child that it touches.
It's made by BratCatcher, all good fairies have one.

GIRL
„BratCatcher?! So that means you're a Witch! Daddy! Mooom!
HELLLP!

WITCH
„I somehow expected this Girl would be trouble!
With ThoughtSWitch she needs to be sprayed on the double!
SPRAY IT ONCE ON YOUR VICTIM TO PUT THOUGHTS IN HER MIND.
But, to be extra sure, I sprayed the Girl twice...

PRESENTER 1
The Girl's running a fever, her hair now a mess,
she mutters „Let's hunt," then „Help, I'm in distress!"

WITCH
Meanwhile I grab the pony, how did the spell go...?

VULTURES
BULLCRAP!!

WITCH
Bullcrap? Fiddlesticks! Mumbo-jumbo's the rap!
The steed's wooden hooves break free of the rockers,
its nostrils aflare, eyes alive in their sockets.
„Onward," I cry, „'tis finally the hour!
I'll have lunch, eat my fill, and regain all my power!"
But enough of this talk, I have kids to devour!
Ha ha ha ha ha!

3.

CORNELIUS THE ROCKING HORSE
...and even though
the little Girl swore
she'd never help nab kids,
there rose up this foul-smelling mist,
and changed her for the worse.

GIRL
„Hi-ho, horsie, we must help the hag!"
and she mounted the nag,
and sped ‚cross the floor...
...to end up in exactly the same place as before.

4.

WITCH
Meanwhile, I went home, mean and hungry and cold,
did I mention I lived at the edge of the world?

VULTURE 2
It takes two years to get there:
first you journey through forests, then through meadows and downs.
You avoid all the suburbs, and you bypass the towns,
there's a power plant next, then you come to the railway,
if you don't see a train,
you scoot under the barrier.

WITCH
And the lorries rattling by
keep me company at night.

VULTURE 1
HGVs, delivery trucks,
speeding past like crazy bugs,
racing to the shops and stores
to deliver more more more.

WITCH
Past people's houses I sneak,
and into their windows I peek.
Besides my rumbling guts, there's just one other sound:
namely, gas-station hot-dogs spinning slowly around.
Then you come to one last meadow,

morbid, blasted, swathed in shadows,
beyond it gapes a yawning hole
when I was young, a frisky troll
shoved me down there – ten years I fell.
My legs broke off, my arms as well.
The next ten years I groped around,
and when my head I finally found,
it wasn't mine, it was a bear's,
who'd crashed beside me. Unawares,
he wore my head for years on end;
it stank so bad, I had to spend
a fortnight scrubbing off the mess.
But don't tell people my address!
They'd swoop down on me with their choppers and drones,
set up camp in my yard, snap at me with their phones.

PRESENTER 2
First there'd come the wealthy, bored out of their skulls,
in palatial houses their lives futile and dull,
and, no matter how much they want more more more more,
there's no way it can fit in their closets and drawers,
so they think that a trip to the end of the world
might bring them some relief, help them be less bored.
They'd take photos and beg to have their fortune told.

VERMIONE U'RINN
„Good news: you won't die, and you'll never grow old."

PRESENTER 2
„That's fantastic," they'll gush „do you heal people too?
I've been feeling so weak, listless, languid and blue…"

VERMIONE U'RINN
„Not a problem," I'll say, „stick this rock down your throat."

PRESENTER 2
„I Was Cured by a Shaman" claims the special report:
„There Is Hope to Be Found at The End of the World."

PRESENTER 1
Once the news got around, the middle-class crowd
would come down here in coaches on their package tours
wanting in on the magic and the miracle cures…

VERMIONE U'RINN
„The crystal assures me without hesitation:
next summer you'll go on a foreign vacation!"

PRESENTER 1
„I don't believe in magic, but that sure rings true!
Costs the same as our coast, plus free drinks, heated pools"

CORNELIUS THE ROCKING HORSE
Then the average Joes would all finally descend,
going, „Yo, where's the lake, where's all the hot-dog stands?"
but they'd drown their complaints with a six-pack or two
play the radio loud, start up a barbecue...
They'd redeem a coupon to get their fortunes by text
message that reads: „YOU'LL HAVE LITTLE AND LESS."

WITCH
So remember to never disclose my address...
Now where's my crystal ball? Did I misplace or lose it?
Here's a broken bottle, let me see, can I use it?
Ah, the spell's working fine and the Girl is obedient,
ThoughtSWitch never fails, thanks to secret ingredients.
It's this potion I found in some big urban sprawl
round about Halloweek, or whatever it's called,
(that's a night when kids wear monster masks on their faces,
which true monsters like us find incredibly racist.
They carouse in our graveyards, try to get us to rise –
I'd not be caught dead wearing a human disguise!)
I remembered my stash of bay leaves had run dry;
and they're crucial for making little-kid pie.
I chanced upon a store, Lidl-Schmiddle, who cares,
it said HALLOWEEK, so I thought: Why not check out their wares?
I was stopped by a guard, „Our store's off limits to tramps"
then he takes a close look, „Sorry, great costume, ma'am!"
(It took hundreds of years to get my clothes this amazing –
they might reek, but they fit every social occasion!)
I step inside and browse through the products in stock:
pumpkins, webs, vampire teeth, and such cheap seasonal shlock,
but what's this here? Why, ThoughtSWitch – a spell in a spray,
„Spray it onto your victim, they'll think whatever you say."
So I take it and make for the exit, stage left,
when some lady cries out: „You must pay, or it's theft."
„You want payment? Here's a groat and three dry old bay leaves,
what the heck make it four, now I bid you my leave."
„That's four-ninety," says the clerk, a mean glint in her eyes.

I spray ThoughtSWitch at her, and start to apologize...
„No harm done! And your leaves and your groat you can keep.
There's no charge, and I'll throw in some old fingernails cheap...
I mean free... freely dig in my fingernail-heap."

WITCH
So I sprayed both Sleep Dust and ThoughtSWitch on the Girl,
who jumped onto her pony, convinced for the world
,tis a good deed to nab that chip-eating churl!!
She'll be bringing him soon, time to hurry, by Jove!
Put some wood in the oven, put the pot on the stove!

5.

GIRL
„Cornelius, make haste," cries the Girl with a shiver.
„The good... Witch is waiting, getting hungry and thinner
We must bring her that plump, tasty child for her dinner!"

PRESENTER 1
Magic potions are fine, if not bought at cut rate,
but that batch of ThoughtSWitch was past its sell-by date,
so it worked for a while, then the spell lost its force,
and the Girl hesitated, surprised at her own words.

GIRL
A CHILD PLUMP AND TASTY?!
Where did I ever get thoughts so evil and nasty?!

CORNELIUS THE ROCKING HORSE
Then the potion kicks in, the Girl cries in my ear:
„Run Cornelius, methinks yonder children I hear!"
But Cornelius who was usually up for a spin,
if it didn't mean leaving the place he was in,
instead of dashing off fast as his four legs allowed,
stands there chewing on grass, and gazing up at the clouds.
„Let's go!" cries the Girl. „We'll go," the horse said,
„but first please remove this rubber heart from my head,
it's ugly and jiggles every time that I move."
The horse furrows its brow, crossly crossing its hooves:
„What's more, it's no fun, I would venture to posit,
when you pile me with clothes that won't fit in the closet.
And, third, let me say it's a sign of bad manners
to glue on my eyes stickers from Chiquita bananas!"

GIRL
„I'll peel them right off, I thought they'd suit you well!
Now let's go hunt some children. Follow that junk-food smell."

CORNELIUS THE ROCKING HORSE
„I'm not done. Third of all," (he could just count to three)
did it sound weird to you, ,cause it sure did to me,
when she said kids were plump, when she said they were tasty?
I'm no expert on kids, this might sound a bit hasty,
but there's three types of kids: first the nice, then the good,
third of all there's the mean, then the totally rude,
but it's grass that is tasty, and not kids, that's for sure."
The Girl is asleep, yet aware, so her thoughts
are slightly confused, but then she says „Hey,
why hunt some chip-eater – we're in DreamLand, let's play!"
„That's the ticket, I say."

GIRL
„How come we're still here? Come, let's fly, dash and soar."

CORNELIUS THE ROCKING HORSE
„No, we're staying right here, that's the way to explore."

GIRL
„What do you mean right here?"

CORNELIUS THE ROCKING HORSE
„In case you forgot, I'm a rocking horse, see?
All this running around is beneath me – that's three."

GIRL
„I'll smack you so hard," the Girl suddenly thundered,
„it'll teach you to count all the way to one hundred!"
„How could I have said something so offensive!
Forgive me, please?"

CORNELIUS THE ROCKING HORSE
The horse just looked pensive....
But when he gazed in her eyes, he saw such remorse,
that, though easily triggered, he forgave her, of course.

VULTURE 2
Because, as the Witch's good-meter revealed,
the Girl was quite good, though not quite ideal,
her three main faults being: hiding food in her room,

so it smelled like a corpse that was freshly exhumed...

VULTURE 1
...and the ladybug farm she'd decided to run,
but most of them died, so it wasn't much fun,
while the others roamed free... And if that weren't enough
she made drawings of her English prof. in the buff...
but that's it.

VULTURE 2
Other than that, she was helpful, and cared,
her candy with others she happily shared.

VULTURE 1
She preferred giving away flavors she didn't like
but, every now and then, she gave ones that she liked...

VULTURE 2
In a word, there's no way she could have been serious
when she said what she said about smacking Cornelius.

6.

PRESENTER 1
Meanwhile, the Witch, broken bottle in hand,
is mad that the hunt isn't going as planned.
The horse still won't budge, the Girl bawls him out,
with foul curses the Witch had put into her mouth.
But then she is gripped by a pang of remorse,
as they stand there, she says, „I'm so sorry, dear horse."

WITCH
By now the hag's hunger is driving her nuts,
and her whole cottage shakes with each growl in her guts.

VERMIONE U'RINN
Then she sees in her shard a gleaming black Volga
with a Witch at the wheel who's practically an ogre.
She's pimply and huge, in a monkey-skin coat,
with a cig in her mouth, and a stud in each wart.
„Vermione U'Rinn" her soggy card reads.
„I'm here to help Witches with their ugliness needs.
I'm the STINKLUX lady, take this brochure – it's free,
all the most evil Witches buy cosmetics from me.
Our best-seller this month is by Nina Reeke,

blending bog-slime and sweat for maximum chic;
good for sabbaths and broom-rides, it's an all-purpose scent
I can offer a discount of twenty percent."

WITCH
Our Witch she just stares at Vermione in awe.

PRESENTER 1
Now it's time to remind you, though it's been said before,
that ThoughtSWitch from Lidl, though a bargain entirely,
was purchased well past the point of expiry.

VERMIONE U'RINN
And just under the name, in fine print on the box,
it said „TWO SPRAYS, AND YOUR VICTIM AND YOU WILL SWAP THOUGHTS."

VULTURE 1
The Witch sprayed her victim two times, as we said,
so the little Girl's thoughts bounce around in her head,
and, while the Girl curses the horse in a rage
because he won't move from his place on the stage,
and she fumes and she spews insults coarse and profane,
all of a sudden the Witch feels the urge to play games...

VERMIONE U'RINN
„See anything you like?" asks Vermione U'Rinn
as she lays out her samples with a buttery grin.

WITCH
And our Witch grins right back, though somewhat improperly
„Now what would you say to a game of Monopoly?"

VERMIONE U'RINN
„Beg pardon?!"

WITCH
„It's easy, you'll catch on in a flash.
Here's the board. Pick your piece, and I'll hand out the cash."

VERMIONE U'RINN
„Have you gone quite insane? Take this STINKLUX brochure"

WITCH
„Hey, you've got a neat car. Ooh, a cat! Does it purr?"

VERMIONE U'RINN
The black mangy collar on Vermione's shoulders
glares at her with a hatred that blazes and smolders.

WITCH
„Here, kitty-kitty! What's his name? He's so nice.
Tell me, has he been spayed? Tell me, does he catch mice?
Wait a sec. Last night mom fried a fish in the pan.
I hid some on the shelf... Or does he eat from cans?"
Let me guess, you must be a good fairy, n'est-ce pas?
I can tell by the warts. Do you also have fuzz
under your arms like my dad? I wish I had some too.
Can you make it grow there if I give you this tooth?
Are those Vultures above us? They're so cute, I can't bear it!
I've a kite here, it's broken, could you maybe repair it?"

VERMIONE U'RINN
U'Rinn drove off jumpy as a bag full of fleas,
and then made a call to the Evil Police:
„Bad day, there's a Witch here that's mad as a hatter
send a squad to arrest her, it's a serious matter!"

PRESENTER 2
„Your report has been filed."

VERMIONE U'RINN
„When can you send a crew?"

PRESENTER 2
„The response time right now is a century or two."

VERMIONE U'RINN
„But that's totally daft!"

PRESENTER 2
„We're a bit understaffed."

VERMIONE U'RINN
„Well that's between you and your conscience, I guess.
See you never, bad-bye, fare-you-ill, and god stress."

PRESENTER 2
„Bad-bye."

7.

CORNELIUS THE ROCKING HORSE
And now back to DreamLand, not to dwell on the ugly,
nor the icky. So, DreamLand was perfectly lovely.
Though the horse had its doubts, it began to relent,
but put in its two bits before giving consent....
„...third of all, I can't see without glasses, you know;
third of all, where was it that you wanted to go?"

GIRL
„In the audience!" screamed the Girl with all of her might.
(„I'm so sorry I yelled, that was most impolite!")

CORNELIUS THE ROCKING HORSE
„I can do that as long as you show me the way."

GIRL
„I'm not sure, but I think it leads through the duvet."

CORNELIUS THE ROCKING HORSE
Cornelius braced himself...
and to get his nerve up
cried „hi-ho and away!"
followed by „giddy-up!"

PRESENTER 1
The Girl suddenly knew which direction to go.
They leaped onto the quilt, dived in soft downy folds,
and each printed pink rose seemed as tall as a spruce
with that fresh laundry smell. They turned left by the juice
stain that she had made once when she had the flu.

PRESENTER 2
They leaped out through a hole Dad had burned with a cig,
then plunged back in the folds, weaving between them quick,
till they spotted a mountain that was pinkish and big....

GIRL
„What's that peak?" asks the Girl, scanning the far-off route.

CORNELIUS THE ROCKING HORSE
„If this map can be trusted, I'd say it's Yourfoot"

GIRL
„Myfoot? Then let's climb it all the way to the top!"

CORNELIUS THE ROCKING HORSE
„That would be pretty ticklish and you'd surely wake up."

GIRL
„What's that plateau, the vast one, that's just up ahead?"

CORNELIUS THE ROCKING HORSE
„Why, I'm fairly certain it must be Yourhead."

GIRL
„Myhead?" asks the Girl, looking across the sheets
under which her huge body rolls about in its sleep,
„But I'm here on your back. Wait, this doesn't make sense..."
CUT THE CRAP – she then shrieks – HEAD FOR THE AUDIENCE!
THERE'S A PLUMP TASTY BOY OUT THERE WE MUST CATCH,
OR I'LL DOUSE YOU IN STINKLUX AND THEN I'LL STRIKE A MATCH!"
„I'm so sorry Cornelius, I don't mean what I said.
Hark! The sizzle of hot-dogs past that curve up ahead!
I have gas-station hot-dogs on road trips with my dad!
I'm so terribly hungry I could eat a horse!
Sorry, figure of speech!" „Hot-dog please... and some grass."

VULTURES
„Would you like your grass dried? Scented? Salted perhaps?"

GIRL
„Just the regular kind, raw and juicy and green"

VULTURES
„There's some growing outside. That's ten zlotys fifteen"

GIRL
„I don't have any money, it's kind of a bummer,
I'm crossing this quilt dressed in just my pajamas,
and my horse is off its rockers, so it doesn't have pockets..."

VULTURE 2
„Well I'm sorry then, miss. Try our bargain cologne....
Do you collect DREAMVOUCHERS?" the clerk mechanically drones.

VULTURE 1
Menwhile a black Volga pulls up at the station.

A lady steps out – she's an abomination.

VERMIONE U'RINN
„If gasoline prices don't start going down,
STINKLUX will go bust!" Her collar says „Meow!"
Then a Girl in pajamas drags herself out the door
on a horse made of wood, looking hungry and sore.
„Mmmmm....not too big, not too small, not too pale, not too blue."
Now Vermione U'Rinn, (yes, it's her – can't deny it)
wanted to wow her coven and had gone on a diet
(this was before a mammoth, nationwide Witches' Sabbath)
she had been human-free for a decade or so,
eating nothing but tadpoles, chicken feet, and rat claws
but the sight of this Girl got her drooling and panting:
„I'm having people for dinner, with a lovely Chianti."
„Why the long face?" she asked, her voice nervous and hoarse,
and glanced at her iCompact to see what was the score.
„They won't serve you for free? Heartless corporate trash!
Have these hot-dogs on me, ring them up with the gas."
And she wheezed and she coughed, sick of being so kind:
„How would you and the horse like to go for a ride?"

CORNELIUS THE ROCKING HORSE
The horse neighed with joy that the running was over,
„Now we'll see more of DreamLand." They got into the Volga.
„And now please buckle up, fasten your seat belts tight."
says U'Rinn with disgust (she hates being polite).
Her iCompact lights up with a series of beeps:
that means magic's at work in the vicinity.
„Now that's strange. What the hex?" thinks Vermione, perplexed.

CORNELIUS THE ROCKING HORSE
But before she can manage to shut the car door,
the Girl's hair stands up on end, and she lets out a roar:

GIRL
HEINEKEN! OPEN AIR! INTER MARCHE! BIEEEDRONKA!

VERMIONE U'RINN
„Where did you learn that spell? This can't be! Mumbo Jum..."
But the counter-spell fails; Vermione lands on her bum.
And a magical rope ties her up in tight knots
like a big hairy roast in an oven or pot.

WITCH
„As regards dinner, I'm already engaged!"

CORNELIUS THE ROCKING HORSE
Cries the Girl in a voice hoarse and seething with rage.

WITCH
„Besides, as of today you're on a zero-food diet,
you've made your resolution – you ought to stand by it!"

VULTURE 2
And she grabbed the StinkLux catalogue with disdain:
„EVENING REEK – what a gyp, doesn't stink, just smells plain,
it's banal and it's dated, so three seasons ago,
and the black dye for cats – you can wash it right off."

VULTURE 1
„This frazzling iron actually straightened my hair,
and my skin wasn't aged by age-cream, au contraire!"
She threw down the catalogue with a look most incensed
and said to the horse:

GIRL
„GIDDY-UP, STUPID,
HEAD FOR THE AUDIENCE!"
„I'm sorry I said that; it wasn't on purpose.
will you please forgive me? I'm hungry and nervous.
This is too much for me, I wish I could rest
a bit in this dream," said the young Girl distressed,
„and not be hunting some boy, no matter how delicious,
out there in the audience, looking bored and capricious.
I'm sick of this place, and I'm sick of you dummies.
I wish I were in bed, and I want my mommy!"

8.

Remember the part when the evil witch said:

WITCH
„See those dark rows full of seats up ahead?
He's there munching chips and tapping his phone!"

GIRL
„But how will I find him?" said the Girl with a groan.
„That's easy, my dear. He'll be formally dressed,

clean pants, polished shoes, and a shirt freshly pressed.
He'll have a bag of chips, and another with wafers
the one chocolate-covered, the other BBQ flavored."

Boguś
„I've got wafers right here!" Boguś gets up to yell
but clams up and decides he wants them all for himself.
There's a bag that says Chips in his other hand, though,
almost empty by now, so he shouts out: „Hello!"
He hasn't been paying the play much attention,
his thoughts idly straying to games on PlayStation,
but he piped up at „Chips."
„This is a theatre, behave!"
said his mom „or on stage you'll be dragged,
and they'll make you eat chips until you almost gag."
And she checks her BlueBerry beeping inside her purse,
while Boguś continues to play Angry Birds.
And then the battery died – Mom forgot to charge it.
„She must pay!" Boguś thinks. Along the aisle he barges.
„What shall I break? What mischief make? Perhaps I'll start a row?"
Not that he meant to be a brat, but that's the way it goes.
These things just happen, sad to say, it's best to be prepared,
no matter what, in trouble deep he'd end up anyway.
In parks, or theatres, or stores, or at a hot-dog stand,
there always was something he'd break or someone he'd offend.
Not that he meant to be a brat, it happened by itself:
„It wasn't me" he would protest „that stupid thing just fell!"
He sometimes cried, he sometimes raged, because the world was cruel,
and he felt sorry for himself, a boy beset by fools.

Boguś' Mother
His parents couldn't comfort him because they were at work:
they had a company to run, called More& More&More:
a PLC,
or Ltd.,
in which their son was made

Boguś
-in charge of lip,
-in charge of sass,
-of never sharing toys,
-in charge of mope,
-and saying nope –
a most absorbing trade.

Boguś' Mother
To offset the losses that Boguś incurred,
his mother and father concurred,
the best thing to do was give him some food
and an iPhone to keep him distracted.
And though that did help to steady his mood,
it didn't make him any more placid.

Boguś
Boguś forged down the aisle, scattering crumbs in his wake,
stepping on toes till he reached the stage.
A Girl in pajamas, face plain, body thin,
was there with a horse. „Let me go for a spin!
Oh, man this is lame. Your horse doesn't move.
You should see the steed that I have in my room,
with colorful lights, and lasers and guns,
if it gave you a blast, you would blow up – KABOOM!"

Girl
„Is that so? There's a kite I have, but it's damaged"

Boguś
„I have one of those. I got it from dad. It's from another planet.
It's got a radar, it's got lights, it's armed with laser beams,
one shot would blow you off your feet and you'd land by that tree.
I kid you not, a single shot and you'd fly though the air."

Girl
„That's pretty far. You mean I'd fly to that tree over there?"

Boguś
„You think that's far? That's nothing, kid!" and he began to laugh,
„One time, I tripped so hard I fell all the way there and back.
You think that's far? One time my dad was whirling me around:
I flew to the end of the earth before I hit the ground.
So how ‚bout you? What brought you here? You sure have lame pajamas.
I bet the kids all pick on you, and you cry for your mommy.
I bet you don't have any friends, and everyone rejects you;
when they choose teams in PE class, I bet no one selects you.
But who needs friends, I always say: they'd only take your snacks,
and once they've eaten all your chips, they'd laugh behind your back!
Now let me ride that horse of yours, I'm getting really bored.
I can't? Well then I'll ask my mom to buy one just like yours.
Only mine will be way more cool, more awesome and hardcore:
more speed than yours, more eyes than yours, like, more and more and more!"

GIRL
„More and more?!"

BOGUŚ
„You've heard of it? My dad's the CEO.
He brings me more home from the office, so I have plenty more:
more in my room, more in the kitchen, more in the garden shed –
there's so much more, I sometimes wish I had much more instead..."

GIRL
„How 'bout you make it Say No More?"

BOGUŚ
„Huh?! Lemme have the horse!"

GIRL
„You let him go!" the Girl protests,

BOGUŚ
but Boguś doesn't flinch.

GIRL
On top of that, he's much too fat and wouldn't budge an inch.
But then the Girl recalls she has BRATCATCHER from the Witch.

VULTURE 2
She nets the boy!

VULTURE 1
A cunning ploy!

AND NOW A WORD FROM OUR SPONSOR: BRATCATCHER – CATCHES
CHILDREN LIKE A CHARM!

GIRL
„Oh Cornelius, let's go home! I've had it with this place!"
the Girl cries out, and frees the horse, and falls into his arms.

BOGUŚ
(„Help!" – Boguś cries pathetically – „Come to my rescue, stat!")
But no one helped the brat.

GIRL
„Why don't we go back to Myfoot and tickle it," said she,
„and then I'll wake, and everything will be as it should be."

CORNELIUS THE ROCKING HORSE
The Girl climbed on the horse's back and though they both were weary,
they trotted off at a fair clip, uneaten and quite cheery.
They thought they might set Boguś free, but that proved hard to do,
so he was forced to follow them, running the best he could.
They saw the headlights of a car a hundred yards away...

GIRL
„That's Daddy's car!" exclaimed the Girl, and she began to wave.

GIRL'S MOTHER
„Why aren't you in bed, my dear?" a voice inquired brightly.
Her jaw dropped low, when she espied her mother, in a nightie,
behind the wheel, pursuing her dream for DreamLand to explore,
Mom honked the horn and flashed the lights, and cried out: „All aboard!"

GIRL
„But you know you can't drive, oh, mother of mine!"

GIRL'S MOTHER
„Well maybe I can't, but I'm doing just fine.
I've been driving for hours; it's as simple as cake!
To turn - spin the wheel, to stop - hit the brake.
And now, my young lady, you're off straight to bed,
or don't you remember there's a school-day ahead?"

BOGUŚ
„Don't forget me!" Boguś cries in a petulant tone.
„Drive me home and I'll let you play games on my phone."

GIRL'S MOTHER
„Should we take him?" wonder mother and daughter alike.
Says the horse: „I won't sit next to that ill-mannered tyke."

VULTURES
The boy kicked and spat, and cursed like a brute
and so, to shut him up, they locked him in the boot.

9.

Two years I roamed, two years in limbo
starving and cold I would peer
into all the windows,
the warm, shiny windows,
and just when I thought a hot meal

was coming my way for real...
...my dinner decided to split,
specifically the meaty bit.
And what good is this wart on my lip
when my dinner just gave me the slip?
In every piece of broken glass,
I can see her making tracks.
Driving fast,
without a license,
low on gas
(they've raised its prices).
You can tell me to be tough
but I've really had enough! Enough! Enough!

10.

GIRL
„Hurry, Mom! I see a gas station. Wow, we made it, hooray!"

GIRL'S MOTHER
They stop by the pumps, and fill up the tank, and go inside the station to pay,
„I drove here in a dream, I don't have any money..."

WITCH
„But we wouldn't even dream of charging you, honey!"
the attendant says sweetly,
covering her features discreetly.
„Company policy."

GIRL'S MOTHER
„That's so kind! Thank you, miss!"
And she leans over to give the attendant a kiss...

WITCH
The attendant starts wheezing and choking – the horror! –
warts bubbling like geysers under coats of mascara.

GIRL'S MOTHER
„Would a slap on the back help?" the mother asks, frightened,
surprised at the Witch's response to her niceness.
„Call an ambulance, maybe!" she cries, unaware
that she's making things worse by showing she cares.

WITCH
The crone's fading fast, she's sick and complaining,

as her spells are all lifted and powers start waning.

GIRL
„No, Cornelius," cries the Girl, „don't turn back into wood!"
She gets him some grass, but it doesn't do him much good.

VERMIONE U'RINN
„Ha ha!" someone laughs like a rusty old ratchet,
it's Vermione, who's no longer bound by BratCatcher.
Freed of the spell, she appears on the scene
sure she'll win the fight, nonchalant and serene.
So she sweeps back her hair, and she pulls at her beard,
then she raises her arms – like a doll's, cold and weird,
like a concert pianist striking an evil chord...
SHE CASTS HER MOST POWERFUL SPELL
HA HA HA HA!

CORNELIUS THE ROCKING HORSE
There falls a silence unbroken by the tiniest word.
With the only sound being the hot-dogs' soft sizzling,
and, once in a while, a little Girl giggling.

GIRL'S MOTHER
„This is not a good time" mom says, edgy and tense,
„be quiet, or else you will ruin the suspense!"

BOGUŚ
Now Boguś shows up with a wheeze and a cough,
when the Witch lost her power, his BratCatcher came off.
He climbed out of the boot, and he saw an old hag.
As she leaped through the bushes, stuff fell out of her bag...
First he wanted to yell „Lady, yo, is this yours?"
for on TV he'd seen finders getting rewards.
But then he saw, among the scattered potions,
the auxiliary warts and the foul-smelling lotions...
„What's this? Something I've never seen:
CHOOSE THE SPELL THAT YOU WANT, THEN TAP TWICE ON THE SCREEN!"
So he took the iCompact that gave Vermione her power,
and cracked all of its apps in less than an hour.
When he came to the station, fearsome weapon in hand,
everyone hid their heads though there wasn't much sand.
Boguś had a PS3, loved to play shooter games,
and though he sucked at PE, he had excellent aim.
„SELECT PROJECTILE: putrid fish, gooey turds,
maggots, mud, smelly socks, or plain old rotten eggs?

What should I shoot you with?" Boguś says, his face grim.

Vermione U'Rinn
Vermione shrieks shrilly „TAKE THAT AWAY FROM HIM!!!!"

Boguś
But it's no use, for the boy is tapping all the icons,
and shoots eggs, tennis balls, cupcakes, insects, and pythons.
The roof buckles, walls crack, and the brake fluid spurts,
coke sprays from punctured bottles, hot-dogs roll in the dirt.

Boguś' Mother
And that might have been where we conclude our narration –
with a great heap of trash filling that service station –
when a woman burst in, dressed in heels and a suit,
yelling into an iPhone at someone less resolute:
„This is Alicia More, from „More & More & Co."
her waist was so laced, so slim front and rear,
she looked like a wasp with a business career.
„The more and the more that you ordered last week
has all been delivered as per the receipt!
So I don't see why... Wait I'll call you back"
she stopped, for the fridge she'd reached inside to grab
a Redbull or something was now a tangle of scrap.
Alicia looked around, yes, something was amiss...
her local gas station had been reduced to this:
a stinking heap of rubble, drenched in wiper fluid.
Alicia cried out „Boguś??! Say you didn't do it."

Boguś
„Do what?" came the reply, and Boguś clambered out
from underneath the trash, chips stuffing up his mouth.

Boguś' Mother
„What are you up to, what's this mess?" his mother gravely queries.
„Just playing, mom." „That's nice, let's go. It's past your bedtime, dearie."

Girl's Mother
„Hold on a mo!" the Girl's mom says, „Who's cleaning up this mess?"

Boguś' Mother
„Ahem, ahem, excuse me, ma'am... Alicia More's the name,
I need to wake and go to work, so don't get in my way,
I'll send our cleaning lady by to clear away the rubble."
and hands her some small bills and says „And this is for your trouble."

CORNELIUS THE ROCKING HORSE
The next scene's one we'd rather not show.
Turns out the mom knew Taekwondo:
her roundhouse kick its target hits,
Alicia More's smashed into bits...

BOGUŚ
Boguś looks on, petrified.

GIRL'S MOTHER
„And as for you, my fine young man,
clean up until it's spic and span!"

BOGUŚ
„It wasn't me!" the boy starts weeping,
but fear of Taekwondo soon gets him sweeping.
(From that night on, in every dream,
he's forced to scrub the station clean.
A chore worthy of Hercules
Dead fish and filth up to his knees.)

BOGUŚ' MOTHER
The doctors are confounded by Boguś' condition:
„At night he sweats and screams, takes mops without permission."
No cure can be found, and the doctors' bills soar
so his mom has no choice but to earn more more more."

GIRL'S MOTHER
„Get your horse," says the mom „it's time we went home."
They speed across the duvet, among the roses roam,
take a left by the juice-stain and, later that morning,
wake up in their beds, lethargic and yawning.

WITCH
The Girl ran down for breakfast as soon as it was light:
„I'm starved!" (one hot-dog was all that she'd eaten that night).
„I had the strangest dream," her mother softly said,
„but I forgot the details when I got out of bed."
„I had also had a dream and, jeepers, was it great!"
the Girl replied, and looked up from her breakfast plate.
„The dream was like... was so... I think it went like this..."
„Dig in," the Girl's mom said, while giving her a kiss.
It soon was time for school, the Girl was by the door,
then saw in her mom's purse a thing she'd seen before.
Her cheeks became all red as if she'd seen a ghost:

yes, the iPowder Compact, the one Vermione lost.
„What's that you have there, mother?" the Girl breathlessly asked,
It's nothing, said her mom, and closed her purse up fast.
The Girl's mom winked at her, and in a hushed voice said:
„It's broken but – who knows? – I might need it when I'm mad."

THE END

BOWIE IN WARSAW

BOWIE IN WARSAW
Bowie w Warszawie

Translated by **Soren Gauger**

ACT 1
SCENE 1

The 1970s, Warsaw. The dead of night.
Interior of a small apartment in a large building.
This is a single space crammed with many spaces.
In the darkness we see the outlines of a life's accumulated clutter.
Baby carriages, scooters, ferns, crystals; wobbly piles of laundry on wall unit shelves.
A piling and contamination of shapes which turns into monsters in the night.
This mess can only belong to someone sloppy, it signifies a multitude of irreconcilable interests and uses assigned to one room, it is a theater and storage space all at once.

A sled. A juicer. Canning jars. On a hanger, next to sheepskin coat and a child-sized duffel coat, there's a military cap with a belt.
Children sleep on fold-out couches with their arms splayed out. On a hide-away couch, under a popular reproduction of a Wyspiański painting, PLATOON LEADER WOJCIECH KRĘTEK tosses and turns, unable to sleep.

A cleaner crosses the stage with a bucket—this is ANASTAZJA ŁADCZUK, hereafter called MRS NASTKA. This character is not entirely a part of this reality, she moves about in it, and alongside of it, somewhat transcendentally; she's real, but she also walks through walls.
She's dressed in a plastic apron that smells of perspiration and lace-up cleats, her spongy arms are dotted with vaccination scars like arcane runes or treasure maps.
She treads heavily, drags her feet, sighing and batting her eyes, she might pick up the odd object and then lay it back down, mumbling something like "Wrecked, abandoned,
gone astray, nothing put back, no respect, never taught to be tidy, it's all because they have too much, we never had so much, you found a stick or a button or some glass, kids had none of this stuff, because they played, kids knew how to play, and now they're drowning in this stuff and they just smash it up...".
She just might, after taking a superstitious look around, shove a thing or two into her apron pocket.

PLATOON LEADER WOJCIECH KRĘTEK doesn't see her. He is a man in his thirties, handsome by the standards of his time: mustache, striped pajamas.
His wide open eyes glisten in the dark. They have a blend of metaphysical suffering and very non-metaphysical, corporal irritation.
Beside him is his WIFE. PLATOON LEADER might even be considering a roll in the hay with her to ease his anxiety, but she is sleeping like the dead. Her face is slathered thickly in cream, emitting a faint, supernatural glow. In the end

the PLATOON LEADER just fidgets there next to her and sighs, like a man fight-ing for the attentions of a rock or trying, by raising an eyebrow and sighing loudly, to make the stone give him a sign….

Something is clearly tearing him to pieces. Something in him is cracking, itch-ing, there is a deep wound that nags and tugs and needs his attention. He gets up. He grabs his cigarettes, casting an accusatory glance through the balcony window at the chimneys and neon signs drifting in the gelatinous dark of the May night. Finally, he lights a small lamp and sits at a collapsible table; he begins poking at a typewriter, shaking out more cigarettes, smoking them, and then stubbing them out carelessly in a giant crystal ashtray. He is an en-thusiastic, though inexperienced writer.

PLATOON LEADER WOJCIECH KRĘTEK:
In private we call him: the Lady Strangler from Mokotów. There's victims, au-topsies, a portrait drawn from memory and report by the boys from the crime department. The case has been dragging on for two weeks, but so far there's been no official bulletin. Lips are sealed, and stretched taut into professional on-duty smiles, to keep the population and the broads from getting all hyster-ical. That has to be snuffed out, or kept under wraps for as long as possible. Because for the time being, a piece of this puzzle is missing. What? Or who, is more like it? The culprit.

This had no business happening in our free people's democracy. The boss has started feeling the pressure, so he puts the pressure on us. Word has it the screws are being tightened everywhere, even up so far as the ministry…. The mood in the station is unbearable, combustible as hell. All you hear is "sh…", "fu…," and even fouler language than that. Our Bad Guy is still on the loose, running amok, and no one knows where he'll strike next, who his target will be, then wham-o. Recently it was a lady working at the cafeteria at a film pro-duction house, yesterday two scantily-dressed girls running out of the Bristol in a flush, all sick to their stomachs. Underage. Someone had let them into the dance hall—we don't know who, probably they greased the palm of the cloakroom attendant.

(Wife wakes up. She sits on the fold-up couch, out of sorts and bleary-eyed, pulls the cotton from her ears. She's a woman of maybe thirty, in curlers and a vegetable-patterned night shirt. These might be parsnips, fennel, thistles, and carrots falling into a juicer. She throws an unaffectionate glance at her husband writing.)

PLATOON LEADER (*not noticing or pretending not to notice, because his writing speeds up, and a shade of irritation creeps into his voice. His notes might be illustrated by technical photos from the autopsy and lab reports*).

Her hair-do a mess, her testimony muddled. With tears and sighs, heavily soused on brandy. One is shaken up,
wounded in the eye, in shock, remembers very little. The other passed out, her knee banged up, an ugly gash on her ear, apparently, he choked her with a scarf. All she remembers is the snowflake pattern and a foreign word: SKI.

She'll heal in time for her wedding. But this goddamn louse is playing cat and mouse with the militia. The boss is racking his brains trying to figure out what to do to keep this from spreading by word of mouth. He's called together a secret intervention and investigation force, he's beefed-up patrols out all over downtown. We're to have eyes on the backs of our heads looking out for some Lady Strangler, so we can start blaring out another triumph and success for the Citizen's Militia. But to do that, we have to overlook all the other, just as urgent....

WIFE (*hesitantly*):
Wojtek...?

PLATOON LEADER:
...evil and degeneracy. (*snarkily to WIFE*) What do you want?

They say being a militiaman makes a man hard. Really? It seemed to me a hundred times I'd become desensitized to all the foulness, the violence, the degradation. So why am I writing? Are these the memoirs of a waif, letting off like some kid who can't stand the enormity of the lies, the indignities, the filth? Is this literature of the gutter?

In the brightly painted and colorful houses, flags flap on their poles, and new condos sprout up...

And meanwhile, the alleyways teem with vermin. Should I have a heart of plastic? Feel nothing, see nothing? The daily life of the suburban garbage dumps where the old people—can we still call them people? — dull their senses with rubbing alcohol....

WIFE (*still softly, but with growing resentment*):
Wojtek!

PLATOON LEADER:
Hothouses for runaway kids, all their ideals and goals gone, drunken away. (*to WIFE, furious*): WHAT?

WIFE:
...may I ask why you've got the lamp on at night?

PLATOON LEADER (*rudely*):
I've taken home a report.
.... Children without guidance or ethical role models sent to the school of the street, where the teachers might be cruel, but they are quick and effective. To toilet stalls where deviants lure kids to be defiled for a couple bucks... to corrupt them both in body and in spirit.

(PLATOON LEADER is irritated that his flow is interrupted, but also embarrassed that WIFE has caught him writing diaries at night, as scarcely befits the iron constitution of the militiaman; he ostentatiously reaches for another smoke, though he has just put one out): What report? What kind? This kind. You think maybe I'm writing a diary here? Dabbling in literature?

WIFE (*reproachfully, also fumbling to light a cigarette*):
All you ever do is work.

PLATOON LEADER:
Isn't that true? And still we struggle to get by *(he theatrically turns out his pajama pockets)*. A new anorak for little Piotr, then some sandals, a pack of cotton balls for you, even though I just got you some. I don't know what you do with that cotton, you must be stuffing it in your ears when I try to explain something to you.

(roughly, as if to restore order and the household hierarchy with a stern command):

Go fetch me a cup of tea.

(Though offended at his tone of voice, WIFE obediently makes for the kitchen annex, weaving gracefully through the piles of stuff. She puts on the kettle)

PLATOON LEADER:
And when I sit here working overtime, wrecking my eyes and my health, that's no good either. Because the lamp bothers you.

WIFE:
We only just got the electric bill.

PLATOON LEADER:
Since when have you stopped adding sugar?

(Wife meekly goes to get the sugar bowl).

PLATOON LEADER (*conciliatory*):
There you go. No more glaring at me now.

WIFE:
But I... we?

PLATOON LEADER:
What do you mean: we?

WIFE:
We hardly ever.... I mean last month barely at all, and this month nothing. You didn't even notice my new house dress.

PLATOON LEADER (*Sighs*):
I did. It's synthetic.

WIFE:
Maybe there's someone else?

PLATOON LEADER:
Get to sleep, dummy... Can't you see I'm dead tired?

(WIFE shrugs. She lies down to sleep, pulling the blanket over her head. If she is crying, it is softly; the bed only shakes with her dry sob).

PLATOON LEADER stares into the abysmal night, to draw inspiration and get back to writing. The timbre of his notes becomes more bitter and scathing):
... what was I...? Oh yes, Warsaw in the new era. The atomic era.

New neighborhoods cropping up, wealthy and modern.

But so what, when in the old flophouses. The dregs. Speakeasies. The moldy back alley rooms, with their fifteen-year-old whores. The pimps keep an eye on them. I call those guys dentists, because they like extracting the girls' front teeth with their fists. But they love their daddies, they're ready to claw up a militiaman to defend them. Somnambulent hippies, they lie in their flower-beds among the gilly-flower and dirty needles. Morphine, heroine, shrooms. Dopeheads. Try to help them? Reach out a hand? They'll just call you a crooked cop, drag your name through the mud.

But what the hell? They may be hideous lowlifes, but at least they're honest, up front about it. Worse are the ones with top-notch poplin coats and poplin faces to match, always ready with a cliché. Their faces shaved a little too clean of stubble and a filthy smile, no scruples, just cold calculation. Flabby parasites drifting by in the murky waters of the tide. Shady, fly-by-night businesses, robbery.

Even at the station, sometimes a stapler, a stack of paper, a drafting triangle, a flashlight, or a gas pipe goes missing.

Mindlessness. Moral depravity. All that matters is the perfect, slick, skin-deep facade. But the thicker the varnish, the less oxygen seeps in, and that is what feeds true REALITY...

But the reality we've got isn't so rosy. Take today for instance. I'm walking. Staring people in the face. I'm thinking.

(Flashback: the action shifts to a bridge on the Vistula. It's a bright, windy day, the sun frolicking in the rolling masses of dark brown water. PLATOON LEADER is in full militia get-up, a whistle bouncing against his chest, strolling contemplatively, when suddenly he sees something that makes him speed up.)

Platoon Leader: I look at the Lady Strangler case from this angle and that one, but it's like trying to tidy up the bits of a kaleidoscope. Snowflakes...a scarf... why a scarf when it's spring outside? And what could be the meaning of that damn SKI? What language could it be in? Was he a serious perv or an impotent creep getting revenge for his failures in the sack? I think and think, search and search, and all at once I find... Hey, it's a balloon.

(The balloon turns out to be a person. It's REGINA)

Platoon Leader: It raises ever-so-slightly and swoons, quivering in the wind, caught on the bridge barricades. I come up closer. This is no balloon, it's fabric. A lady's dress, puffed out in the spring wind...

(REGINA is a young woman, undoubtedly beautiful and full of effortless grace. Yet she carries her beauty as if someone had forced her to sling a warm blanket over her shoulders, one that might come in useful but which hampers her movements and is heavy, tedious, and smelly. Her eyes are always a bit disoriented and wary, as if she'd been summoned from the hereafter, caught in absentia, as if forever awkwardly explaining: "here I am, I was here all the time, I just stepped out for a moment!" There is no shade of coquetry here, only a vigilance, a distance, a kind of challenge.)

Platoon Leader: The owner of the dress is a creature of around twenty, ready to jump to her death. From close up she's easy on the eyes. Makes a guy feel bad, a pretty face like that. And why shouldn't he? No doubt one of those dumb geese who visit the capital city to take care of some urgent formality, but actually she wants to stroll around and haunt the coffee shops until some PLAYBOY notices her and starts pouring the rowanberry vodka. And she shines... for one night. With no cash or home address, she's looking for an American adventure film, but she often gets a Polish low-budget drama, or even a b-film. Now pregnant, she's ashamed to go back to Pasym or Garwolin, and the playboy has vanished in the tangle of unfamiliar streets.

Another victim of a collision between the dreams of spring and the realities of a man's world, in brokenhearted despair, she goes to the river...

(Here we see badly dressed village and small-town girls, full of all-too-obvious dreams, tumbling en masse into the Vistula, between the age-old ships and the royal treasures, the chests filled with necklaces, gold coins, pearls and Jagiellonian scepters; scattered swarms of glittering fish, staring rationally and disillusioned, lugubrious river catfish. The water immediately decomposes their unflattering hairdos, molded with hairspray into extravagant rural styles. It opens their purses, out of which tumble their meager wages, photos of their fiancés, lucky carp scales, combs, tissues, sunglasses, and unwinding chains of sausages. Their legs in tight flared pants transform into corduroy fish tails, and the girls turn into schools of mermaids. REGINA turns from the sight in horror.)

Platoon Leader: Though she herself does not know. Does she want to die, doesn't she? Maybe not entirely. Because when she's grabbed by the wrist, after a moment's flimsy struggle, she lets herself be pulled back onto the bridge, generously agreeing to live a bit longer.

(PLATOON LEADER pulls a weakly resisting REGINA off the barricade and, with a salute, demands to see her ID)

She's carded, she stumbles through an explanation of why she was so desperate.

(This might be done as a pantomime. PLATOON LEADER cards REGINA; she is stubborn and reluctant, but gives her responses more and more indifferently, her eyes drifting in boredom, fidgeting with her purse)

Pregnant: she says she's not. She's a student. Except she was expelled from Teacher's Studies some time ago. She kept her mother in the dark, naturally, because that's her meal ticket. But then the letter came from the college. That's when the shit, as they say, hit the fan. Mother fell into a pit of despair. What to do with the prodigal juvenile—who knows. Now she might even lose her benefits from her dead father.
Why was she kicked out? She gets in a tiff. She hedges badly. Finally she loses her way in her own bluff.

Regina *(irritated, clearly wanting to leave):*
Who cares. Anyway, I'm in a rush. That's my business! What are you trying to prove, what's the point? Why should the police care? Have I killed someone? Or stolen something? I've done nothing wrong. Nobody's been, you know. Ev-

eryone's free...

(*REGINA breaks down and cries. She turns on her heel and tries to make off, but PLATOON LEADER grabs her by the hand*)

I ask her about what she plans to do now: nothing. Lips luscious, waist slender, legs not bad either, I guess the thing to do here is....? It was like I'd just stomped right on her bladder.

REGINA: Are you all...

PLATOON LEADER: —she shouts all at once—

REGINA (*suddenly raging*):
...ganging up on me? It's always the same. Husband, apartment, furniture, boy and girl. I don't give a shit! I won't live like that. I'd rather die! Alone, without any furniture! Without any mushrooms. You can shove your mushrooms up your ass. I'd rather sleep at Central Station....

PLATOON LEADER: Central Station's closed for renovations.
REGINA: So Gdańsk Station! Makes no difference.

(*PLATOON LEADER hugs REGINA, who hammers on his chest with her fists*)

REGINA: I want to live! I don't want to be always faking it. Faking myself, playing a part in some cheap flick on command. Get in the line-up for happiness. And beg, pander, flatter, seduce, serve coffee, just to make someone want to be mine! And what if I don't want a husband? Not him or anyone else!

PLATOON LEADER (nestling his face in her head and covering her with kisses): Her hair was fragrant of the wind and... the swelter of the kitchen. Her name was....

SCENE 2

MOTHER'S IRATE VOICE:
Regina!

The voice is coming from an open window, behind a curtain. It's a May afternoon. We see an urban courtyard with a scratched-up statue of the Virgin Mary, the gaping maw of a trash bin, the inevitable bench and a stumbling, mumbling drunk. Kids are kicking a hacky sack, playing with a live bomb, or chasing the cats with an ax. The cracked walls are made somewhat less discomforting by the lush May foliage; the white flowers of the treetops look like discarded gowns of escaping brides, lacy and torn.

At the side of the stage, somewhat in this courtyard, yet in her own parallel reality, MRS. NASTKA is on her knees scrubbing the sidewalk. For the first time we see her in daylight; we now can tell she is the kind of tired women who has spent years bombarded by misfortune and cruel fate, and now seems to be both 40 and 80 years old.

We take a closer look at her rag, we examine the structure of its cheap felt. It is made up of multicolored threads, tangles, strips, and spots, scraps of colors, shattered atoms of sweaters and dresses, slips and stockings of dozens of women, thousands of designs and colors melding into the eternally dun rag.

NEIGHBORS sit on the bench, turning their endless TIME and ATTENTION into POWER over the whole courtyard. They twiddle their chubby thumbs; bouquets of sausages or smoked pig trotters wrapped in wax paper protrude from their shiny purses.

NEIGHBOR 1:
Have you heard the pervert is on the prowl?

NEIGHBOR 2:
Who's he looking for?

NEIGHBOR 1:
What do you mean, women of course.

NEIGHBOR 2:
Mother of God.

DRUNK:
Heard he strangles 'em.

NEIGHBOR 1:
Strangles 'em with a necktie.

NEIGHBOR 2:
Well, I never. What's happened to the world.

MRS. NASTKA *(cuts into the conversation, looking up from her rag):*
Ahh, she'll be fine.

NEIGHBOR 1:
How can she be fine if she's strangled? I guess God hasn't given you children.

MRS. NASTKA:
Don't know how many times my old man has strangled me.

NEIGHBOR 2:
What would your children do by themselves? It's them I feel sorry for.

MRS. NASTKA:
I was washing a floor back when I was young and foolish, I hadn't wrung out the rag enough. It was slippery. Then along he came, carrying two bottles of vodka, one for him the other for him too. One to drink, the other to wash it down with. One for him, the other to get off the first one. He wouldn't have stumbled and broke those bottles, he wouldn't have flown into a rage if he hadn't had a thing for me. Because I gave him such a look that it made the bottles just drop from his hands. A dark force, he cries, a kind of delirium got him. I even prayed, just let him go ahead and choke me. Sweet Lord Jesus I said in my mind, because I couldn't go saying it out loud, couldn't say much of anything with him strangling me like that.
But those softest prayers, whispered inside the heart, are what He hears the most. I offer these sweet strangulations, oh Lord, to Thee, I give them to you in sacrifice...
And I was more and more blissful, and I saw the hands of a sweet and transparent void coming to get me. And then I heard a voice....

VOICE FROM BEHIND THE CURTAINS IN THE WINDOW:
Regina!

SCENE 3

Interior of an apartment, the one the shouts were coming from. It's tiny, its layout absurd and impractical, carved out of some long-gone space and splendor. Meager basic furnishings, among them, in a place of honor, an antique, wrecked table with chipped varnish and crooked legs and drawers.

MRS. NASTKA (*crossing the stage, kicking along the bucket and finishing her story about being strangled*):
... a voice that rang out like a bell, yet soft and delicate as muslin, like the ear of an infant child...

HOLY VOICE FROM THE HEREAFTER:
ALWAYS PICK UP THE RAG AFTER WASHING LIKE YOU WERE GATHERING UP A CRUSHED PIECE OF CAKE, ONLY THEN WRING IT OUT. THEN WILL THE FLOOR ALWAYS BE DRY, AND THY SWEETHEART SHALT NOT SLIP UP.
MRS. NASTKA falls to her knees, but it turns out to be a kid with a paper bullhorn, he runs away squealing, and MRS. NASTKA heavily gives chase, trying to slap him with her rag. REGINA is sitting on the sofa bed, sedentary as usual. In a state of undress, in a slip and one stocking. Hard to say if it's despair or boredom. It is simultaneously the boredom of her great despair and the great despair of her boredom. She is consumed by such enormous inner emotions

that in coping with the banalities of everyday life she is left with a disoriented and discouraged stare, as if someone is forever yanking her out of sleep.

Around her bustles MOTHER, a forty-something woman whose gestures and posture are old before their time. She sighs and grumbles, maybe purposefully acting out a weariness with life and an infinite suffering, seeing them as a kind of investment with which she may yet draw dividends. Every day she composes a tally of wrongs she has been done. Waiting for a person or institution to whom she will deign to submit it. Yet the longer they refuse to turn up, the deeper she slides into anxiety.

This she invests in various ineffectual projects; she is forever sprucing up her dismal lodgings. She minces and bustles, wiping micro dust and trailing a moistened thumb on a scratch in the varnish, straightening up things that will swiftly slump back down. She moves about for herself and for her daughter. In this odd imbalance of movement and exertion, both are, in their own way, waiting for someone.

The table is sumptuously laid with meager dishes whose dreariness MOTHER has hidden under decorations made with the skill of a pantry chef. The plates are bigger than the food. From one side of the stage, we see Mrs. Nastka's tush; in a position of anal submission, she is monotonously and listlessly washing the floor somewhere in the hereafter.
A crackly SONG FROM THE RADIO, the dissonant hiss of an old record, an old woman sings;

Such lovely flowers bloom here
I see those days, the Cafe pod Różą, in Lwów back then,
you kiss my temple, clasp my hand in yours
my eyes faint but when I open them again
I know it's not spring, no no, my dear

it's your tomb
it's your tomb
it's your tomb, darling
it's your tomb

(the song fades into the background)

MOTHER: A woman must be clean.

REGINA *(laying her head on a pillow):*
Mama turn off that radio. Are they coming to see us or to check if we scrub? *(gets up heavily, yanking up her stocking)* Will they be checking me with their dirtometers?

MOTHER (*pretending not to hear, humming, looking ungrudgingly at the table and the spread, primping and shifting nothing from one empty plate into another*):
Your hair will get tangled again.

REGINA: Wash and wash. Is there a point to any of it, will I ever be blessed as clean enough?

MOTHER: The fleas will get you in the end.

REGINA: They can come and get me. I'll start a Flea and Louse Circus and tour the world.

MOTHER: You don't know what you're saying! Wacia and I had awful lice after the liberation.

(*MOTHER'S eyes drift toward the window. They light up, you can tell her inner tail is wagging as she retells this story. This begins the dynamic flashback of the wartime fate of MOTHER and her sister WACIA in postwar Warsaw. REGINA'S face tells us this is not the first time she has heard these stories.*)

MOTHER: A lady lets us sleep it off on her divan. We sleep the sleep of the dead... Then I look at Wacia, and her head is pulsing and crawling like an anthill. I laugh at her till I burst, but then I look, and the same thing's happening to me. I'm fed up with the war, and starving, and they itch, and soon they'll be devouring my head. One lady had a cup of vinegar, you rubbed your face in vinegar, then wrapped it in rags... It burned and stank. But in hell everything stinks, we were used to it. It didn't matter what stank and how it stank, we just wanted to get to Warsaw, to get home, to our parents, our friends, school and fun. We were as dumb as a pair of left shoes. We'd seen so much evil that we were going round the bend. We no longer know what was up and down. We laughed till we burst and clapped out of time. One guy saw this and put us in a car... and he started making sweet talk and wooing us, and we ate it up. Nice ladies, lice ladies, heads all wrapped up in vinegar... We'd have been good for soaking headcheese. The whole way we sang him the filthy songs we learned in prison, until our throats were raw.

(*MARYJKA AND WACIA'S FILTHY SONG. It has a primitive, childish tune, played on a dead cat, a live bomb, and a fake jaw stolen from a dead body.*)

Basia went for a walk, after her class,
then she fell down right on her.......leg,
she stands there thinking, what a stunt,
then she fell down right on her......back.
She walks along, she sees a stick,

then she fell down on a…….boy.
They walk along, the boy sees a rock,
so then he fell down on his…….mother.)

There it is, finally… the house is there… warm, inviting, built by Dad, solid, directorial. At the sight of it we left that guy without even saying goodbye, we just ran in a jiffy to that desert mirage… Except that, just like a mirage… it was all empty… Only walls. Burnt, black. The rooms soiled. The pictures, carpets, tapestries, birch wood, stripped bare…

(MOTHER bustles about talking, meanwhile REGINA turns to the audience and mouths her words, she knows the story word for word. This is what she always does.)

…in our girls' room, by the wall, someone had left their excrement and wiped himself with a white lady's sweater. No sense in looking, I say, but it's Wacia's mock turtleneck, the one she wore under an apron. Seeing that she begins to laugh. She laughs and laughs, louder and louder, and suddenly she changes her mind and begins to cry and cry, again louder and louder, as if she herself were surprised… stop it! Stop it! Don't look…Oh, some fuckers must have lived here, they didn't know what a bathroom was. But don't you give them this satisfaction, come on, look, they left the piano.
The piano stood there covered in ferret crap, the keyboard gruesomely bent out of shape, like a sarcastic grin.
Wacia sits down, wipes away the guano with her apron, and plays… and plays… But every note is not what it should be, it is twisted, hideously warped, grating like an old lush who, after a hundred years on the bottle, has opened his parched and reeking mouth… But she plays and play, she hasn't played for so long, how could she have? She can't stop, but when she plays a waltz, it comes out a dirge, and when she plays a polka, it turns into a funeral march, she plays "Let's All Go to the Manger" and "Dreary Silence" comes out, she plays "Happy Teddy," and it becomes "The Last Horse to Croak Is Making Its Death Rattle"…. *(This might be expressed in the music.)*
It was like it wasn't her, as if someone or thing was suddenly playing her, letting out all the hideousness of those days, which had turned us from girls into vampires, werewolves, from people into ghouls that know only blood and vinegar, and shrieks, inhuman shrieks, and dismal dirt, drudgery, despair, and a dreary death…
At that point, something tells me to open the servants' quarters… I do it, and there…. I can't believe my eyes.
It's there? *(she sheds a tear)* Can eyes that have seen so much misery and horror be deceived?
(In the servant's room MOTHER opens we see a fine table, shining and exuding a former life of comfort.)
I trace my astonished fingers across the tabletop… I pull out the drawer—

there's a dust kitty, a thumbtack, a cross, a knife for paring grapefruit, a drill for figs, clippers for trimming boot leather... As if someone had left them there only a second ago... Or maybe the table was enchanted? Charmed? Or cursed? Wacia was playing the whole time. I say: Wacia, look. Hey have a look, Wacia, over here. "Don't bother me when I'm playing." I carried it out of there on own back. And she says: "What are you taking that for, dummy, think how it'll look!" I carried it all the way to Otwock by myself. Like a hump. Like a cross. She walked beside me, laughing at me, shrugging her shoulders. "Carry it if you want, I sure won't!"
"Wacia, take it for a bit, I'm going to pass out!"
"I don't give a damn!"
"But it's all we've got left."
She just took off her kerchief, waving to men as she walked and laughing.
"Wacia, come on!"
"What do you want? It's bad enough you look like a donkey, a pack mule, a laughingstock! You just make us look crotchety, you wanted it, so carry it, I'm young, I want to live, play, laugh, love, dance!"

It was a lovely nightstand. Everyone said so. They wanted to buy it! With little drawers, a nifty handle for an ashtray on one side, it kept popping out and whacking me on the head, I got lumps, bruises, ecchymosis. My head swelled up, grew deformed, wider and thinner by turns, as if someone had been kicking it like a ball.
But I got it there.
I sanded it, buffed it.
I always put something under one leg to keep it from wobbling; I spoke to it like a dear friend. Gently, sweetly. It replied with soft creaks, and at other times with silence, with the sagacious silence of old wood.
In Otwock we were taken in by a distant aunt. The winter came, I got a cough. The doctor said it was tuberculosis. I went to be cured. So, I'm getting better and better... In comes a telegram: Maryjka—stop—auntie.
It should have said "is dying," but Wacia claims she didn't have enough money. Not for frills like that.
When I got back, it was all over. Cancer. By what miracle she signed the whole home over to Wacia, even though Auntie always preferred me, that I'll never know.
Studies were out, I applied for work, I rented a room in Warsaw. Everything was packed up, the driver was waiting,
and suddenly Wacia didn't know where the nightstand was.

WACIA:
The one we found after the liberation, and we took turns carrying on our backs?

MOTHER:
What's this tall tale you're telling me?

WACIA:
Oh, it's the god's honest truth; I had bruises from carrying it long after.

MOTHER:
What carrying? After I carried it the whole way? That's what gave you bruises?

WACIA:
You carried it? You carried it?

MOTHER:
I carried it! I carried it!

WACIA:
Poppycock. We carried it together, I remember it well.

MOTHER:
The devil's muddled your head. I carried it by myself, or my name isn't Maryjka.

WACIA:
I carried it by myself, you just walked beside me.

MOTHER:
What: walked beside? Then how'd I get this scar from the handle that kept banging me in the head? The blood poured in buckets, my brain started poking out from my wounds, some good folks helped me shove it back in, bandaged it with rags, gave me a shot of pepper vodka for my fever. Don't you think you'd better run and get it?

WACIA:
Well, I better check.

MOTHER:
Check what?

WACIA:
Just check. I don't know right now, because we're doing the pickling.

MOTHER:
So go look.

WACIA:
How can I look when I'm standing in a bucket of cabbage!
(As she says this, Wacia hastily jumps into a bucket and with mock enthusiasm stomps on the pickled cabbage)

MOTHER (*deriding Wacia's laments*):
"It must have gotten lost, I don't see it anywhere. Maybe Jurek put it some-where, who knows? It's a miracle we found it back then. Oh, this pickling, when I pickle, all this pickling is going to make my knees crack."

How many years I couldn't get her to give it back! Finally, we'd stopped talking to each other because of her crookedness... First, I stopped talking to her, and then, in revenge, she stopped taking to me. And when I saw she was taking re-venge, I got tight-lipped in revenge, because since it was her fault, she should be coming to me on her knees, but she just started claiming and spreading all around that I had lived so long at their place, she'd shared everything with me, her last potato, I owed everything to them, and I was making such a fuss about some little piece of furniture that was so shitty that when you were watching TV you could only stick one foot on top of it, and only when you weren't wear-ing a slipper, and...

(*The flashback comes to an end, we see that REGINA, taking advantage of MOTHER being lost in her memories, is picking at the food from the table; she is presently gobbling up a big rose carved from a carrot, a garnish from one of the platters.*)

REGINA:
And what, it just suddenly turned up after a while?

MOTHER:
Maybe they were doing some cleaning?

REGINA (*skeptically*):
I see.

MOTHER:
And why do you care all of a sudden? You've got eyes. Where'd those stockings come from?

REGINA:
They were under the sink.

MOTHER:
You know, that's where I put the old ones into a sack to give your cousin.

REGINA:
My cousin?

MOTHER:
Trudka makes them into carpets! Comb your hair!

Mrs. Nastka *(watching as REGINA pretends to comb her hair, but only grazes the surface):*
Either she thinks too much, or her hair isn't combed. Or someone cursed her and put her hair in knots. Too many thoughts in the head; the thoughts tangle round and round, they spin and whirl like shit in a blowhole, they knot into a knot. Four fingers of pure vodka, three nettle leaves, mix with a handful of ribworts, a handful of ash and sweeten with plenty of sugar or honey, cross yourself, pray hard. Fall to your knees, grab a stick, a ruler, or something straight, and pray to Mary of the Raging Heart, to the Weeping Jesus, for the knot to untie, for the girl's mind to untangle from befuddled thoughts, and free the foolish ones…. And cleave away the knot, before the first length of winter grain should grow forth….

Mother *(suddenly seeing through the window that guests have arrived):* Jesus and Mary, Regina, they're here! Nothing's prepared! Quiet! They've come. Arrived! They're here…

SCENE 4

Still in the apartment. MOTHER is eavesdropping at the door. Raised voices coming from the staircase: Careful now! Careful! Not like that. Dammit, come on! Do you want to completely…., damn good-for-nothing… You big lunk, meathead…What an oaf, a goddamn pain in the ass. Jesus and Mary…

MOTHER wants to open the door and run out. But she stops herself, seeing her excitement as gauche, she strikes a pose that is calm and aloof, combing her hair and primping a little lock.

A tug at the door. Then an irate pounding. MOTHER haughtily unlocks it and removes the chain. AUNT WACIA comes tumbling into the apartment, followed by UNCLE JUREK. They are carrying a large package together, wrapped in a sheet or packing paper.
UNCLE JUREK is a fairly heavy-set man who tends to fade into the background. Around 50, roughly similar to anyone; one look at AUNT tells us that he plays third, fourth, or even fifth fiddle here (maybe he's forced to, maybe to keep from rocking the boat). AUNT, in turn, is a relatively young woman, but quite ahead in the process of becoming matronly. Chunky and heavily made up, her fur coat that makes her look like a yeti with a perm. A thousand tiny rabbit eyes stare out from its multitudinous folds; they are, as it were, an extension and multiplication of the piercing, appraising stare of their owner. She looks around ostentatiously, as if examining everything, the people and the furnishings, for where she can spread her toxic energy. She strolls about in a cloud of heavy, sweet, communist-era perfumes, and her kisses on her relatives' cheeks leave traces of pink Yardley. Her way of being is full of sweetness yet laced with venom and psychotoxins. The love which she swiftly snuffed out, the

beauty she was unable to hold onto, have left her alone with her bitterness and a longing for destruction:

AUNT:
My my, I see we've bolted ourselves up tight to keep out the killers? *(handing MOTHER a package)* Here's some tea; I know how much you like it.

MOTHER *(inviting her in and scooping up the parcel)*:
Oh, you shouldn't have, imagine what it cost. But why linger on the staircase, come in, come in...

Behind AUNT and UNCLE slouches their indifferent daughter, BOGUMIŁA, chewing gum, about 20 years old. She is also a large, chunky girl in a sheepskin coat, turtleneck, and too-short skirt, exposing her panties and stressing her overt eroticism. Her face is a blank. She looks around, yawning, she emanates nonchalance and modernity.

AUNT WACIA *(starting her nosy inspection, and extravagantly patting the parcel she brought)*:
Well, here's our bane. Our furniture of contention! A real Trojan Horse.

(Everyone greets and kisses each other. There is a nervous chaos of hanging coats and removing shoes, overlapping pleasantries which we might choose from the list below:

You've only got one family, after all. Isn't that a beautiful hair-do! Maryjka, well aren't you slim! And what was all that fuss for then? I wish you'd tell me what diet you're on, because I've been gaining weight again. Diabetes, ha-ha! Mama can drink all the juice from the bottle in one go! What an imagination. How long has it been!
Bogumiła, God in heaven, the nonsense you tell people. Maybe don't unwrap it! What for! Plenty of time for that later. Soon enough! Oh of course. Oh of course. The food's getting cold, Maryjka spent all day cooking. Jurek give us a break, no smoking in here for God's sake. Let's be seated, be seated, Jesus, it's cramped in here!)

MATKA looks fondly at the package, we see her hesitating, then deciding not to unwrap it, wanting to celebrate the reunion with her beloved object in private. The family is still in a flurry of small talk:
O Regina, how you've grown, and so beautiful! You were so small. Oh sure. What a lovely fur! Oh thank-you, Jurek bought it for our anniversary. Spot of liquor? It's made of our chokeberry. Chokeberry?? From the garden. What garden? And Bogumiła is a young lady. She just got back from England, working for a family as a governess, as they say over there...)

Bogumiła *(gloomily, fed up with the women's idiotic babble):*
Au-pair.

SCENE 5

An apartment. The family meeting is still going. Everyone is eating in silence. Meanwhile REGINA, as far as possible at such an unplentiful meal, is osten-tatiously chowing down, smacking her lips and annihilating all the rules of table manners; she stares at the tablecloth the whole time to avoid the gaze of MOTHER, who, seeing this etiquette, has a series of all-too-visible heart palpi-tations. She clears her throat sophisticatedly and wipes her lips with a napkin, but her eyes scream: THIS IS NOT A ROADSIDE INN FOR YAHOOS!!! AUNT WACIA observes all this with pleasantly raised eyebrows, noting every consecutive rape of etiquette with open, badly concealed satisfaction. Uncle Jurek can't find his feet in this complicated multilevel psychodrama.

Uncle Jurek *(naively, to relieve a bit of the tension in the room):*
And maybe the girls would like to listen to some records?

The adults remain at the table; without looking at one another, REGINA and BOGUMIŁA put down their cutlery and move toward REGINA's chair-bed. There is a tapestry, a few postcards. The young women seem too big for the furniture and the cute decorations; they sit in awkward silence.

Regina:
Wanna listen to something? I've got some new platters.

Bogumiła:
O'key.

REGINA puts on a record. BOGUMIŁA shows no special interest in the record player, she pulls a compact electronic calculator from her purse and begins nonchalantly calculating. Her equations appear on the screen:
$2+2+3+4+5=16$
$1+1+1+1=4$

The record plays the sounds of a big-beat hit, "Morning time" by Shabadaba-da:

*"When I loved ya you were lovely like the morning,
like the dawn you just came up without a warning,
smelling like lilac and May, but since I stopped lovin' you one day,
you smell like nettles and cabbage stew
the kind you mama liked to do
your face is so drab, in my dreams you're a nag,*

you doodle hearts in notebooks and dream of the curtains
you'll hang in apartments to stop your hurtin'
your apartment, husband, kids, furniture, and you

o'key, you ain't gettin' nothin' ba-by
o'key, I don't love ya no more
o'key, you're bored my little la-dy
o'key, so now I guess you know the score

etc.

The sound of a bouncing ball is heard through the window.

REGINA (*pointing to the calculator*):
What's that?

BOGUMIŁA (*bored and disappointed that her cousin's so out of touch*): Don't you know? It's a cybernetic personal calculator.

REGINA:
Calca...later?

BOGUMIŁA:
You can count things on it. Any number you like.

REGINA:
Really?

BOGUMIŁA:
In England everyone's got one of these. It's so smart. It's a real-life hack. Here they make you learn math by heart. But there, whenever you have to count something, you just pull it out, even in the bus, and count away.
REGINA:
Mama said you lived in London?

BOGUMIŁA (*still counting*):
Eh, first I lived in Leeds. That's a worse shithole than our Otwock. I was there with one family, then another. Just don't tell mum. I broke too much. Porcelain, I mean. And supposedly it was me who wrecked the carpet. O'key.... Except it wasn't totally me.

REGINA:
You could have got it out with baking soda. Or citric acid.

BOGUMIŁA:
Dummy. They don't have stuff like that there. All they've got at the self-serve supermarket is a whole shelf of various powders and shampoos specially for carpets. For big ones, small ones, whatever you want. Wanna fag?

REGINA:
I don't smoke.

BOGUMIŁA *(taking out a pack of foreign cigarettes and lighting one up)*:
Players. There was a girl and a boy. But English kids sure are daft.

REGINA:
More so than ours?

BOGUMIŁA:
Heaven and earth. And totally rude, *blimey*! I got so bored I started teaching them Polish. But the boneheads couldn't understand a thing. The girl couldn't even say *dziewczynka*. That's a problem bordering on the ontological, don't you think?

(unexpectedly, BOGUMIŁA remembers the LITTLE GIRL in question)

BOGUMIŁA:
Repeat after me: Dziew-czyn-ka!

LITTLE GIRL *(helplessly)*:
Jev-ka-chin!

BOGUMIŁA *(unexpectedly harsh)*:
Wrong, one more time.

LITTLE GIRL:
Chin… jev…. Jeev-ka!

BOGUMIŁA *(revolted, enraged, tugging at LITTLE GIRL'S ear)*:
Wrong! You can't do it!

LITTLE GIRL:
And why is your name like BOG?

BOGUMIŁA:
My name is Bogumiła, not bog.

LITTLE GIRL:
I've heard your name is bog-o-mila.

BOGUMIŁA:
Who told you that?

LITTLE GIRL:
Mama. Because you're from a country where they haven't got bog paper.

BOGUMIŁA:
Who told you that?

LITTLE GIRL:
Mama.

BOGUMIŁA:
That's what your Mama says? *(she thinks a moment; her eyes mist over vengefully)* It's true what your mother says. When we have to go to the john in Poland, we don't have to use paper. Cool, huh?

LITTLE GIRL:
Really?

BOGUMIŁA *(showing how it's done):*
Everyone just uses their hand, wherever they happen to be, and then they bury it in the ground with their nails.

LITTLE GIRL *(totally surprised and inspired):*
Even on the carpet?

BOGUMIŁA:
Of course! Just go ahead next time you've got the urge.

(LITTLE GIRL runs off skipping merrily and vanishes off-stage. After a moment's odd silence a scream is heard, then right away the sounds of an argument, lament, sobbing, and the mother spanking LITTLE GIRL.)

SCENE 6

At the table again: MOTHER, AUNT WACIA, and UNCLE JUREK. UNCLE eats monotonously, deep in thought, while MOTHER and AUNT chatter away in high, sickly-sweet voices, though we can sense the buried tension of long-estranged sisters. They are making every effort not to kill each other at once. Thus, they sit next to one another, a bit stiffly, trying not jostle one another with their gazes. As if by looking unwarily into the other's eyes they could see what they know about themselves all too well! Their conflicts and long separation have allowed them to rebuild themselves. New versions of their lives and family hierarchies, never questioned and never confronted, had perfect conditions to flourish. Yet now both feel threatened. A confrontation and audit could occur at any moment. Chopin is playing on the radio, something grand and strident, such as the Revolutionary Etude.

MOTHER (OR VOICE OF MOTHER):
I have no regrets before my death, only that I won't be going to the philharmonic. To watch a pianist hang there over the keyboard... like a falcon over its prey.... Then come crashing down, crashing, scattering into a cascade of sounds. Did you hear that luscious arpeggio?

AUNT WACIA (OR VOICE OF WACIA):
Arpeggio, shmeggio. I stopped playing ages ago. Why we still have that old upright, I'll never know, it's just gathering dust.

MOTHER:
Watching those slender hands race about the keyboard like two hares, hunted down and in their death throes! Thrashing about, fainting, only to... live, and find another moment's harbor in silence, another....

AUNT WACIA:
Bogumiła's got a real tin ear. She's got it from Jurek. We hired a teacher, he ran away screaming, his sheet music scattering after him. But I sometimes dream of that old upright at home, remember? How we went in back then, back when we were girls... The wreckage, the ravaged home, only that untuned upright, covered in cat shit. And you started to play. And you kept on playing, I was all bored, I started looking around... And that was when I found that nightstand, I said: Look Maryjka, isn't that....

(UNCLE JUREK, who knows about this nightstand business better than he'd care to, yet unable to find any other stimuli at this meal which has prematurely concluded for lack of food, slips into a reverie. A young lady wearing skimpy underwear appears in the front hall. She creeps up to the coat hanger and snap! snatches AUNT WACIA's rabbits. With the seductive gait of a strip-tease dancer, cuddling the fur like the hairy chest of a lover, she creeps up to UNCLE JUREK, who stares at her hypnotized, suddenly beaming. With a nimble hop the woman lands in UNCLE JUREK's lap; he is blissfully unaware of the endless babbling of MOTHER and AUNT WACIA)

UNCLE JUREK:
All right, all right. Just don't whip it around like that, it might get caught on something.

WOMAN:
How do I look?

UNCLE:
Very pretty. Just go easy on the perfume, or I'll be in trouble driving from here to Grójec.

MOTHER (*seeing this, discreetly*):
Who's the girl?

AUNT WACIA (*waving a hand dismissively*):
Some girl from the local post office. Miss innocent with a child. Total guff. If she's so innocent, where'd the kid come from?

WOMAN:
She gets a fur, and all I get are some dumb nylons. When are you going to get me one?

UNCLE:
Oh don't be silly, it's a bargain-basement coat rejected for export. (*cuddling his face into her cleavage*) Anyway, first I have to see if you deserved it, if you washed yourself nice and clean, if you've got a clean…. heart, wait, wait…

(*The voices of MOTHER and AUNT WACIA interrupt their fling again. They are still talking over one another, in a know-it-all tone of "and this, and that, and how, and why, of course," not hearing each other. They have their whole lives to tell each other; they both want to brag to the other that she, despite the burns and affronts by fate and loved ones, has come out on top. Each wants to triumph over the other, at least in her stories. But the censored and souped-up versions of the facts they depict, once free of their control, start to crack wide open and let in the truth. As a result, they "end up saying" things they hadn't intended.*)

MOTHER:
I told Regina, you like books, go study medicine. You always recited poems so nicely

(*a child's voice from the microphone:*
"…a moribund mare gave its last sigh…
…and from the blood and suffering grew flowers
…poppies will bloom from the blood that was shed
…celebrating the blood in the summer")

MOTHER:
I tell her: you always recited poems so beautifully, go to the polytechnic, they've got professions there that always come in handy. But she insisted on the Teacher's Studies. And what came of that?

AUNT WACIA:
Bogumiła was supposed to study dentistry. Jurek had already got her signed up. She says: times may change, but there will always be rotten teeth. So what if she couldn't even pass grade nine?
Composed and modest, yet bratty as hell. Morally rudderless, physically too voluptuous, she is a bad example to others. Teachers couldn't praise her enough. So clever and quick, yet so dull, cynical, her studies took a back seat to cutting classes, coffee shops, flirting and boys. Often much older ones. One was even Jurek's age.

MOTHER:
Regina's just the same—top marks. One day we even got a letter from the school...

(MOTHER recalls being happy and excited as she cut open the letter.)

Hand me my glasses, I can't see a thing without them. Not those, the other ones, the ones your father used to wear! She studied so hard, no doubt this is some kind of special distinction, a medal for her grades, or a scholarship... *(reads)*
" ...owing to the recurring absences... crossed off the list of students...".

(MOTHER paces the room, faints, loses her wits, reads the letter time and again in disbelief)

Where are these absences coming from, when I see her getting up and going to school every day? Maybe they've made a mistake? Maybe there's someone there who looks similar, or with a similar name, who's always skipping out, and Regina's been mistaken for her, and all this is her fault? So much for her benefits, so much for everything...

AUNT WACIA *(pretending to listen politely but remaining focused on her own story)*:
A boy Jurek's age! I say thanks but no thanks to boys like that. A steward on the SS Batory. No thanks to that kind of studies! That's just shame and anxiety. The doctor charged a mint for the operation, and when she got back she ate a whole loaf of bread. She lost her chance to study dentistry, and on top of it all, we had to shell out for a ticket to England.

MOTHER:
I say: "You'd better explain this at once, write an appeal...." She just went ballistic; she hid my jacket. "Mama don't go there. I never want to go back there! NEVER! If you go there I'm going to go jump in the Vistula." Of course she was just bluffing, she'd never do something that dumb.

AUNT WACIA:
Bogumiła's just the same. She can forget about that dentistry! And it gives you the chills to go somewhere with your tooth when you know they take any old person to study for two cups of coffee. So, she saw a bit of the world, just dipped her toe into it. She would have even brought home an English husband, except she said, "Blech mama!" Because they're all redheads. Each one of them a redhead. Apparently, that's why no one wants to make friends with anyone. Every child has to be alone in a one-person classroom. First, because they're redheads and nasty, and second, so that other nasty redheads won't hassle them, and third, so that they don't gossip about them and hurt their feelings, and fourth, so they don't get bullied and beaten up. And vice versa.

MOTHER:
Oh, of course. Regina didn't want to even look at those "professors," she had no such craving, and even if they begged her to come back she wouldn't. Anyway, let them ask. She's not going back to studying. I've already started applying for her jobs.

AUNT WACIA:
Oh, of course. Because they're oddballs. They're a stuck-up generation. Waited on hand and foot, they have everything without having to pick their ass up off the couch. We were lashed with rods and belts, and rags, and pokers, and did it hurt us? We understood why they were beating us; we felt they were beating out of love. We asked them to beat us some more.

(now they might start speaking at the same time)

MOTHER:
Work in the bookshop.

AUNT WACIA:
She gained 20 pounds! But I tell her it's all for the best. She can be slimmer when she's young, and now it's better she puts on weight for marriage.

MOTHER (*unpleasantly knocked off balance by news of BOGUMIŁA's marriage, she speaks louder and louder. She takes her niece's wedding as the final insult, reminding her of what a failure REGINA is as her peer. This explains her blathering on, trying to cover up this inconvenient news with a landslide of words*):
Books are always books. Whether they're presents, or whatever. Gałczyński. Ovid. Hemingway. Conrad. Mickiewicz.

AUNT WACIA (*who also starts speaking louder and faster, trying to drown out REGINA's successes in response. These "successes" are, of course, only the names of writers whose books she might one day sell, but the sisters' jealousy*

has nothing to do with common sense):
She looks more serious for the wedding, and in the bureaus, and in the line-ups, a thin girl gets pushed aside, shoved, elbowed and soars off like a balloon, she never gets anything done.

MOTHER *(barreling on):*
First pick of all the new releases! Aretin. Saganka, of course. Sholokhov.

AUNT WACIA *(now almost shouting):*
And now that they're about to get married in October, she's going to look more stately for the wedding as well.

MOTHER *(evidently unsure of how to escalate things; she shouts, desperately trying to bury BOGUMIŁA's wedding under a violent deluge of varied and unconnected bits of information):*
Bulgakov. Hłasko.
Krempiński, he's got talent. But also, the older generations: Reymont, Prus. Eat, eat. Mushrooms are the new meat. We serve them every day. They're great for frying in the pan. OUR friend has a great mushroom farm....

AUNT WACIA *(shouts):*
Anyway, her man is an engineer. Hard-working. Tough. He's got a place to live. He's thinking of buying a car.

MOTHER *(shrieks):*
He's also got his own greenhouse, he has hotbeds.

AUNT WACIA *(shifting gears: she now speaks softly, with class):*
He is also serious, but not exceedingly, he also likes to joke and have a good time. He's taller than her. That's good. The man should be a bit taller.

MOTHER *(a bit terrified that she's lying, but going for it):*
Her man is also... well built. Stockier. But also very decent, responsible.... He makes a few thousand on those grocery vegetables alone in the winter.

AUNT WACIA *(irritated to the extreme at these high earnings from grocery vegetables, wanting to end the whole argument by changing the subject):*
JUREK ARE YOU EVEN LISTENING TO THIS CONVERSATION?

UNCLE *(woken from his stupor, the scantily-clad woman in the fur coat scampers from his lap in fright):*
... Uh... He's definitely a guy with assets. *(the conversation about the virtues of this unknown man gets bogged down, so he turns his attention to the food)* So I guess I'll eat... while we're on the subject... a mushroom!

SCENE 7

Meanwhile, the girls on the couch have sunk into a sad awkward stupor. RE-GINA sits there lethargically, BOGUMIŁA keeps calculating things, sometimes looking glum, shaking her head in wonderment, other times even giggling at her sums.

BOGUMIŁA *(conceding that maybe it's not so kind to have such a good time without sharing):*
Wanna try?

REGINA *(abashed by the wonderful device):*
I always sucked at math...

BOGUMIŁA *(not seeing this as an obstacle):*
There's nothing to it. Just think what you want to add.

REGINA *(cautiously accepting the super modern device):*
It only adds?

BOGUMIŁA:
No way. It does everything. Subtraction, multiplication...

(REGINA pokes at the calculator with pious respect, trying out small numbers at first)

BOGUMIŁA:
Careful. The batteries aren't cheap. Mmmm... *(stretching out on the couch)* This is the same sofa you had when we were little! We stuffed cotton balls into our bras. And hour after hour: What's your husband's name going to be? Mine's gonna be Irek, and yours will be Waldek. Mine is Andrzej and yours Romek. Mine is Krzysztof, and yours is Zygfryd. And the kids? Bożenka and Pawik. Hala and Krystek. Małgosia and Wacek. Ela and... Pankracy! You got so mad that your son would be a Pankracy! Ew, so ugly! You shoved me into the bushes and there was a skull and some old, barbed wire, I tore my skirt. And now: abracadabra! We're older girls, and men are eating out of our hands.

MRS. NASTKA *(crossing the stage to wring out her rag in the bucket):*
During the war all thirty-three of us lived in Zagródek. Marauders came in the night, dragged everyone out in front of the house and whether a body was small, big, young, old, every last one got shot. And I was shot with them. They dug a ditch. When we were all there lying in the ditch, dead, I saw something strange. It was like the coat of my neighbor Karpiuk had a hole, and the hole was getting wider. Out of it came the Gorgeous Girl.

(The dead NEIGHBORS from Zagródek are lying on MRS. NASTKA, she alone moves.)

GORGEOUS GIRL:
The Lord has had mercy on thee, because thy soul is pure, and thy heart fervent. Merciful He is, and among them all he hast chosen thou among all those who testified with their suffering.

MRS. NASTKA:
So, I think to myself: Am I alive or aren't I?

GORGEOUS GIRL:
You are alive. But the life before you is hard and fraught with pain.

MRS. NASTKA:
Will the war end?

GORGEOUS GIRL:
It will.

MRS. NASTKA:
And will I find a husband?

GORGEOUS GIRL *(sighs):*
You will.

MRS. NASTKA:
And I'll have children.

GORGEOUS GIRL *(sighing even more heavily):*
Oh, will you ever. Your husband will be of vodka born, and so too will he drink vodka. Your hut of vodka shall be built, vodka shalt thou breathe, for vodka shalt thou labor. Thy fate shall be writ in vodka on broken glass. Thy sons of vodka shall be born, and to vodka shall they be drawn. Yet woman must suffer, and in silence thy hardships and thy vodka, confiding thy complaints in the Lord, and he shalt take from thee all that is evil, and grant his gifts in exchange.

(GORGEOUS GIRL vanishes. REGINA and BOGUMIŁA again on the couch)

REGINA:
And you? Have you been with a guy?

BOGUMIŁA:
Bah. *(counting on the calculator: 1+1+1+...2...+1+1....)* Fourteen or maybe

twelve times. I stopped counting. No biggie. Anyway, it depends. The male penis looks like a severed goose head that suddenly woke up and came alive! If you like a severed goose head squirting between your legs, then sure, you'll get a real kick out of it.

REGINA:
Why should I? Boys bore me. Their puppy-dog eyes, their sighs, their bullshit. And those mushrooms.

BOGUMIŁA:
Mushrooms? What are those? *(She looks at REGINA with uncertain though watching eyes, after a moment's reflection deduces with satisfaction that RE-GINA has said something wicked)* That pig... Maybe you just don't know how to fondle them right? Silly. Come here. I'll show you. Not like that. You've got to get closer to him.

REGINA *(reluctant to be instructed):*
Closer how?

BOGUMIŁA *(embracing REGINA like a pro and wrapping her legs around her tight):*
Like this, so your smell covers him, so that your eyebrows and eyelashes, your lip hairs tickle him... But when he's thinking God knows what, you push him away. Let him think you're easy, you're a whore or a slut, that you like it. Let him wait, and again he'll respect you, do this... so that he thinks... and when he's totally insisting, then you pretend to surrender to him for a moment... So that he thinks that he's finally got what he wants.... But then you quickly push him away, because actually you don't want to, why should you? What's in it for you? If he jokes, you giggle. If he tells a story, you listen to what he says as if you're totally interested, because he's older and so wise. They really like that. And when he's drunk and gets mad and crude, and he berates you starts pawing and grabbing at you, you know there's nothing to be done, you can let him kiss you... *(demonstrating)* Part your lips. PART 'EM. And with your tongue... First gently, like you're licking a cloud... and after a while, harder... like you're biting an undercooked hunk of beef. Sigh to show it's more and more pleasant... more and more pleasant... Harder, so that he thinks that this is it.... And then again drop it, you're not interested, as if you never wanted anything in the first place... He's no Clark Gable, you can have him or someone else! You can give him a bit, but not too much, so that he doesn't think you like it. But not too little either, or he'll find a better chick, not some chaste medieval nun. Why the dopey face?

REGINA *(pushing her away):*
Because it tickles... weirdly.

BOGUMIŁA:
I'm not tickling, I'm fondling. You've got to be ready for that. Breasts are very important to a boy. He's gotta touch them, knead them, flip-flop them around. You've got to get used to it. They're like children. *(Miffed at how dense her pupil is, she starts adding on her calculator, changing the subject)* I don't know why Mama didn't want to give Aunt Marysia that bloody table, you know something about that story??

(REGINA is still unpleasantly surprised at the lesson, trying to fix her dress and bra)

BOGUMIŁA:
She kept it in the pigsty, water dripped onto it from the roofing, and... But she didn't want to give it up, "Maryjka's a real sly one. I carried it all the way from Warsaw to Otwock, she rode in a cart alongside of me. And that was an antique." But now at the swap meet they told her that it wasn't worth a thing, it was trash, "better to buy a new one." So dumb. Anyway, it totally doesn't match our new flat, because it's in a new building, and we're doing it up all modern, the way we like it...

(REGINA falls silent, but in her silent aggression she does some impossible calculations, e.g. 19082080753475037585839: 209808385075)

BOGUMIŁA:
Well, and it's so much hassle. You've got to stand in line-ups in the shopping centers till late, and then it's dark and scary, *gives me the willies*... How many times have I had to take the night bus home from Warsaw. I wanted to stay overnight with you, but mama forbade me to even call. And you know how dangerous it is now. Have you heard about that pervert that attacks in the evening, raping women, then killing and strangling them?

REGINA:
That's what they say.

BOGUMIŁA:
Everyone in Otwock is talking about it.

REGINA:
A militiaman told me about it.

BOGUMIŁA *(perking up a bit):*
A militiaman? Is he handsome? They say the Lady Strangler strangled a friend of a friend. I mean, her mate from her childhood.
Apparently, he cut off both her ears with nail scissors, because she was wearing valuable earrings. And I just happen to wear earrings. Now she gets so em-

barrassed, she always walks around in a kerchief, like an old lady... Apparently a world-famous professor has already checked her out, he says he might be able to sew those ears back on... *(miffed that REGINA doesn't react to her revelations, she decides to take back her treasured gadget)* Why are you punching in so many numbers? You'll break something. It's not a toy. Give it back.

Blackout. Again we see the stage, UNCLE JUREK is helping AUNT WACIA on with her fur.

MOTHER:
That's a beautiful fur.

AUNT WACIA:
Ahhh, this old thing. These shabby rat skins. It's all coming apart.

Everyone exits, BOGUMIŁA immersed in her calculator, forever adding something, AUNT WACIA ties her shoes for her.

BOGUMIŁA *(looking up from the screen with her glum, meaningful stare):* Ciao, ciao Bambina!

REGINA and MOTHER are left alone. MOTHER ceremoniously walks over to the package. She trembles as she touches the fabric wrapped around it. Finally, with one gesture, she tears it off. Underneath is a nightstand in a comical state of disrepair.
Blackout.

ACT 2
SCENE 1:

We see the BOOKSHOP DIRECTOR'S room, stuffed with books, darkened by the pulled curtains; he is snoozing or resting off a headache with his legs stretched out on his desk.
On his face is an ice pack, so we can't see that the masculinity and symmetry of his features is beginning to give way to the puffy face of an alcoholic.
Once he loved literature, he longed to be a writer himself, but he lacked the talent or wit; today he sells books.
He himself says, "I only sell them." But should anyone else say that "only selling them" he's liable to go nuts, liable to launch into a rant about how that "only" is worth so much. SO MUCH! And that a bookshop is a far loftier pursuit than writing some damn book for nothing and no one.

He is a bitter and unhappy man. It happens that when you plan great things in life they take so long and meander so much that along the way they manage to turn into medium-sized or small, insignificant things. His dreams began to go foul. The compromises he struck up and the unpleasant deals he had to make to keep afloat in life meant that he projects constant unease, discontent, gloominess. He'd like to snuff out people's spark, especially when they're carefree and smiling. A little kid chasing a hoop with a stick, girls with bare knees waiting for a tram, a guy with a SKI scarf despite the warm weather, a heavy overhang of lilac blossom blocking the window, a kissing couple... He'd blow it all out like birthday candles, watching it go black and give smoke.

Bulgarian cognac glistens gold in a shot glass. A calendar with naked women hangs on the wall. MRS. NASTKA is on her knees, scrubbing the floor.

MRS. NASTKA:
Our wedding didn't raise the roof, it was modest. People said Ładczuk, he's a good guy, but he's a lush. Be his wife, good plan, you'll come out on top. A husband pretty as a picture, but gets royally sloshed, he's drunk up his mother's hut, he beats her, but she's old and sick, you're young, healthy, you'll adapt. And there'll be children, you'll have nothing to cook in the pot. For Ładczuk is a good man, but all he likes is vodka. He's a good guy, but when he's all tanked he likes to give a good lashing, he'll treat you right. What could you do, you had to get married. God had already blessed us, we were on our way home from the church. At first it went so-so. I'd heard the warning of the Gorgeous Maiden, so I says to him: don't go drinking so much. Don't drink so much, and put down that ax, why bring an ax to your own wedding. So he went and put it down. But all at once he was holding it again. And he was looking at me good and hard... it seemed he was looking at me, but in fact he was looking

inside of himself, rummaging around within him, searching... but he didn't find a thing, so again he looked at me... He crawled around on the ground, got up... Now he's forgotten why, who, and what, who I even am and he just says: it's my wedding, we have to dance. And when he started dancing with me....

(The Ładczuks dance destructively.)

PRIEST:
Pray to the Lord to accept your sufferings, and he will repay them a hundred-fold with his gifts.

MRS. NASTKA: Wonder how, when he's broken my arm. How am I going to forage for undergrowth without it.

PRIEST:
Oh you see Mrs. Ładczuk? You don't even see that God has rewarded you already. Don't you know that foraging for undergrowth is now considered poaching? It's a steep fine you have to pay, maybe even go to court. And what does undergrowth get you? A few bucks. And the court will set you back a few hundred or even a few thousand.

To drown her out, the DIRECTOR cranks up the radio. He might even dance a bit or just with his feet, to fool himself for a moment that he's on top of the world, he's got untapped imagination, yet it looks sad and pathetic. The radio plays a big-beat tune with the following lyrics:

"Don't say you don't wanna
don't say you don't wanna, at last tell me o'key!
When you look that way when you look that way
oh I know that you wanna

oh you're so foolish you don't know
you're tryin' to fight it
you're makin' faces and goin' through the paces
but now you can't deny it

you love woogy-boogy and you love cha cha cha,
you love kissy-kissy and na-na-na-na
you love hanky-panky and the flies of tse-tse-tse
and my fingers on your boobies is what you love to see

RADIO:
Attention attention! This is a bulletin from the Head Station of the Citizen's Militia. We now have a description of the man suspected of assaulting women in the Mokotów and Downtown regions this April, his motives impure. Height:

medium. Posture: hunched, frame: slender. Hair: a light shade. Forehead: low, Mongoloid. Jaw: outcropping, slack... Numerous small scars, pock-marks from teenage acne.... Stare: terrifying. Wears a trademark scarf with a winter pattern... Citizens, should you have any information about this suspect, telephone this number at once... or write to this address....

From behind the door, we hear how Karolinka, the Director's secretary, is trying to shoo an applicant from the office. This applicant is Regina.

VOICE OF KAROLINKA:
If you please, just hold on a minute. The director has not yet asked you in to his office.

VOICE OF REGINA:
Since I've been waiting so long...

VOICE OF KAROLINKA:
The director is busy right now.

VOICE OF REGINA:
But I have a referral.

VOICE OF KAROLINKA:
Who's referred you?

Now the office door opens, and in slinks a nervous, cowering Karolinka, fearfully clutching a file. She is a nice young woman with no special distinguishing features.

KAROLINKA *(in a sweet and extremely soothing voice):*
Boss...

DIRECTOR:
What?

KAROLINKA:
...this woman has been waiting over an hour and a half. Referred by someone named.... (whispers).

DIRECTOR:
Oh for Chrissakes. Might as well send her in.

Regina enters the room. Karolinka slips out. The director does not remove the ice pack from his face.

REGINA:
I'm here about a job. I've been sent by....

DIRECTOR (*as if wanting to rewind a reality that is unspooling too fast*):
Right, Stępnia.

REGINA:
Tadeusz apparently called you about me.

DIRECTOR:
For what job?

REGINA:
As an intern salesperson.

DIRECTOR (*hopelessly*):
Nice idea he had. Am I a shelter for distant relatives? Got an application form?

REGINA:
Here it is. *(opening a file)*. There's a photo... and a resume.

DIRECTOR:
Put it down. Wherever. Education?

REGINA:
I've been studying at the Teacher's College. Except that...

DIRECTOR:
Except what?

REGINA (*sadly lowering her gaze, silent for a long time*):
Dad went to war... And then.... And when... things started to get unpleasant, and then.... There were absences and...

DIRECTOR (*disgusted with these confessions, he brushes them aside impatiently*):
... Languages?

REGINA:
Russian.

DIRECTOR:
I'm not asking about that. English?

REGINA:
In a manner of speaking.

DIRECTOR (*irritated*):
Listen, this isn't a discount shop where you'll be selling soap and rotgut. Our customers are foreigners, and non-natives, and guests from abroad....

REGINA:
I had lessons at the Methodist Church.

MOTHER (*appearing in some inexplicable way, as if by the power of her prayers and incantations she teleported here for a moment*):
She recited poems more beautifully than anyone in her whole class!

(we hear a child's voice through a microphone, with the echo of a school gymnasium
"...a moribund mare gave its last sigh...
...and from the blood and suffering grew flowers
...poppies will bloom from the blood that was shed
...celebrating the blood in the summer")

DIRECTOR (*not noticing MOTHER*):
...for this work you also need a bit of prestige, sometimes you have to converse or discuss with the customer. Here she is sitting with me in a nice atmosphere, and she's trembling hard, even making the table shake, I can feel it. What's got her so rattled? What's she so afraid of? Nothing's going to bite her. Am I supposed to believe that if a Yankee strolls in here she'll be able to chat with him? Show off the pearls of our culture, suggest the right book or record, so that he knows we're no slackers, that our culture is as rich as... like... that is....

(*clearly DIRECTOR has reached the limit of his hangover vocabulary. Disappointed at being so inarticulate and generally at the futility of his actions, he decides to turn this interview with REGINA into a master class in recruiting*)

DIRECTOR:
Imagine this scene... Here we go. I'm that Yankee who comes in here, sees the bookshop, I say to myself I'm going in, let's see what the Poles can do... Out in Oklahoma we got some interesting books... we writes with our eyes closed... We don't even know where this whole Poland thing is on the map.

(*REGINA sits there embarrassed, not knowing what to do*)

DIRECTOR:
So, are you just going to sit there? Take him something and show him... (*holding the ice pack to his face, he grabs a "Śląska" record from the pile*). Here's

a brand-new record that just came out. *No? Please... This is Polish music...*

REGINA:
This is Polish music...

DIRECTOR:
From Silesia...Folk music.

REGINA:
Folk music.

DIRECTOR:
Why the long face? Perk up. You want him to buy the record or to give him a fit of depression?

REGINA (*livelier*):
This is folk Polish music...From Silesia...

DIRECTOR (*bored with this lame performance*):
Well...looks like we don't have any openings right this minute, I won't be needing to hire anyone.

REGINA (*comes alive, terrified at the thought that she'll have to return home defeated*):
But Tadeusz...

DIRECTOR:
To tell the truth, the only reason why I've wasted time with you here is because of Tadeusz. He helped me a lot during the war years... But that doesn't matter, what could you know about that? You young folks don't know much about anything. Born with a kite in one hand and a balloon in the other! A balloon generation! One prick and pop! Empty! Nothing! What are your plans? Dreams? Aspirations? Dig your heels in here for a time and wait until Lord Michorowski appears. And he'll sweep you off your feet, first to the altar, then to the bedroom. Maybe in a Fiat 126p? Hmm? Are you married?

REGINA:
Single.

DIRECTOR (*bitterly*):
Oh how modern! An independent woman. Get yourself a husband, bear children, hang up curtains. Let your husband earn the money, why are you jostling for work. You'll only get bored, tired, and sick of human inanity. You need a husband. Cook for him when he's hungry, spread your legs when you've got to, that's all there is to it! Oh no, what am I saying! Why, you've got your own

personality, your own passions. Books, am I right? Hmm? *(imitating a chirping girl's voice)* In prose, I mostly read Mniszkówna…. And of the modern poets I like Courts-Mahler.

I can read your applications with my eyes closed. It's a magic trick I've learned over the years. Anyway, tell me, what have you read lately?

REGINA *(uncertainly, clearing her throat):*
Spring Isn't Coming by Wojciech Krempiński.

DIRECTOR *(with sarcastic surprise):*
Ha ha! I forgot. Of course, that atomic cherry on the cake of stupidity—Krempiński. And what do you think? Will the spring come or won't it?

REGINA:
It will. Except I believe the book is a failure. Too chatty. Cheap and gratuitous. And pointlessly vulgar.

DIRECTOR *(pricking up his ears. He sips his cognac. He thinks. He smokes his cigarette.):*
You think so?

REGINA *(sneakily reading from the notes in the file on her lap):*
The author takes no risks. He might only cause a few churchgoers to faint. Does casual sex shock anyone these days? The style is insipid. Compared to his earlier novels, it merely seems derivative.

DIRECTOR:
Indeed! All too true. A flash in the literary pan. His second book showed this all too clearly. Let me tell you, what he had that was formally innovative a few years ago turned out to be just a copy of what we wrote in the 1950s, now served up as a great new discovery. But why should that hurt sales? Or keep him from picking up two or three awards from the SPS… Do you know what the SPS is?

REGINA *(she doesn't know):*
The Society….

DIRECTOR *(grimacing, gesticulating, as if this was the only subject that got him going):*
…of Polish Scribblers. Or better yet: Polish SHIT-LICKERS? Shit-lickers! Butt-kissers! They make him out to be the new Henry Miller! The salons will whisper: Krempiński said so-and-so. Write it down, note it down! Note it, note it, note it! *(pretending he's a Scribbler furiously noting things down, making writing noises):* Note it, note it, note it! Oh, how Krempiński farted gorgeously

in *Modern Life magazine*! What a sound, what painful depth, what guts! The truth of his digestive winds came straight from his guts! Oh, don't sniff so much, you'll sniff it all for yourself, leave some for me! Knowing all the time, of course, that he's not making literature, only piddly-shit literature for little girls like you to pleasure yourself under the blankets. I bet you were first in the bookshop, you stood in line to sip the fresh nectar of the ink of the still-warm pages of Wojciech Krempiński's immortal work! What a success!

Meanwhile, there he sits in his Zakopane sweater, in his parka that he got from the Americans, and he dishes out to the titillated housewives who love to lap up this nectar. And all the time, he's cooking up his next pseudo-icono-clastic three-penny porn-novel, which your generation will of course be utterly enthralled by. You and your friends, the excitable girls and the bearded boys in filthy sweaters dangling down to their knees, you'll have fodder for your heated discussions long into the night!

(DIRECTOR, worked up from his rant, tears the ice pack from his eyes. The light comes on in the room, and for the first time he sees REGINA's beauty. DIRECTOR is somewhat shaken at the discovery.)

DIRECTOR *(a bit ashamed of himself and his whole tirade, he suddenly slips into depression. He goes weak.):*
I... maybe I shouldn't have gotten so carried away. I might have implied that the career of that... What was his name?

REGINA *(torn from her lethargy):*
Who?

DIRECTOR:
You know that...The whole... Krempiński.

REGINA:
Yes, his name is... exactly, Krempiński.

DIRECTOR:
Or whatever... Nevermind. *Tout égal.* I really don't care what happens to him. NO. Three days from now, no one will remember his name. Maybe only in washrooms, where he'll be passed around as toilet paper. I say all that only from the perspective of someone who has been around the block and knows his literature has no depth. He might be a highly talented man. MAYBE. But he lacks experience, depth, the truth of the experience of someone who has truly lived. Formal virtuosity is not enough. All this praise, declaring him the Polish so-and-so only does the guy harm. The result is he's the darling of some and the whipping boy for others, you might say: A HOSTAGE of his own talent... And you must not criticize him. Oh no no... Just try!

(DIRECTOR blathers on and on, gesticulating, but REGINA is not much interested. She nods absently and makes empathetic faces, but his words increasingly fade into the background. In her thoughts we see:
- 1+2+3+4+5+6+7+8+9=?
- she forgot to bring in her stockings to have the runs darned again
- her belly rumbles—she dreams of bread with headcheese
- MR. KOZEŁKO's hands with their thick sausage fingers)

MRS. NASTKA steps out in front once more.

MRS. NASTKA *(imitating a priest):*
Give your suffering to the Lord, bear your cross, as the Lord Jesus bears his. First I thought: a fat lot of good are God's rewards. What kind of rewards are those when he hasn't got any money? The wedding was over. The guests went home, leaving me with Ładczuk. Maybe things would have been good if they weren't so bad. Maybe sometimes he didn't drink, but that was just because he'd only finished or was right about to start, and when he got going, then he kept on doing it. Sometimes he wasn't totally drunk; then he was nicer, kind of a log that lay on the stoop, a doorstop. He didn't get mad, he only sometimes lashed out at the dog when it was in heat. But it just so happened that I was standing on the doorstep in the place where he saw the dog.

(MRS. NASTKA is hit with a club)

Then I saw a great flash of light, blinding, crackling like water from a siphon. And when I rubbed my eyes, I was seized by something that made me feel I saw through everything. I see a tree, with all its roots, and its rings, and then later, how it burns in a stove. I see the earth beneath my feet, but every grain of sand is separate, spinning in a cement mixer, and new apartment buildings going up in the background. I see chickens, and through their feathers and skin I see their stomachs, lungs, livers, and everyone eating chicken soup at a table, because it's Sunday.

That was my second vision. And then I opened my eyes and saw that everything checked out. Eight chickens, because I was with child eight times year after year, and five rails from the fence because I brought forth five children, one rake, because one was stillborn, and one horse because one girl died of the croup. Those people came out of me like products from a factory. I'd barely gotten over one, come to my senses, and lo and behold my belly was growing again. His hangover was dragging him out of bed, he was all hallucinating and spasmatic, and I was giving birth to another brat. But I loved each and every one of them, though they weren't much fit for studies...

NEIGHBOR 1:
Thieves! Damn skunks! Your names are cursed from Szmulki to Pelcowizna.

NEIGHBOR 2:
They robbed my shed, took the rake, scythe, hoe, tore the antenna from the radio, and swiped twenty boxes of matches!

NEIGHBOR 3:
They threatened my youngest son with a monkey wrench. They snatched away his balloon and let it go.

NEIGHBOR 4:
They raped my chickens!

MRS. NASTKA:
Shut your faces! Who cares about your chicken? They were only playing around, and it wouldn't have laid eggs without them. What kind of thieves are they, they're too dumb; they couldn't pick their own pockets. Of course, a mother never lets anything bad happen to her children. She suffers, but she loves them. Baring her teeth and her claws she'll go to the militia, to the gendarme, to the prosecutor, all the way to the top if she has to, if they come to take them away!

SCENE 2:

REGINA returns from the interview in the bookshop. Pressing her file to her breast, deep in thought, she goes to the tram. Suddenly someone catches up to her, throws a scarf around her neck and starts strangling her.

KAROLINKA *(in the scary voice of the Lady Strangler):*
IT'S ME, THE LADY STRANGLER FROM ŻOLIBORZ! I attack defenseless women! I strangle way better than that loser from Mokotów!

REGINA *(terrified for a moment, struggling and panting):*
Congratulations! You've got your first victim.

KAROLINKA:
Aw, he sucks at strangling and molesting! Me, on the other hand—I'm a crackerjack!

We can see the girls instinctively like each other. They laugh and go to the tram stop together.

REGINA:
I just died of heart palpitations. All you can do now is grope me.

KAROLINKA:
Are you going downtown? Me too. Hey, listen... Don't be mad at him.

REGINA:
At who?

KAROLINKA:
The manager is something else.

REGINA:
You can say that again.

KAROLINKA:
There's worse ones out there! He's frustrated. He'd like to be a brilliant writer, but he's just average.
Krempiński stole his dreams. Now he's going through a rough spot, but it'll pass, then he'll change.

REGINA:
Like how?

KAROLINKA:
When his hangover passes, he'll be gentle as a kitten. You could hang him in the window for curtains or serve him with cheese as a cracker. You'll see! Basically he's a gentleman. He lies, curses, slanders, then doesn't remember a word of what he said.

REGINA:
I don't even know if he hired me.

KAROLINKA:
That's because he fell asleep. But when he woke up, He asked a lot about you. "A very resolute creature," "You'd never know from her voice she was so handsome." And then studied your application very carefully. I mean, your photo. You're a shoe-in.

REGINA:
I hope so. Otherwise I'm jumping into the Vistula.

KAROLINKA:
What?!

REGINA:
That's what. I don't want to gas myself. And I detest the sight of blood. I guess there's always nitrobenzene, but...

KAROLINKA:
You're a total fruitcake. I'm Karolinka.

REGINA: And I'm Regina.

KAROLINKA:
I heard you talked to him about Spring Isn't Coming? Have you read it?

REGINA:
No.

KAROLINKA:
Get out. I was listening at the door. The old man's got a thing about that book. He always forbids me to order it, but they always mess up at headquarters and send a few copies. Then he rages, he thunders! He won't have me reading it! He writes out some fake receipts, that it's sold, and he takes it home. Then he burns it or some damn thing. Stuffs it down the toilet. He must have done that to half the print run. Got a boyfriend?

REGINA:
No. I mean...

KAROLINKA:
Weeeellll?

REGINA:
Mama and I have... she and I have got... for me.

KAROLINKA *(amused):*
You're awesome!

REGINA:
It's hard to explain.

KAROLINKA:
Brunet or blond?

REGINA:
Not really sure. Blond, except he's bald. His hands aren't so hot. He's got these goofy little fingers... He dances them up and down me like a deaf pianist.

KAROLINKA:
Brrr, stop it! What are you looking at his hands for? Mrs. Nastka, who cleans up our bookshop, told my fortune and said I'd find a brunet. But that was six months ago and neither hide nor hair of him. She'll read your cards cheap, and the quality of the fortunes matches the price. Maybe she should tell yours as well? Just keep far away from her sons. They don't mean anything wrong; they just like to grope. *(puts a parcel in her hand)* Catch!

REGINA:
What's this?

KAROLINKA *(running for the tram):*
It's liverwurst! I'm on a diet, but I keep eating like a hog! Ciao.

SCENE 3:

The same day. Afternoon. REGINA and MOTHER's apartment, the famous wreck of a nightstand is on display, carefully bound with string, held together with tape, and trussed up. The faraway ring of a tram, the sound of a carpet being beaten, the bouncing of a ball, and the shrieks of a tortured cat come through the window. REGINA is eating a sandwich.

MOTHER:
And did you say what he suggested?

REGINA:
About Krempiński? Yeah.

MOTHER:
That he was a lame poser? That after the war his father...? Where'd you get that sandwich?

REGINA:
From a friend.

MOTHER *(following REGINA around the room):*
Who's this friend? Tell it to me straight, did he hire you or no? (suddenly sees something through the curtain) Sweet Jesus Regina, he's coming.

REGINA *(still eating):*
Who's that?

MOTHER *(quickly tidying the very tidy room):*
He's parking... He'll be here any moment. Who do you think? Who? Why are you playing dumb, sitting there like an ass? He's opening the trunk! Your hem on your skirt is falling.

REGINA:
Big deal. What is he, some kind of master tailor, you think he's going to notice?

MOTHER:
Also, you smell bad.

REGINA:
If he loves me, he'll put up with it. I've said a hundred times: he's mama's fiancé, not mine. Why should I wash for him, just for fun?

MOTHER:
You really don't know? He'll take one look at this weirdo, this demon-spawn and he'll say: hang on, hang on. I think I'll find myself another lady friend, maybe one a little less pretty, but without any screws loose.

REGINA:
Sounds good to me. Maybe he can see a bit of truth for once. Not just facades, veneer, Yardley and Vogue make-up. Theatrical staging orchestrated by mama. Maybe I should recite him a little poem? Which one?

MOTHER:
How you got so immature I'll never know. Don't put that there, you'll scratch up the tabletop, you'll slop water, you'll wreck what's left of the varnish!!

REGINA: *(moves the bowl and angrily scrubs her armpits. She doesn't care for obedience, however, and she decides to get back at MOTHER with some impromptu poems, recited with the enthusiasm of a schoolgirl)*

"Mushroom, oh mushroom, what a fungus you are.
They're great in a sauce or straight out of the jar.
In the sun how you change, how red in the pot,
and then from a plate I gobble you down hot!"

(the atmosphere heats up. MOTHER walks in REGINA's footsteps, as if wanting to bite her or at least whip her with a rag)

MOTHER:
Cover it in talc. A few stars have had that kind of bright idea. They had that idea, got all choosy, hemmed and hawed, looked aloof, and ended up alone. Or better yet: now they're prowling the alleyways and dives.

REGINA:
Maybe that's a plan?

MOTHER:
One guy's dull, another one's mouth smells weird, that one starts groping me right off the bat, the other has ears so big he can tune into Radio Free Europe.

REGINA:
I'm going to prowl the alleyways. Maybe that's where I fit in? A girl deluxe! Foreign creams, vintage clothes... apparently you can eat pretty well for one

sucker. Meat every day, not just once a week like us....

MOTHER *(this remark about meat pushes her over the edge and she gives RE-GINA a sharp slap):*
Oy nothing good will ever...

The cheeks throb. Suddenly, the doorbell. MR. KOZEŁKO is standing in the doorway with a bouquet.

He is an unhandsome, heavy-set, charmless man, painfully pragmatic. His life of physical work and various pursuits has never allowed him to develop any manners or subtly. This he makes up for with effort, broad gestures, which only exude his fumblingness and great sense of shame. His skull glistens helplessly from under his prim combover, his suit sleeves are too long, only the tips of his chubby fingers poke out from under them. His eyes are an abyss of terror and love.

Seeing him, a trembling MOTHER shoves the basin under the couch. REGINA freezes with her red cheek, suds in her armpits, and her sandwich in her hand. MOTHER tries to cover all this with confusion, chaos, and empty chatter. She is servile, awkward, and, hard to say why, suddenly erotic,
as if trying to compensate for REGINA's indifference with her own flirtations.

MOTHER:
Oh my! Well, this is a surprise! You here? But we're so unprepared, the whole house is a mess, we're a mess, we never expected, what a sty, please forgive us...

MR. KOZEŁKO:
Oh, I was just passing by, driving along, and I thought: I'll pop in! I'll see what Mrs. Maria is up to, drop in on little Regina, steal a kiss, I'll stroke her alabaster hand, or maybe both of them...

(he starts doling out the bouquet to the ladies, having had it behind his back, pointing downwards)

MOTHER:
Oh, you shouldn't have, so expensive! And daffodils, how gorgeous, and twine, and what good, thick new cellophane. Gorgeous flowers, blossoming away, running rampant. The muslin of their petals cries out: Spring! LIFE! By by-and-by they must wilt; they last for a moment, then plump! Rotted, black, undone, spent. The flowers may wither, but the cellophane—remains.

MR. KOZEŁKO:
Apparently it lasts forever.

MOTHER:
What's that you say?

MR. KOZEŁKO:
Plastic sticks around for a hundred years. At least that's what the latest American science research tells us.

MOTHER:
Really! Maybe a stiff drink?

MR. KOZEŁKO:
Oh, no no no…

MOTHER:
But it's homemade liquor from my own chokeberries.

MR. KOZEŁKO:
I'm driving.

MOTHER:
This won't go to your head.

MR. KOZEŁKO:
Well, if it's homemade, maybe just a sip.

(MOTHER thinks a bit and we can see she has a plan. Suddenly she begins getting ready to go, tying on a kerchief.)

MOTHER:
Regina, pour. In shot glasses, not those big ones! We're celebrating. Regina began working….

REGINA *(gloomily burping):*
We still don't know if I'm hired yet.

MOTHER:
As a… you know, on Komuna Paryska Street!

REGINA:
Apparently my resume was missing job references. But I…

MOTHER:
That's no obstacle. Your aunt will give you a reference from her company.

REGINA:
A fake one?

MOTHER:
A real one, she's got stationery!

REGINA:
I hope she's got a round stamp. He said he won't take any with oblong stamps.

MR. KOZEŁKO:
Round or oblong, and if he doesn't take it, what's the problem?

MOTHER:
To your good health.

(they drink)

MOTHER *(heading for the door):*
Well. I'm terribly sorry to be leaving, but you young folks know how to get along without me. I'd stay, but it's time for...

REGINA:
The Great Love.

MOTHER:
"The Great Love of Balzac." A new film in installments. Yes! I feel foolish admitting it.

REGINA *(glumly):*
I want to watch too. Maybe we could all watch it together?

MOTHER *(explodes, irritated to the extreme at this attempt to sabotage the date she's arranged):*
It's a shame to watch it on our set! We've only got black-and-white. And it's blurry and the faces are stretched out! Watching a beautiful film like that on our set is nonsense, it's a crime. Those noble faces, those hair-dos! The men are all sophisticated, honorable. Counts and lieutenants. In color it's as if I was there dancing at the ball with them. Forty-five years old and I see that, and wham, I'm just a girl. The legs just itch to start waltzing, the breast heaves. But I'm an old biddy, I have no clue how the world's changed. The only dress I've got left is a black one for the coffin, and the only ball on my calendar is my funeral. (takes a slice of headcheese from her purse and gives it to REGINA)

Regina, slice it up! (in a harsh whisper) Not in thick chunks, you'd think it was bread the way you're cutting it! It's too salty, you'll dry out your tongue!

MR. KOZEŁKO:
Now now, Maria, you look so young and spry, you haven't let yourself go, you don't even look your age, to say nothing of...

MOTHER *(watching REGINA slice the headcheese as nervously as if it were her own body being cut!):*
Well, aren't you the old flatterer! Regina took all my good looks. And grace. And now she's ungrateful. So sarcastic. Young folks today are so cynical. They've got no ideals. But as I always say, they never lived through a war... (Don't cut it like that!) They were born in a free, democratic people's state, they think life is just a fun fair, you spend a few bucks, and you ride the elephant, then the motorcycle, then the teddy bear, and then the airplane... I'll dim the lights for you two. Hurts the eyes.

(The lights are turned romantically low. REGINA sticks out her tongue at MOTH-ER behind KOZEŁKO's back. MOTHER takes her coat, goes out, the door slams, we hear footsteps on the stairs)

MR. KOZEŁKO:
I'm not afraid of your sarcasm, Regina.

REGINA *(hiccups):*
Beg pardon?

MR. KOZEŁKO:
Something tells me it is only a mask, behind which beats a tender and yearning heart.

REGINA *(making a move for the headcheese):*
You think so?

MR. KOZEŁKO:
It longs to be caressed, like mine. I remember your eyes when we last said farewell. As if you could no longer bear to look at me.
... *(waits for this to be denied, in vain)*

I neither wrote nor telephoned, to make you miss me. But he who lives by the sword. I very nearly wilted away without you. Truly, I kid thee not! There I was at the Polish expo of grocery producers, among those booths for various initiatives and innovations, and I only sighed and thought what a pity you weren't with me and how you would have liked it there in the mountains. So modern. An expo hall for 500 people! I brought you something back. Cups for drinking the spring water in spa towns...

REGINA *(sadly):*
Oh, wicked cool... *(silence)* And what a funny little spout. *(awkward silence)* And how are your...greenhouses? I mean your, you know. Mushrooms??

MR. KOZEŁKO *(flustered, sensing nastiness behind the question):*
You... you're asking me about...

REGINA:
You know, the things you grow. I wanted to ask how your... I mean, is it true that you use horse manure...

MR. KOZEŁKO *(regaining his senses after a moment's confusion):*
If I must. Oh, Regina, if I only knew you were truly asking out of curiosity, not to mock a simple man heavily burdened with a heavy, unsophisticated, manual job.... Then I'd be all too glad to tell you, even though, as they say: it is not the most romantic activity.
Well, some speak for hours about roses, others about mushrooms and fertilizer. Roses wilt swiftly, while the latter you can monetize, and can turn a very tidy profit. Not to brag, but my future wife will be pretty pleased with herself. I've just bought an automobile, and things are only looking up. A house is in the works. A bungalow. With a terrace and attic. The fence is made of metal rods on a wall foundation. After that: thujas, roses, a foyer. Down below, a kitchen with white tiles with navy-blue windmills, ships, and stormy seas, a hot plate and an oven, an electronic clock that tells the time without being wound up...

It will be right next to my office, my desk, across from the salon, where... *(KOZEŁKO's voice grows faraway and blurry, REGINA's mind is wandering)* ...I'll keep the library. That is, the books.

REGINA *(absently):*
You don't say.

MR. KOZEŁKO:
Isn't there so much to be done?
REGINA:
Mniszkówna is a fashionable writer right now.

MR. KOZEŁKO:
Rings a bell.

REGINA:
And the poetry of one Courts-Mahler. Quite interesting, apparently.

Mr. Kozełko:
So they say.

Regina *(playing with his tendency to agree):*
But others say he's not so interesting.

Mr. Kozełko:
You know… Interesting, uninteresting. You want my opinion? One person says one thing, another person something else. One person likes it, another doesn't. What's it all mean? Why the big discussions? Everybody can discuss things. I'm sure you could be of assistance in making a suitably chic collection of books. Just as you like it! Oh, and the record library, the cassette tapes. The record player will be stereophonic. The speakers made by Fonika. I'm quite certain you know your way around records. Indubitably while working at the bookshop, just about everything that is being currently printed and pressed has passed through your hands.

Regina:
I sometimes get the feeling that I'm not interested in anything at all.

Mr. Kozełko:
Small wonder! You're too pretty to be interested in things. You're what people should be interested in! And whoever denies it should be abducted and strangled by the beast of Mokotów….

(MR. KOZEŁKO sits down by REGINA and gropes her passionately, as BOGU-MIŁA did before him. She tries to respond to his advances as per instructions, but in the end she leaps away and bursts out laughing.)

Regina:
Oh no! Oh, it can't be!

Mr. Kozełko:
Something wrong?

Regina:
Oh no, just your hands are so incredible.

Mr. Kozełko *(looking at his hands, abashed):*
They're what?

Regina:
I don't know. They're so silly… It looks like five village idiots masturbated on a turnip.

(He sits there offended, sips his liquor. REGINA's mood improves at once, vampirically feeding on his pout, prattling to win him over.)

REGINA:
You know, let's leave that alone; I really do like mushrooms. I never ate them much, because Mama and I have a modest diet. At most vegetarian dishes, or just a bit of meat. Sometimes headcheese, liverwurst, or blood sausage. In the summer there's fruit soup or dumplings, because we have a garden plot. But mushrooms are a clever idea.

(silence)

Apparently tomorrow's going to be meat.

(Silence. MR. KOZEŁKO pours himself more liquor)

They say in China they eat lots of mushrooms. They're a real delicacy.

MR. KOZEŁKO *(disgusted, put off, mad)*:
In China, they... you know what they eat? Dogs!

REGINA:
Well, there you go! Dog grilled with mushrooms! Or snake in a creamy mushroom sauce! Stew.

(Silence, unable to appease MR. KOZEŁKO, REGINA slumps into a sense of guilt)

REGINA:
Mama does the cooking at our house, because I only know how to cook up trouble.

MR. KOZEŁKO:
Oh, that's not mandatory. It's not mandatory that you cook. The housekeeper will agree. And all the more you shouldn't trouble yourself with work. In a bookshop? What for? A woman like you shouldn't be selling books to strangers, slaving away in a shop, you should have your own books, and whenever you please.

(increasingly feverish and incensed)

I'm quite certain they're lining up at that bookshop just to get a good look at you, to feast on you with their eyes. The ones with the Master's degrees, the shithead professors! Doesn't take a rocket scientist to haul home some books and slap them on a shelf. And every last one of them thinks they're got the copyright on brains. The wisdom just pours down on them every day from the shelves, so they can dazzle and impress, prancing around in front of the girls, showing off how educated they are. Meanwhile, those days are over. These are modern times, and they demand a new kind of intelligence and wisdom. I'd call it a material wisdom. Two packs of sheet music, cries the customer, but only because he knows it's tucked away down low. And of course it's you that's got to turn around, bend over, and he stands and stares, devouring you with his eyes. With his X-rays, he pierces through the thin material of your skirt, right to the corset, the panties, and beyond. By night, when everyone is asleep, he recalls this sight and in his thoughts enacts—no offense—his darkest desires and... he defiles, he desecrates...

REGINA:
They see that well?

MR. KOZEŁKO:
Oh, believe me, men know how to see. They see whatever they want.

REGINA:
Well, then I envy them, because I don't see anything! Mama's always turning the switch so as not to use up the light, and she skimps so badly that I'm going to have to get glasses soon.

(A sad silence. MR. KOZEŁKO nervously paces the very small room, at one point he swivels around, as if to say something vital and conclusive, but to give his words even more gravity, he leans on the demolished table.... Seeing his intentions, REGINA instinctively darts toward him, but for some reason changes her mind with a wave of the hand. There is a great crash—hard to say if it is the final crash of the defeated nightstand or of dreams and illusions nurtured for so long.)

SCENE 4:

The same apartment, the same day, now later evening.
MR. KOZEŁKO is gone, and above all, so is the nightstand. There are flowers. MOTHER stares tearfully out the window. REGINA lies on her stomach, her face in a pillow. Suddenly, without knocking, as if it is her home, a panting BOGU-MIŁA enters, all hung with shopping bags. REGINA and MOTHER raise their tired, heavy eyes to see her; they are so immersed in their disappointment and despair that neither greets her. BOGUMIŁA, however, is not attuned to such subtleties.

BOGUMIŁA:
Why so down in the mouth? What if someone were to break in here? Supposedly there was another attack today. They say it was a doctor from the city hospital. It was even on TV. A hundred militiamen on the case. A hundred! And an

award for whoever identifies the culprit. I was shoulder-checking all the way here. I thought: ah, let him go ahead and attack me. Go on! Attack all he likes! Know what I'd do! I'd knee him in the balls, that's what! Then lead him by the balls to the police station. For how much money? Here you go. Auntie? Regina? I got some toilet cleaner. And cotton. I bought a dozen bags. I'll give you two. Or no, just one. *(putting down her bags)*

I waited five hours at the counter in the furniture store. Finally the shipment came, but what could they do with only three counters and a hundred twenty-five customers? I put us on the waiting list. I gave the manager two packages of coffee. That's enough, right? Huh? What's with all the long faces? I sense some blocked chakra here.

It's getting late. *(takes out a loaf of bread and bites into it without slicing)* Mama told me not to wear myself out on the bus, that I can crash with you guys. Where can I lie down?

If Regina bunks with Auntie, then I could sleep on her hide-a-bed. Or the reverse... Whatever works for you guys.

(No one responds. She shrugs, undresses, lies down in REGINA's bed. MOTHER also lies down and begins snoring gently.)

BOGUMIŁA:
Where's Mom's nightstand?

(long silence)

MOTHER *(suddenly awake, like a zombie):*
It's gone.

BOGUMIŁA:
It's gone?

MOTHER:
He destroyed it.

BOGUMIŁA:
But who?

REGINA *(faking a conciliatory tone of voice):*
He said he'd have it repaired.

MOTHER:
He annihilated it completely. All the legs fell off.

REGINA:
He took it with him. To be renovated!

MOTHER:
The drawer snapped off. Not even splinters left.

REGINA:
When it's renovated it'll be even prettier than it was.

MOTHER *(vengefully):*
Truck farmer.
Prince of Mushrooms.
Nouveau riche.
Overgrown toddler!

BOGUMIŁA:
Oh, I wouldn't worry, Auntie. It's like Mama says: to hell with it, better off without it. A person only feels bad looking at old junk. The bad memories come flooding back.

(MOTHER, cursing MR. KOZEŁKO, drifts off into a well-deserved sleep, snoring gently)

BOGUMIŁA:
Are you sleeping?

REGINA:
Yes.

BOGUMIŁA:
Can I show you something?

REGINA:
What?

BOGUMIŁA:
What you do every night when you're married?

REGINA:
What? No!

BOGUMIŁA:
It's not what you think. Lie down more on your back. On your back, dahling, I'll show you.

SCENE 5:

The apartment of PLATOON LEADER WOJCIECH KRĘTEK, not a bit cleaner than in ACT 1. The children are sleeping, piles of laundry wobble, PLATOON LEADER is making love to WIFE, trying to minimize the creaking of the couch.

WIFE:
Just be careful...

PLATOON LEADER:
What if I am being careful....

WIFE:
You were careful?

PLATOON LEADER:
I said I was careful.

(Finishing, he gets off the couch. WIFE straightens her vegetable-patterned nightdress. PLATOON LEADER touches his face and lips with disgust)

PLATOON LEADER:
What's that slop?!

WIFE *(her face shining with cream)*:
Calendula cream.

PLATOON LEADER *(wipes his face)*:
Ugh... Brrr...

WIFE *(amused at his aversion)*:
Watch it, you're going to turn into a broad!
This prompts PLATOON LEADER to put on her house dress and pretend he's "turned into a broad."

PLATOON LEADER *(in a girly voice)*:
How do you like it? Tell me I'm pretty. Would you buy me that? Buy me a fur? Gimme a kiss. It's been so long since you kissed me...Irenka kisses her husband.

WIFE *(in retaliation, lowering her voice and pretending to be a very stern and harsh husband)*:
Quiet, I've got an important report to do. Hand me that folder. Not that one, dummy!

PLATOON LEADER *(smothering her with sweet kisses)*:
Oh, all you do is work… And what about love and flowers? You know… Little Piotr has grown out of his anorak. And we have to pay the cafeteria. Oh look… see what just passed by! Those new Fiats are so nice… They've got steering wheels, and lights… and wheels. And not just one—four in all. And look at them go! So fast! And even forwards! Ohhh! Go, go, ha ha!

Their mutual joking slowly spirals out of control. They increasingly hit at each other's soft spots.

WIFE *(pretending to be her husband in a literary pose)*:
You and your low-brow affairs! The tragic banality of everyday life, whose arid swamp I drag myself through every day. This year spring will not come, and the flowers will bloom in gray!

PLATOON LEADER *(laughs uncertainly, beginning to suspect WIFE is reading his diary)*:
OK, that's enough. You're getting up early tomorrow.

WIFE *(still pretending to be her husband, reciting like a child at school)*:
The ash-gray morning line-ups, gray people, vacant eyes, hostile, abusive, wolfish stares… The stupified, underslept throng is semi-consciously pushing their way into the tram. The stink of damp clothing and wet rubber. Someone sneezes, another murmurs, another somnambulently wipes his nose…

PLATOON LEADER *(losing control, enraged)*:
Put on your glasses. You're all ugly. When you take them off you look funny, like a mole. (tears off her house dress and begins folding it up with furious attention, like a costume for a performance he suddenly hates, in which he no longer wishes to take part) It's like someone smeared up your face with a Pink Pearl eraser!

WIFE *(about to cry)*:
You want me to sleep in my glasses?

We can see the spell is broken; the carriage has turned into a pumpkin. Reality is back.

WIFE *(frosty)*:
Give me a few bucks for tomorrow. I've got to do the shopping.

PLATOON LEADER *(vengefully)*:
Take a hike. I'm broke.

WIFE:
What do you mean, broke? How am I supposed to buy vegetables, meat...

PLATOON LEADER:
Get a job.

WIFE:
I haven't got one.

PLATOON LEADER:
Then get one. *(hearing her sob)* SLEEP!

WIFE (sobbing): What about you?

PLATOON LEADER:
I still have to…. Bah, you wouldn't understand it anyway. Sleep. *(sits down to the desk. Opens his notebook)* Even here, in this stupid notebook, I can't feel fully at ease. This vestige of freedom… it's not worth a hill of beans. It's bad here, cramped, we're always tripping over each other's asses, and at the station it's worse. It's sultry, the rooms are full of the smell of nervous sweat and badly tanned leather on the bands on the new caps sent from HQ. And everywhere those eyes: dull, dismal, dreary. They look how they've been trained to look: forward and at nothing. But as soon as you turn around, you feel things intensifying behind your back; a strange and surreptitious movement: a groping, sniffing, inquiring, snooping. Let's have a look in those pockets and panties, maybe there's something of interest? But when you turn around again, it's lips sealed, eyes forward, ears at attention… This is the proud and free man of our times.

The atmosphere around the Lady Strangler is getting really thick. The air is strangling, so to speak, because we've got our first corpse. Denatka, 65 years of age, according to the autopsy dead not from the injuries, but of a heart attack, from the shock. She had a sick heart. She was employed mending stockings. Her funeral was attended by a handful of geezers, but we were still sent there undercover to scope things out, get the word on the street. Didn't learn much. The official and unofficial price of Dutch kakaa, and all the discomforts that come with a rectal prolapse. The Beast struck again yesterday, on Rose Street. Luckily, a car was driving by. If we believe the driver, the assailant literally dissolved into the air. The rheumy corporal, who was first on the scene of the crime, says the victim was totally nonplussed. Slightly scratched, a head wound, skirt torn in a strategic place, which the woman claims she can easily have restitched at her own cost. A nurse had finished her shift. She was most concerned about the cream cake she was bringing home after the ward director's birthday party.

The old man was chewing the carpet. He took her in person to his office to make a statement. Didn't squeeze anything interesting out of her. She only gave him an off-the-cuff diagnosis of high blood pressure and prescribed a relaxing stroll in the Royal Gardens. That was too much! He just flew into a rage. I can just see him chasing the swans give them a kick and cussing out Chopin.

They're threatening to cut bonuses for a lack of investigation results and the general obstruction of other activities. After the press bulletin, the station was swamped with anonymous calls. No time to verify them. Instead of real clues, we get human pettiness, miserable nastiness.

Somebody's cousin is living with no housing registration. Another person's cousin got two chicken legs from the countryside, maybe he's the strangler? A woman's getting it on with the mailman like he's her husband, some florist cuts back on the number of freesias in a bouquet. Two students of the sewing school are always fooling around on the moving staircase at the shopping center between the hours of 5 and 7 pm, riding it up and down. A guy walks Wera Kostrzewa Street in the evening, holding a box and wearing a scarf, 90% chance he's the strangler. Another one writes that the Lady Strangler is her brother-in-law, a member of the opposition, a real brute to her sister ever since they've been married, showing an unhealthy interest in homoeroticism, and his whole description checks out.

They could have stared at the clouds. They might have sniffed the chestnut blossoms.... Instead, they sat down and wrote.

As if they were captive, overgrown midgets. Twisted cellar creatures, stooped over permanently, mangled, limping. Freed from their chains, they shriek horribly and cheer. But someday their cheers will end, their banners will sag. Then all of a sudden they won't know what to do with all that freedom. They feel kind of off when they aren't bumping their heads on the ceiling... When there's no one whipping their ass into shape they have no urge to fly. Why should they? What for? So they can talk, so they can fire their slingshots and BB guns? They took aim, tying up their legs, dropping them in the mud, sticking them in a vice, pulling a bag over their head and strangling and strangling. Look at her struggle! How she kicks her funny feet!

In a few minutes they'll miss the prison walls, they're even ready to start making their own bars. They need no guards. They'll do fine trailing themselves, keeping watch, guarding, giving themselves measured doses or rations. One leg is crooked, the other limps, something's up... The bars are made from the stares, and the whip of filthy and cruel words. They'll keep themselves in check, no one's needs to jump on them. They'll smear themselves thick in the shit and finally it'll be the way they know it, the way they like it, the way they need it.

ACT 3
SCENE 1:

Morning. Downtown. A dark figure is fiddling around behind a trash container. Eventually he throws himself on a woman passing by. He attacks her, choking her with a scarf that reads SKI! SKI! SKI! pulling her offstage. A moment later, REGINA comes out of the building gateway. She goes down the street in the opposite direction of a First of May procession, which is eyeing her carefully, waving flags, holding balloons and banners. It has all the characters who have appeared in the play, as well as two Huge Mushrooms.

DRUNK *(stumbling):*
Hey, is that a head or a toilet brush? No answer even. Isn't she high and mighty! Thinks her shit smells like roses.

GIRL RUNNING BY:
How old is she? They say she's 21 already! So old and loony. Beauty fades, and what remains? Only a few screws, because one's loose!

BABY IN A CARRIAGE:
Her mother carts her around to doctors like a Gypsy does a bear.

MOTHER:
All she does when she gets home from work is lie down with her face in her pillow and stays there till evening.

DOCTOR:
Blood pressure's fine, textbook pulse. Blood fine. Listening through the stethoscope revealed nothing.

MOTHER:
For her fiancé—nettles. She's sad and cranky. Any day now she'll discourage him entirely, though he's very persistent.

MR. KOZEŁKO *(following MOTHER, hauling a modern table of cheap tile):* Here's the cause of our worries.

MOTHER *(unpleasantly surprised):*
What's that supposed to be?

MR. KOZEŁKO *(winking):*
A table. Wouldn't you say it's rather, oh, I don't know: lovelier? It set me back a pretty penny, I know you wouldn't have wanted me to put myself out. I have certain connections at the Meblotex, I happen to know the director, who was

once in close relations with a certain well-off sweets shop saleslady. Let's just come out and say it: he was her lover, she had a fabric buttons workshop, during the war she loaned a Jewish woman money, who in turn left for Sweden some time ago *(his voice goes soft and indistinct)*, and began sending citrus fruits and clothes, which the saleslady sold with a mark-up at the Różyc Bazaar, while….

MOTHER *(highly distraught, yet not wanting to upset MR. KOZEŁKO she tries to find the good sides of the table):*
A decent piece of furniture… more modern. It stands up straight, you don't have to prop it up. What happened to the old one?

MR. KOZEŁKO:
You'll never believe it, but I managed to sell it, or in fact trade it for… look!

(He pulls a surprise from behind his back, a plucked goose, which he holds like a bouquet of flowers, its head dangling dolefully.)

DOCTOR:
Regina is as healthy as a clam; the problem is in her mind. She needs to go on walks and listen to some good old rock'n'roll.

MOTHER:
My daughter a mental case? I beg your pardon.

HIPPIE *(taking a shot of heroine):*
Statically speaking, intelligent folks have more metaphysical problems. Just look at America. There practically everyone has their own private psychoanalyst, and nobody thinks they're crazy for it.

MOTHER:
But maybe she….? She was doing her studies, but no one saw her in class for the whole semester. Maybe… maybe she takes dope?

HUGE MUSHROOM 1:
Give me a break. She spent the whole semester in cafes nursing a coffee and nibbling an eclair. She was adored, even offered money. They accosted her, sent cognac to her table, she drank it half-conscious, she boarded a tram at the time she usually returned from school.

HUGE MUSHROOM 2:
Every day she swore to herself that her days of cutting classes were over. Yet when the tram arrived at her stop the next day and it was time to hop off, some strange force held her to her seat.

NURSE *(with a sack full of chocolate cream cakes):*
She was spotted in the International Press Club. She was capable of sitting there all day with a single newspaper. It was a paper from Pernambuco. Or Honolulu.

RIVER CATFISH:
She threw her report card into the Vistula River. I watched it float away. Methodology: Absent. Descriptive Grammar: C minus.

SCENE 2:

A familiar bookshop on Komuna Paryska Street; sales room. Not many customers. MRS. NASTKA is watering the rhododendrons and dusting with a rag. KAROLINKA and REGINA are behind the counter, doing some accounting.

KAROLINKA *(suddenly grabbing REGINA's hand with an engagement ring):*
Groovy! Oh, you sneak, why didn't you say anything!

REGINA *(hiding her hand in embarrassment):*
What's there to say? He proposed. And the way he was looking at me, what else could I do? And now it's too late. Anyway, who cares.

MRS. NASTKA:
Show your hand, I'll tell your fortune... The death line, the love line.... This is real gold! But the ring he bought is too tight, your finger swelled and now you can't take it off....

(MRS. NASTKA eyes REGINA's palm like a pro, studying her lines. Her eyes grow strangely misty and suddenly she sees everything that happened in REGINA's life recently.)

...because you have a broken, festering heart.

(The reality of the bookshop gives way, becoming the arena of a flashback. MRS. NASTKA, buffeted by an attack of superconsciousness, relates the events of last summer in a strange voice and language):

In the summer she went to a camp for students. There was a certain girl there, let's call her Judyta. A country girl, her lips eternally pouting, twisted, giving her words a now fashionable touch of irony. Regina thought the girl disliked her for some reason. Whatever she said, the girl just raised her eyebrows, rolled her eyes, or gave her a steady, sarcastic stare that gave Regina the chills. It was awful, strange. Regina pretended to ignore it, but in a quiet place in her heart she was terribly pricked by this needling.

One day, under the shower, someone pulled back the curtain.

JUDYTA:
I'm so sorry...

That was Judyta. Her voice was friendly, conciliatory.

JUDYTA:
I think I've got a tick and I can't pull it off all by myself.

Why was she so docile all of a sudden? At first, Regina washed off the suds and went under her shower. It turned out that the tick had burrowed itself in the pubic mound of her adversary.

JUDYTA:
Twist it so that the head comes out, otherwise the tick spits toxic poison into the bloodstream, I know what I'm talking about, I study at Nursing School.

Regina vainly tried to remove the insect. Her nails were pared short, as was mandatory for camp staff. Unable to dispatch the pest in the gloom, she thought it might be better to take it out with her mouth. She knelt in front of Judyta and, trying to discreetly avoid the shameful place with her gaze, she put her burning lips to the tanned skin. Not far away, Judyta's pubes lurked there like a dark, moist, one-eyed animal, vigilant, steaming, greedy, as though waiting for someone. Regina tried to tactfully avoid looking, yet the pink eye sparkling amid the abundant moss of hair stared straight at her. Not thinking much, moving by instinct, she took it in her mouth. It seemed to her she was eating it, and in response, it was eating her. It ate her, first tentatively, inquiringly, then ravenously, sloppily, tenaciously. It was all so dreadful it seemed it would never end...never end... until the water ran out in the shower, and the camp leader called for an assembly.

JUDYTA (*incensed, or cynically pretending to be, grabbing a towel*):
Enough. How could you do that to me? That's totally sick, it's revolting. Goodbye!

Regina was so afraid that Judyta would blab about what had happened between them and they'd be severely punished, even expelled. She decided they should talk. Because the other campers were constantly around, she had to steal into her bunk at night, lie down silently beside her and put her hand on her mouth so hard it crushed her like a pulpy, bloody fruit, inadvertently sticking a finger inside. The tarp whispered softly, the repellent gave a strong odor, the wind carried the song of scouts and the fragrance of sappy pine needles from across the lake.

Scouts' Song *(sound of the guitar from far away, a choir of yearning voices in the vein of "Turn, turn, turn")*

Judyta:
You wish, I'm telling them everything, that's my final word, they'll strip you down and dunk you in the cesspit.

Yet it just so happened that the cook, whose shift was over, hadn't managed to eat supper and had a long, juicy cucumber in her bed she'd swiped from the storehouse. The cucumber fell between them and got jammed between their legs, so that neither could get rid of it. They tussled in dismay, in the heat and the stickiness, the putty of bodies that seemed all too close, not wanting it, but feeling how a dreadful powerlessness gripped them, as if, beginning somewhere below their bellies and rippling throughout their bodies, there came a sound that was not a laugh, nor the shriek of a madman, nor its echo. They could not tear themselves apart, and finally, after, a long struggle, Regina managed to break the embrace. She arrived to the morning assembly worn out, sore, and weak...

Regina:
Cheeks flushed, evidently feverish...

They were prescribed a shot of pepper moonshine and both were soon back on their feet. But after that they avoided each other as far as they could and refused to keep watch together, until the camp leader noticed and, to break down the girls' animosity, sent them off to gather kindling together.

They walked the meadow in spiteful, angry silence, when Regina suddenly tripped over a stump, pulling the other girl down with her. As a result, the two both fell in an unfortunate way, so that Judyta's head found its way under Regina's skirt and got stuck between her legs. She tried to get up, to flee this awful and embarrassing predicament, yet all at once she was hit by a terrible fatigue... a helplessness... a weakness so horrible that her body succumbed to gradual bifurcation. It forked and spread, to become great and spacious as the whole earth, yet so tiny, no larger than a red pearl; fiercely powerful yet delicate as well, helpless and transparent as an infant. It went on so long that three two-person patrols were sent from camp to comb the forest! They met on a path. They said they'd gotten lost, yet revolted at themselves and their lie, they didn't breathe a word to each other until the camp was over.

Finally, everyone went off home. The summer was over, only memories remained. On the surface nothing had changed, and yet everything was totally different. Regina got out of bed and lived aimlessly, robotically doing her duties. She paged through life like a book full of lush and enticing illustrations, yet colorless and insipid, dull and bland; she read it faster and faster, just to get to the end. She was engulfed in tedium. But not the ordinary tedium, the cosmic tedium, the universal tedium, which could not be overcome. As if she were hungry but did not want to eat. She was thirsty but did not want to drink. She went somewhere but then forgot where she was going, people seemed like irritants, and their words reached her as if through a pane of glass

(here we have dreamlike flashbacks from this period, sharp and intrusive like a fever dream)

MR. KOZEŁKO:
Your lips are like two pieces of tomato, and your eyes shine like the lights in a radio....

REGINA *(disoriented, jostled out of her reverie):*
What?

MOTHER *(wiping off the nightstand):*
Why did you put that on my table?

REGINA:
It's only a handkerchief.

MOTHER:
You know how easily it scratches, how easily it gets ruined, I carried it on my back from Otwock... *(she is still speaking, but her words grow inaudible).*

LADY FROM THE SECRETARY'S OFFICE *(with the sound of rubber stamps hitting the desk):*
Here you are, your student card and your benefits certificate.

Any day now school was starting again, the monotonous daily lessons at the Teachers' College on soft and hard consonants and the eternal scritch-scritch of fountain pens. One day, returning the long way home from the secretary's office, through the Praga district, whereby chance, as she had discovered through the Address Bureau, Judyta lived, she saw a familiar face in the crowd. Yes, it was her!

REGINA *(suddenly springing to life but getting a handle on herself and feigning calm):*
Judyta!!

Judyta was walking along radiant, sassy, in a fashionable organdy blouse with buttons and a jacquard ruffle tossed onto flared pants, a charity-store trench coat of khaki poplin and leather demi-pumps, her hair was done into a modern triple wave, dangling jauntily on her bold, high forehead.

REGINA *(panting, having chased Judyta):*
Judyta?! What a surprise!

JUDYTA (somewhat more reserved, as if unpleasantly surprised):
Regina?

REGINA (euphorically):
What brings you here?!

JUDYTA (cautiously): I live here, and you?

REGINA:
I'm on my way home from the secretary's office, I was picking up my student card.

JUDYTA (gently ironic):
From the college? You took the long way around.

(Regina only now notices a man urinating in some nearby bushes. This is Roman, Judyta's boyfriend. He steps up and slings a proprietary arm around her. He drinks up Judyta with his eyes, as if to say: hurry up and finish talking to these other people, I don't even know why they exist, isn't it awesome when it's just you and me, you and me, you and me, you and me? Regina senses this and eyes him warily)

JUDYTA:
It's been so long! Meet my fiancé. Roman, this is Regina, we were at the camp together in Krusajny.

(Roman mutters a few words in greeting. Then he pulls out a switchblade and practices throwing it into a wall. Hot damn, he sure can throw!)

JUDYTA *(neither to him, nor to Regina):*
We got lost together looking for kindling! I was scared silly. *(making her escape)* Give me a ring sometime, we'll meet for coffee!

REGINA *(trailing her, unpleasantly surprised at this chilly reception):*
Why not right now?

JUDYTA *(hanging off of Roman's brawny arm):*
We're going to look at furniture, apparently they're getting in some sofa-shelving combo units, any minute now...Ciao!
Regina is left alone among the roaring Fiats, Nyskas, and trams, the indifferently hustling passers-by. She sings the finale song:

REGINA:
This spring's no good to me. It only pains and stings. Bring the winter back.
I'll murder the spring. It hounds me with its buds and leaves and with the awful lack
of your eyes when you say: no I can't. Your lips breathe a chill
when you toss me a kiss like a tip, and say: why don't you pick up the bill

I still can't believe I walked through fire for you
like a firefighter in an asbestos jumpsuit
going in and knowing there's no walking out
walking and going up, up, up... And after this hellish route

it's not like I lie down and die. Worse than that
I'll live on, with these smoldering embers for a heart.
May will come round, and the plump lilacs will droop low.
Is someone coming? Or knocking? Is it you? The answer's no.

I still can't believe I walked through fire for you
like a firefighter in an asbestos jumpsuit
going in and knowing there's no walking out
walking and going up, up, up... And after this hellish route
it's the end... the end.

Regina stops singing. The bookshop reality returns. Customers mill around, MRS. NASTKA is cleaning. Out of nowhere appear her three sons: Cross-eyed Amorous Whipper-Snappers age about 20. At the sight of them, KAROLINKA slips behind the counter and discreetly covers REGINA, as if to protect her from something.

MRS. NASTKA *(warily, sensing trouble):*
And what brings you here?

CROSS-EYED WHIPPER-SNAPPERS *(with brass knuckles and knives):*
We's here ta protect mumma.

MRS. NASTKA:
What from?

CROSS-EYED WHIPPER-SNAPPERS:
Ya know, from dat Lady Choker guy, who goes around chokin' broads. We ain't lettin' him git our mumma.

MRS. NASTKA *(tenderly coddling them to her breast, wiping their noses. As she does this, the WHIPPER-SNAPPERS turn their heads and greedily eyeball REGINA, licking their lips):*

But I tell you and swear before God: if you swipe something here I'll kill you like dogs, hear me? I'll kill you and throw you bare-ass naked out of the house, all right?

(MRS. NASTKA goes out, wringing a rag. CROSS-EYED WHIPPER-SNAPPERS gape at REGINA and drool, as though in a trance)

CROSS-EYED WHIPPER-SNAPPER 1 *(to REGINA):*
I wanna see dat book... over dere. Up high. On the highest shelf.

REGINA (icy, staring into space):
Which one specifically?

CROSS-EYED WHIPPER-SNAPPER 1:
You know, dat... one up dere.

REGINA:
What title?

CROSS-EYED WHIPPER-SNAPPER 2:
Ahhh, damn this bad eyesight. Firgot my glasses.

KAROLINKA *(covering for her):*
Would you gentlemen care to see Durrenmat's A Dangerous Game?

CROSS-EYED WHIPPER-SNAPPER 2:
Yep. I mean... dat one first. We kin helps da lovely lady on da ladder. Oh, we wanna read so bad we jes can't stand it!

KAROLINKA:
Then read that.

(points to a sign: "THE SALES CLERK DOES NOT GET ITEMS FROM UNREACH-ABLE SHELVES." The WHIPPER-SNAPPERS blink, unable to read it)

MRS. NASTKA *(returns and, seeing a heist brewing, drives them off with her rag):*
You're twerps, one and all of you, take a hike, right this second, or I'll whip you with my rag. And the neighborhood cop better not be waiting for me when I get home! Or I'll set fire to the house and you'll roast like pigs on a spit, and I won't even feel sorry for you.

(Tosses the WHIPPER-SNAPPERS out of the bookshop, she is surprisingly strong and effective, and then gets back to work)

KAROLINKA *(to REGINA):*
Hey there bride-to-be, the manager's calling you. (REGINA goes out. Meanwhile PLATOON LEADER Wojciech Krętek appears at the counter in plainclothes, clean-shaven and perfumed)

PLATOON LEADER WOJCIECH KRĘTEK *(lowering his voice conspiratorially):*
I'd like a copy of Krempiński's Spring Isn't Coming.

KAROLINKA:
We're all out.

PLATOON LEADER:
Well an acquaintance said he bought two copies here.

KAROLINKA:
It's out of print.

PLATOON LEADER:
Have you read it?

KAROLINKA:
More than once. But in secret, because I sleep in the hide-a-bed with my kid brother. I waited till he fell asleep, and then I slipped my hand under the dress with torn armpits I use as a nightgown to rip it open and I touched my breasts to see if there weren't any lumps forming like Mama had. There weren't. So I started checking out the belly, and lower down, and below that in my panties. There I found a little lump that I began exploring and rubbing in circular motions, and it began growing bigger and bigger... It grew bigger and bigger, while I was smaller and smaller. It was bigger all the time, and I was small, tiny, and light as the bladder of a fish, and strange, so strange, until finally I was so small and strange that I couldn't even move for all that strangeness! I just lay there outlandish in the mud of a terrible and paralyzing impure ecstasy, waiting and praying for it to pass at once.

PLATOON LEADER:
Well then, maybe I'll take a Polish-English dictionary.

KAROLINKA:
A big one? Small one?

PLATOON LEADER:
Well, in fact I only need to look up one word: SKI.
KAROLINKA:
Well, if it's just one little word you're after, I guess you only need the pocket-size dictionary, right?

PLATOON LEADER:
Yeah, I think the small one will do.

KAROLINKA:
I'll just write you out a receipt.

PLATOON LEADER:
By the way, is there a woman working here...

SCENE 3:

Office of the bookshop DIRECTOR. He is clearly drunk, and the look of the interior suggests this is not a rare event. The room is in a state of chaos; among the books and manuscripts are scattered empty cognac bottles. The DIRECTOR is lurking by the window with binoculars. He is doing a spontaneous investigation, and REGINA has been called under some pretext, to be a witness, hostage, and to force her to join the investigation.

DIRECTOR *(passing REGINA the binoculars):*
Take a look.

REGINA looks indifferently. In the binoculars she sees David Bowie in the park, looking with the idle curiosity of a stranger, walking toward the bookshop.

DIRECTOR:
You see him?

REGINA:
That guy? Sure. What about him?

DIRECTOR:
What about him? He's just strolling along!

REGINA:
But who?

DIRECTOR:
That gait, I tell you! Those hips. Look how he shakes them! Like this! *(shows how he seductively shakes his hips)* Is that literature? No way. Who is it? I mean that's his jacket, it's HIM. He's coming here. Just dropping in. Like nothing was going on. You know, apparently he's been spreading about town that I don't want to sell him that... what's that damn book called. That I'm hiding copies, sabotaging sales, that I don't want it to get a second printing! That's a good one, how would I do that? Like I've got nothing better to do than ram some shitty book down the crapper to keep it from selling? Haven't I got other things

on my mind? Does he think I've sunk so low? That I'm so petty?

Doesn't he know what I'm writing? That I'm a writer? And by the way, have you read my novels that I happen to have lying around? *The Moss Whispers? The Gawker Didn't Scream? Peter? No? None of them? What about The Hoar Frost?*

(DIRECTOR rifles through the room, overturning furniture noisily. Not everything he says makes sense, but he pays this no mind, not entirely sure if he's thinking these things or saying them. He searches the shelves and piles for books he's written. He keeps finding the wrong ones and tosses them around, forcing REGINA to duck. She politely dodges the missiles coming at her, bobbing up and down, terrified, yet fascinated by this scene of destruction she is witnessing.)

If you don't mind, I'll just read you... one passage... One passage from my Peter, which is oddly and suspiciously similar to the beginning of the TIMELESS NOVEL Spring Isn't Coming, whose author, one Krempiński, probably just LIFTED it, just swapping all the individual words for different ones, but the rhythm of the sentences, the images, he just stole right from me... *(flipping through books, pages in amok)* Just wait till I find it. Just wait till I find it. Just wait till I find it. Just wait till I find it.

"It dawned. Peter awoke bitter and mad...." And in his book? Let's see. Here we go, it begins: "It was morning. The chimneys of Żerań..." No. That's not it. Want to have a drink with me? Are you just going to stand there?

(hollers)

Karolina!
KAROLINA!!!

KAROLINKA *(enters panting, worried):*
Yes Mr. Director?

DIRECTOR *(collapsing in an armchair, utterly exhausted from the drinking and himself):*
Where's that short story I published in The Literary Review? You know the one. Find it.
(KAROLINKA exchanges knowing looks with REGINA and begins slowly pretending she's looking)

SCENE 4:

This whole scene is acted without a word.

Drunken screams come from the director's office, and the soothing voices of KAROLINKA and REGINA trying to soothe the DIRECTOR, and the general sounds of demolition and walls crashing down. MRS. NASTKA is alone in the whole bookshop. She is scrubbing the floor when David Bowie enters.

She gives him the once-over, especially the unseasonal scarf around his neck, because the radio is playing a familiar bulletin.

RADIO:
Attention attention! This is a bulletin from the Head Station of the Citizen's Militia. We now have a description of the man suspected of assaulting women in the Mokotów and Downtown regions this April, his motives impure. Height: medium. Posture: hunched, frame: slender. Hair: a light shade. Forehead: low, Mongoloid. Jaw: outcropping, slack... Numerous small scars, pock-marks from teenage acne.... Stare: terrifying. Wears a trademark scarf with a winter pattern... Citizens, should you have any information about his whereabouts...

MRS. NASTKA looks at David from behind a pillar. She begins putting two and two together. It's the Lady Strangler himself! She goes red and pale, her rag drops from her hand. She does not know what to do, only that time is of the essence. She makes the sign of the cross. She grabs the first Śląsk record from the shelf and walks as if hypnotized toward Bowie, holding it like a shield to protect herself. David Bowie asks her something, and she, in an act of chaotic self-defense, pushes the record into his hands. Having done this heroic deed, she swiftly passes out.

Now we see Komuny Paryskiej Square and David Bowie, clutching the Śląsk record to his chest, trips out of the Bookshop mildly terrified, trying to make off discreetly, but breaking into an unnaturally quick pace. A second later the dishevelled DIRECTOR comes running out after him in a drunken amble. And behind the DIRECTOR, an alarmed KAROLINKA comes running with a mournful "Mr. Director! Mr. Director!" having noticed him slipping a large exacto knife up his sleeve. Her ruffly collar flaps about as she runs. Regina also steps out, of course, but she only watches them run, seeing this as her chance to eat a sandwich. BOGUMIŁA approaches her, sensing something's up.

BOGUMIŁA:
Whatcha eating?

REGINA:
Goose leg, and you?

BOGUMIŁA:
Is that the perv they're always talking about?

REGINA *(shrugs)*

BOGUMIŁA:
Oh, I'll be damned, just you wait, you deviant, I'll give you a whuppin', give back my hundred bucks.
She starts running.

David Bowie runs faster.
PLATOON LEADER joins the race, pulling his never-before-used pistol from its holster and giving a feeble "stop, or I'll shoot," which gets lost in the general confusion. He fires, but the pistol only produces a dry fart. Behind him, her robe flapping in the wind, comes his cream-slathered wife, who spotted him flirting with KAROLINKA.
They all tear after the fugitive, each for their own reason. The pack is joined by MRS. NASTKA's sons, waving their machetes and hand-axes, doing karate moves, and a Mother of God heading for her altar, waving her scepter like nunchuks, and at the end is the Warsaw Mermaid, brandishing her sword. The calculator counts up to the highest numbers, reaching UNCOUNTABLE. At the tail end, the nightstand hobbles along on its broken legs.

David Bowie breaks into a sprint. He is barely keeping ahead of the chase, and at the last minute, grabs on to the door of a train.

His pursuers grind to a halt, watching the tail of the train as it pulls away with a hoot, listening to the clatter and rumble of the wheels. A Great Choir of Mushrooms and River Catfish sings "Warsaw."
A bit disappointed at the lack of carnage, the protagonists grumpily hang their heads and go their separate ways.

THE END

Dorota Masłowska is a Polish writer, playwright, journalist and singer/song-writer. She was 19 when her debut novel, *Wojna polsko-ruska pod flaga bi-ało-czerwoną (Snow White and Russian Red)*, was published and garnered massive critical acclaim in Poland. The book was translated into more than 20 languages, it won the prestigous Paszport Polityki Prize and was made into a movie directed by Xawery Żuławski. Since then, she has written several novels and plays, and she became a celebrated literary figure in Poland. Her second book, a rap-poem, *The Queen's Peacock (Paw Królowej, 2005)* won the Nike Literary Award. In 2006 Masłowska's debut play, *A Couple of Poor, Pol-ish-Speaking Romanians,* was commissioned and staged by the TR Warszawa theater, and it has since been produced in London, Berlin, Prague, Moscow, Chicago and New York. Her second play, *No Matter How Hard We Tried,* was commissioned by TR Warszawa and Berlin's Schaubühne and premiered in Berlin at the Internationales Autorenfestival in March 2009. These two plays received early readings at the Segal Center. Masłowska also wrote a poem for children, *How I became a Witch*, which has been sucessfully adapted for the stage. Her 2012 novel Honey, *I Killed Our Cats* was Masłowska's second novel translated into English and published in 2019 by Deep Vellum.

Her latest novel *Other People* has been translated into a multi-media perfor-mance by Grzegorz Jarzyna at TR Warszawa and was adapted for a motion pic-ture directed by Aleksandra Terpińska and released in 2021.

In 2014 Masłowska released her first music album, *Społeczeństwo jest niemiłe (Society is Mean)*, and introduced audiences to her alter ego "Mister D". In 2023 she retured with her next musical incarnation "Dorota" and released the album *Wolne* produced for the SBM label (QR Code below).

More info:

Facebook

Instagram

Spotify

DOROTA MASŁOWSKA | FOUR PLAYS

The Polish Cultural Institute New York - Co-Producer
https://instytutpolski.pl/newyork/

The mission of the Polish Cultural Institute New York is to share Polish heritage, history and art with American audiences, and to promote Poland's contributions to the success of world culture. The Institute does so through initiating, supporting and promoting collaboration between Poland and the United States in the areas of visual art, design, film, theater, dance, literature, music, and in many other aspects of intellectual and social life. The Institute's main task to ensure Polish participation in the programming of America's most important cultural institutions as well as in large international initiatives.

The Institute works with renowned cultural and academic centers and opinion leaders operating on the American market. Its main partners include such prestigious organizations as Lincoln Center for the Performing Arts, the Brooklyn Academy of Music, the Museum of Modern Art, PEN American Center, the Poetry Society of America, the National Gallery of Art, Yale University, Columbia University, Princeton University, the Harvard Film Archive, the CUNY Graduate Center, the Julliard School of Music, the New Museum, the Jewish Museum, La MaMa E.T.C. and many others. For more than fifteen years, it has presented Americans the achievements of outstanding Polish artists, including the filmmakers Andrzej Wajda and Jerzy Skolimowski; the writers Czeslaw Milosz, Adam Zagajewski and Wislawa Szymborska; the composers Krzysztof Penderecki, Witold Lutoslawski and Mikolaj Gorecki; theater artists Krystian Lupa, Jerzy Grotowski and Tadeusz Kantor; the visual artists Krzysztof Wodiczko, Katarzyna Kozyra, Alina Szapocznikow and many other important figures in the arts. The Institute initiates and actively participates in debates around the humanities in the broad sense, including those concerning history and the today's most important social and political occurrences.

Co-producers

This volume Dorota Masłowska: Four Plays has been created and produced by Martin E. Segal Theatre Center with close collaboration with Tomek Smolarski (Polish Cultural Institute New York), July 2020

The Martin E. Segal Theatre Center is a non-profit center for theatre, dance, and film affiliated with CUNY's Ph.D Program in Theatre. The Center's mission is to bridge the gap between academia and the professional performing arts communities both within the United States and internationally. By providing an open environment for the development of educational, community-driven, and professional projects in the performing arts, The Segal Center is a home to theatre scholars, students, playwrights, actors, dancers, directors, drama-turgs, and performing arts managers from the local and international theatre communities. Programs include staged readings to further the development of new and classic plays, festivals celebrating New York performance (PRELUDE) and international plays (PEN World Voices: International Play Festival), screen-ings of performance works on film (Segal Film Festival on Theatre and Perfor-mance), artists in conversation, academic lecture series, televized seminars, symposia, and arts in education programs. In addition, the Center maintains its long-standing visiting-scholars-from-abroad program, publishes a series of highly regarded academic journals, as well as single volumes of importance (including plays in translation), all written and edited by renowned scholars.

www.theSegalCenter.org

The PhD Program in Theatre, The Graduate Center, CUNY, is one of the leading doctoral theatre programs in the United States and is The Segal Center's de-partmental affiliate at The Graduate Center. The Faculty includes distinguished professors, holders of endowed chairs, and internationally recognized schol-ars. The program trains future scholars and teachers in all the disciplines of theatre research. Faculty members edit MESTC publications, working closely with the doctoral students in theatre who perform a variety of editorial func-tions and learn the skills involved in the creation of books and journals.

www.gc.cuny.edu/theatre

The Graduate Center, CUNY, of which the Martin E. Segal Theatre Center is an integral part, is the doctorate-granting institution of the City University of New York (CUNY). An internationally recognized center for advanced studies and a national model for public doctoral education, the school offers more than thirty doctoral programs, as well as a number of master's programs. Many of its faculty members are among the world's leading scholars in their respective fields, and its alumni hold major positions in industry and government, as well as in academia. The Graduate Center is also home to twenty-eight interdisci-plinary research centers and institutes focused on areas of compelling social, civic, cultural, and scientific concerns. Located in a landmark Fifth Avenue building, The Graduate Center has become a vital part of New York City's intel-lectual and cultural life with its extensive array of public lectures, exhibitions, concerts, and theatrical events.

www.gc.cuny.edu

THE SEGAL PUBLICATION WING

Journals
Segal Center publications include three open-access digital journals, all available for free online to a global readership. After three decades the final print editions of The Journal of American Drama and Theatre (JADT), Slavicand East European Performance (SEEP), and Western European Stages (WES) were issued in 2013/2014. JADT is now exclusively online and WES continuesonline as European Stages (ES).

The Journal of American Drama and Theatre (JADT) publishes thoughtful and innovative work by leadings scholars on theatre, drama, and performance in the US—past and present. Provocative articles provide valuable insight and information on the heritage of American theatre, as well as its continuing contribution to world literature and the performing arts. www.jadtjournal.org

European Stages (ES) combines the activities of WES and SEEP to reflect the contemporary realities of a more integrated continent. Each issue contains a wealth of information about European festivals and productions, including reviews, interviews, and reports. www.europeanstages.org

Arab Stages (AS), a new addition to the Segal Center portfolio of digital theatre journals, focuses on contemporary Arab theatre from around the world. It is devoted to broadening international awareness and understanding of the theatre and performance cultures of the Arab-Islamic world and of its diaspora. www.arabstages.org

MARTIN E. SEGAL THEATRE PUBLICATIONS

Segal Center has published over twenty-five individual volumes of international contemporary and classical plays in translation (French, Spanish, Romanian, Polish, Catalan, Arabic) as well as theatre resources, all edited and translatedbyprominentscholarsinthefield.Thefollowingisonlyapartiallisting. A full listing may be viewed online at www.theSegalCener.org/publications

Four Melodramas by Pixérécourt; Shakespeare Made French: Four Plays by Jean-François Ducis; The Heirs of Molière; Seven Plays by Stanisław Ignacy Witkiewicz; Czech Plays: Seven New Works; roMANIA AFTER 2000: Five New Romanian Plays; Jan Fabre: The Servant of Beauty and I Am a Mistake; Four Millennial Plays from Belgium; New Plays from Spain: Eight Works by Seven Playwrights; Barcelona Plays: A Collection of New Plays by Catalan Playwrights;

Josep M. Benet i Jornet: Two Plays; BAiT-Buenos Aires in Translation: Four Plays; Contemporary Theatre in Egypt; The Arab Oedipus: Four Plays; Four Plays from Syria: Sa'dallah Wannous; Four Plays from North Africa; The Trilogy of Future Memory: Jalila Baccar and Fadhel Jaïbi; Theatre Research Resources in New York City; Comedy: A Bibliography of Critical Studies in English on the Theory and Practice of Comedy in Drama, Theatre, and Performance.

IN MEMORIAM:
Jack Rudin (1924–2016)
Martin E. Segal (1916–2012), MESTC Founder
Daniel Gerould (1928–2012), MESTC Director of Publications

For more information, please visit www.theSegalCenter.org/publications

www.ingramcontent.com/pod-product-compliance
Lightning Source LLC
Chambersburg PA
CBHW061432030726
47503CB00005B/1385